Clint Burnett has written a necessary introduction to inscriptions for New Testament students that has been lacking for some time. The opening chapter offers a very useful and appropriately detailed survey of the topic, and the following chapters offer helpful studies of various sorts. Each of these studies is directly relevant to the study of the New Testament and not only offers insights into these particular issues but suggests how inscriptions may be used for interpreting other passages and topics. I warmly recommend this work.

Stanley E. Porter
President, Dean, and Professor of New Testament
Roy A. Hope Chair in Christian Worldview
McMaster Divinity College

Anyone interested in the civic life and religions of first-century CE Greco-Roman cities will treasure this book. It provides fascinating snapshots of that vast world of letters that were not confined in books and libraries but written on buildings, monuments, gravestones, coins, and even graffiti. Burnett has chosen some special examples in which this evidence sheds important new light on the New Testament. To encourage others in studying this underused resource, the appendices provide guides to the published collections of inscriptions as well as the extensive system of Latin abbreviations.

Pheme Perkins
Joseph Professor of Catholic Spirituality
Theology Department, Boston College

With this book, Clint Burnett builds a bridge between two disciplines that have long ignored each other, epigraphy and New Testament studies. Inscriptions are and, with hundreds of new finds every year, will continue to be a crucial source for illuminating our understanding of many aspects of antiquity. Through five case studies ranging from lexicography, to onomastics, and to social history, Burnett demonstrates the relevance of considering epigraphic evidence for the language and social realities of the New Testament. As such, this book is a must-have for any student dealing with the study of early Christianity within its social, cultural, and political context.

Cédric Brélaz
Professor of Ancient History
University of Fribourg, Switzerland

Clint Burnett's remarkable book, *Studying the New Testament through Inscriptions*, explains how inscriptional evidence sheds fresh light on the values, thoughts, and beliefs of early Christians. In a variety of examples, he deftly demonstrates how this heretofore neglected evidence helps to solve *real*—philological, historical, and theological—problems. This book demonstrates not only the underappreciated role of inscriptions in the study of the New Testament, but also how they can enlarge our understanding of the life and witness of early Christianity.

B. H. McLean
Professor of New Testament Language and Literature
Knox College, University of Toronto

Dr. Burnett's work fills an important void left by many contemporary studies. This book on inscriptions stands in contrast to those more dominated by anachronistic, theoretical models as well as those that toss around artifactual references with little hope of readers understanding the nature and function of the particular artifact. Dr. Burnett's work is truly a vade mecum for inscriptions, primarily Greek and Latin. In this work the author both teaches about the nature, types, functions, etc. of inscriptions relevant for NT studies and also includes specific chapters with the application of inscriptions to NT topics and texts. The indices are extremely valuable both for those wishing to whet their appetite for this topic and also for those wanting to broaden their present skills.

This important work provides a major foundation stone in an approach to Scripture that believes the NT was not given birth in the empyreal realms of Christian doctrine, but rather in the workaday situations, experiences, and life of congregations of God and their leaders. These churches were filled with old and young, women and men, slave and free, ill and healthy, loyal and seditious, faithful believers as well as the faint of heart. Dr. Burnett's point, and his instinct is correct, is that many of the beliefs and experiences of the NT authors and the audiences written to and written about in the NT are far better understood by means of epigraphical resources and studies.

Inscriptions provide an indispensable and clearer lens through which we can view the larger world of these churches. Greek and Latin epigraphy provides the quintessential primary resources for an improved appreciation and understanding of the religious, political, and social contours of Greco-Roman civilization, without which one is doomed to view the NT through a besmudged lens.

Richard E. Oster
Professor of New Testament
Harding School of Theology

STUDYING *the* NEW TESTAMENT *through* INSCRIPTIONS

STUDYING *the* NEW TESTAMENT *through* INSCRIPTIONS

— D. CLINT BURNETT —

An Introduction

an imprint of Hendrickson Publishing Group

Studying the New Testament through Inscriptions: An Introduction

Published by Hendrickson Academic
an imprint of Hendrickson Publishing Group
Hendrickson Publishers, LLC
P. O. Box 3473
Peabody, Massachusetts 01961-3473
www.hendricksonpublishinggroup.com

ISBN 978-1-68307-137-2

Printed in the United States of America

First Printing — April 2020

Library of Congress Control Number: 2020930624

Cover Photos by D. Clint Burnett

To my beloved Gerilyn, who is to me as I am to her,
and she is indeed עֶזְרִי

Contents

List of Illustrations xi

Preface xv

Acknowledgments xvii

Abbreviations xix

Introduction 1

1. Engraved for All Time: An Introduction to Inscriptions 9

2. Jesus, the Royal Lord: Inscriptions and Local Customs 58

3. "Devour" or "Go Ahead with" the Lord's Banquet? Inscriptions and Philology 77

4. Imperial Loyalty Oaths, Caesar's Decrees, and Early Christianity in Thessalonica: Contextualizing Inscriptions 97

5. Benefactresses, Deaconesses, and Overseers in the Philippian Church: Inscriptions and Their Insights into the Religious Lives of Women in the Roman World 121

6. Calculating Numbers with Wisdom: Inscriptions and Exegetical Impasses 140

Conclusion 163

Appendix 1. Important Printed Collections of Inscriptions 167

Appendix 2. Online Search Engines and Collections of Inscriptions 169

Appendix 3. Abbreviations in Inscriptions 173

Glossary 177

Bibliography 179

Index of Modern Authors 207

Index of Subjects 211

Index of Ancient Sources 213

Illustrations

1.1. Warning inscription from the temple of God in Jerusalem from the Istanbul Archaeology Museum, Turkey (© D. Clint Burnett)

1.2. Altar dedicated to "the subterranean god" from the Archaeological Museum of Philippi, Greece (© D. Clint Burnett)

1.3. Sketch of a Greek graffito from Rome's Palatine Hill depicting a Christian worshiping Jesus drawn as a crucified donkey (© Wikimedia Commons: Public Domain)

1.4. Statues on top of Mount Nermut on the backs of which Antiochus the Great of Commagene placed an inscription (© Wikimedia Commons: Klearchos Kapoutsis)

1.5. Greek inscription (*Corinth* 8.3 534) (267–668 CE) with guidelines still visible from the Archaeological Museum of Ancient Corinth, Greece (© D. Clint Burnett)

1.6. Sketch of late first century CE funerary altar of Cossutia Arescusa and Cnaeus Cossutius Cladus depicting the tools that stonecutters used to make inscriptions from the Musei Capitolini, Rome, Italy (sketch by Robert Singler and used by permission)

1.7. Inscription from the architrave on the Baths of Caracalla (212 CE) in Sardis, Turkey (© D. Clint Burnett)

1.8. Copy of Table Number 9 from the bronze tablet containing the municipal law of Taranto (89–62 BCE) from Museo Nazionale Archeologico, Taranto, Italy (© D. Clint Burnett)

1.9. Archive wall from the theater at Aphrodisias, Turkey (© D. Clint Burnett)

1.10. Pantheon, Rome, Italy (© D. Clint Burnett)

1.11. Statue of the Pompeian benefactress Eumachia from a niche in Eumachia's building, Pompeii, Italy (© D. Clint Burnett)

1.12. Latin inscription from Eumachia's statue base, Pompeii, Italy (© D. Clint Burnett)

1.13. Boundary marker set up to solve a territory dispute between the city of Sagalassus and the village of Tymbrianassus from the Burdur Museum, Burdur, Turkey (© D. Clint Burnett)

1.14. Boundary marker establishing the extension of Capua's *pomerium* from Museo Archeologico Nazionale di Napoli, Naples, Italy (© D. Clint Burnett)

1.15. Agricultural calendar (first century CE) from Rome depicting the months of July, August, and September from the Museo Archeologico Nazionale di Napoli, Naples, Italy (© D. Clint Burnett)

1.16. Architrave inscription from the temple of Athena and Augustus, Priene, Turkey (© D. Clint Burnett)

1.17. Tomb of Titus Flavius Zeuxis, Hierapolis, Turkey (© D. Clint Burnett)

1.18. Inscription from the tomb of Titus Flavius Zeuxis, Hierapolis, Turkey (© D. Clint Burnett)

1.19. Gate of Mazaeus and Mithradates at Ephesus, Turkey, with a dedicatory inscription to the imperial family (© D. Clint Burnett)

1.20. Mosaic from the vestibule of the House of the Tragic Poet in Pompeii, Italy, with a dog and the message "Beware of the dog!" (*cave canem*) (*CIL* 10.877) (© Wikimedia Commons: Public Domain)

1.21. Scratched graffito from Ephesus, Turkey, warning against public urination (© D. Clint Burnett)

1.22. Curse tablet from London, England (© Wikimedia Commons: Marie-Lan Nguyen)

3.1. Drawing of a Pompeiian dining room from Henry Thédenat, *Pompéi* (Paris: Renouard, 1906, 77: Public Domain)

3.2. Fresco from Pompeii, Italy, dating 50 CE from the north wall of the dining room of House 2, Room 4 in Regio V (© D. Clint Burnett)

4.1. Golden Gate of Thessalonica (© Wikimedia Commons: Public Domain)

6.1. Leonteus's votive with an iron sickle containing three sets of equal calculations (© Wikimedia Commons: Public Domain)

Preface

This book is an attempt to introduce mainly Greek but also Latin and Semitic inscriptions from the Hellenistic and Roman periods to graduate students, seminarians, and pastors for the purpose of using these sources to interpret the documents of the NT and to reconstruct the history of early Christianity. It is divided into two parts. The first part consists of the first chapter, which introduces inscriptions and the methodologically appropriate way to approach them, treating inscriptions as archaeological artifacts. The second part consists of five case studies in which I demonstrate this approach to inscriptions and the underappreciated benefits that await the interpreter of the NT who uses them. This book's thesis is twofold. First, inscriptions allow for a fuller portrait of life in the early Roman Empire because, unlike Greco-Roman literary texts, inscriptions provide windows into the values, thoughts, and beliefs of individuals who are not elite men, such as artisans, slaves, women, etc. Second, inscriptions are contextual data, representing localized religion, politics, culture, and ideologies, so they help contextualize certain NT texts and events in early Christianity in ways that literary texts cannot. My hope for the reader is that this book will unlock a world of incalculable historical, philological, and theological potential for the study of the NT.

Acknowledgments

This book would not have been possible without the giants on whose shoulders I stand: Richard E. Oster, James C. Walters, Laura S. Nasrallah, and Pheme Perkins. Each of these erudite scholars not only demonstrated how to use inscriptions in interpreting the NT, but also interacted with, engaged with, and influenced my own work with inscriptions and the NT during my graduate work. Richard Oster introduced me to inscriptions by graciously offering an elective course on Greek epigraphy during my graduate coursework at Harding School of Theology. In addition, he read and provided insightful feedback on every chapter of this book (any errors the reader may find are my own fault and not his). While I was a graduate student at Boston University School of Theology, James Walters introduced me to the concept of inscriptions as archaeological artifacts, facilitated and led an on-site archaeology and NT class in Turkey, and even paid for my trip to Turkey from his personal funds. Some pictures in this book are from that trip. Laura Nasrallah honed my work with inscriptions and allowed me to join her on-site archaeology and NT class in Greece and Turkey under the auspices of Harvard Divinity School. Some pictures in this book are from that trip as well. Pheme Perkins, my doctoral mother at Boston College, refined my approach of using inscriptions in the interpretation of the NT, pushing me to consider the limitations and possibilities that inscriptions can have for the NT.

My beloved wife, Gerilyn Burnett, has graciously given up large parts of our family vacations to allow me to peruse museums and archaeological sites in Europe in addition to giving me to the time and space to write this book. The interlibrary loan staff at Boston College's O'Neill library is one of this book's unsung heroes. They have hunted down many of the inscriptions, some of which are obscure, that I use in this book, regardless of the time, cost, and energy. Their tireless efforts are appreciated. A wonderful and unexpected outcome of writing this book was my acquaintance with Cédric Brélaz, Professor of Ancient History, University of Fribourg in Switzerland. Cédric generously read my manuscript and with his immense firsthand knowledge of epigraphy, most notably from Philippi, enhanced and improved my discussion of inscriptions, especially that of Philippian epigraphy. Finally, I would like to thank my wise editors at Hendrickson Publishers, Carl Nellis, Jonathan Kline, Patricia Anders, and Tirzah Frank. Carl, Jonathan, and Patricia allowed me to undertake this project, Tirzah and Patricia provided helpful and valuable feedback on my manuscript, and Tirzah piloted this project all the way to publication. Carl, Jonathan, Patricia, and Tirzah: thank you for all your hard work!

D. Clint Burnett
Knoxville, Tennessee
Advent 2019

Abbreviations

General Abbreviations

ASV	American Standard Version
BCE	before the Common Era
CE	Common Era
cf.	compare
ed(s).	edited by, editors, edition
e.g.	*exempli gratia*, for example
=	other important publications of the same inscription
esp.	especially
ESV	English Standard Version
ET	English translation
et al.	*at alii*, and others
ibid.	in the same place
KJV	King James Version
LXX	Septuagint
m	meter(s)
MT	Masoretic Text
no.	number
NIV	New International Version
NRSV	New Revised Standard Version
NT	New Testament
r.	reigned
repr.	reprinted
trans.	translated by, translator
vol(s).	volume(s)

Ancient Sources

Ancient Near East

ANESTP *The Ancient Near East: Supplementary Texts and Pictures Relating to the Old Testament*. Edited by James B. Pritchard. Princeton: Princeton University Press, 1969

COS *The Context of Scripture*. Edited by William W. Hallo. 3 vols. Leiden: Brill, 1997–2002

Deuterocanonical Works

1 Macc 1 Maccabees

Pseudepigrapha

Sib. Or. *Sibyline Oracles*

Josephus

Ant. *Jewish Antiquities*
J.W. *Jewish War*

Philo

Abraham *On the Life of Abraham*
Embassy *On the Embassy to Gaius*
Flaccus *Against Flaccus*
Joseph *On the Life of Joseph*
Moses *On the Life of Moses*

Dead Sea Scrolls

1QapGen ar Genesis Apocryphon
4Q202 Enb ar
11Q10 Targum of Job

Apostolic Writings

Ign. *Eph.*	Ignatius, *To the Ephesians*
Ign. *Magn.*	Ignatius, *To the Magnesians*
Ign. *Phld.*	Ignatius, *To the Philadelphians*
Ign. *Pol.*	Ignatius, *To Polycarp*
Ign. *Smyrn.*	Ignatius, *To the Smyrnaeans*
Ign. *Trall.*	Ignatius, *To the Trallians*
Pol. *Phil.*	Polycarp, *To the Philippians*

Church Fathers

Irenaeus, *Haer.* Irenaeus, *Against Heresies*

Pagan Works

Aristotle	
Rhet.	*Rhetoric*
Artemidorus Daldianus	
Onir.	*Onirocritica*
Cicero	
Verr.	*In Verrem*
Lucian	
Alex.	*Alexander the False Prophet*
Pliny the Elder	
Nat.	*Naturalis historia*
Strabo	
Geogr.	*Geographica*
Suetonius	
Aug.	*Divus Augustus*
Claud.	*Divus Claudius*
Dom.	*Domitianus*
Jul.	*Divus Julius*
Tib.	*Tiberius*
Vesp.	*Vespasianus*
Tacitus	
Ann.	*Annales*

Inscriptions, Papyri, and Coins

AE	*L'Année épigraphique*
IIasos	*Die Inschriften von Iasos*. Edited by Wolfgang Blümel. 2 vols. Bonn: Habelt, 1985
CID	*Corpus des inscriptions de Delphes*. Edited by Georges Rougement et al. Paris: de Boccard, 1977–
CIG	*Corpus Inscriptionum Graecarum*. Edited by August Boeckh. 4 vols. Berlin, 1828–1877
CIIP	*Corpus Inscriptionum Iudaeae/Palaestinae: A Multilingual Corpus of Inscriptions from Alexander to Muhammad*. Edited by Hannah M. Cotton et al. 6 vols. Berlin: de Gruyter, 2008–
CIL	*Corpus Inscriptionum Latinarum*. Berlin, 1862–
CIPh II.1	*Corpus des Inscriptions grecques et latines de Philippes. Tome II La colonie romaine, Part 1 La vie publique de la colonie*. Edited by Cédric Brélaz. Athens: École française d'Athènes, 2014
CIS	*Corpus Inscriptionum Semiticarum*. Paris, 1881–1962.
Corinth 8.1	*Corinth VIII, Part I Greek Inscriptions 1896–1927*. Edited by Benjamin Dean Merritt. Cambridge: Harvard University Press, 1931
Corinth 8.2	*The Latin Inscriptions 1896–1926*. Edited by Allen B. West. Princeton: American School of Classical Studies at Athens, 1931
Corinth 8.3	*Corinth VIII, Part III The Inscriptions 1926–1950*. Edited by John Harvey Kent, Princeton: American School of Classical Studies at Athens, 1966
GIBM	*The Collection of Greek Inscriptions in the British Museum*. Edited by Charles Thomas Newton. 5 vols. London: British Museum, 1874–1916
GLIA	*The Greek and Latin Inscriptions of Ankara (Ancyra)*. Vol. 1, *From Augustus to the End of the Third Century AD*. Edited by Stephen Mitchell and David French. Beiträge zur Alten Geschichte Band 62. Munich: Beck, 2012
H	*The Nabataean Tomb Inscriptions of Mada'in Salih*. Edited by John F. Healey. JSSSup 1. Oxford: Oxford University Press, 1993

IAph2007	*Inscriptions of Aphrodisias* (2007). Edited by Joyce Reynolds, Charlotte Roueché, and Gabriel Bodard. http://insaph.kcl.ac.uk/iaph2007
IAssos	*Die Inschriften von Assos*. Edited by Reinhold Merkelbach. Inschriften griechischer Städte aus Kleinasien 4. Bonn: Rudolf Habelt, 1976
IEph	*Die Inschriften von Ephesos*. Edited by Hermann Wankel et al. 8 vols. Bonn: Habelt, 1979–1984
IG	*Inscriptiones Graecae*. Berlin: de Gruyter, 1903–
IGRR	*Inscriptiones graecae ad res romanas pertinentes*. Edited by René Cagnat et al. 4 vols. Paris: Ernest Leroux, 1901–1927
IHierapJ	*Altertümer von Hierapolis*. Edited by Carl Humann et al. Jahrbuch des Kaiserlich Deutschen Archäologischen Instituts Ergänzungsheft 4. Berlin, 1898
ILabraunda	*Greek Inscriptions*. Edited by Jonas Crampa. Labraunda: Swedish Excavations and Researches III.1–2. Lund and Stockholm: 1969, 1972
ILS	*Inscriptiones latinae selectae*. Edited by Hermann Dessau. 3 vols. Berlin: Weidmannos, 1892–1916
IMylasa	*Die Inschriften von Mylasa*. Edited by Wolfgang Blümel. Inschriften griechischer Städte aus Kleinasien 34–35. 2 vols. Bonn: Habelt, 1987–1988
IPergamon	*Die Inschriften von Pergamon*. Edited by Max Fränkel. Altertümer von Pergamon 8.1, 2. 2 vols. Berlin: Spemann, 1890–1895
IPriene	*Inschriften von Priene*. Edited by Friedrich Hiller von Gaertringen. Berlin: George Reimer, 1906
MAMA 4	*Monuments and Documents from Eastern Asia and Western Galatia*. Edited by W. H. Buckler, William Moir Calder, and William Keith Chambers Guthrie. MAMA 4. Manchester: Manchester University Press, 1933
O. Claud.	*Mons Claudianus. Ostraca graeca et latina*. Edited by J. Bingen et al. 4 vols. Cairo: Institut Français d'Archéologie Orientale, 1992–2007
OGIS	*Orientis Graeci Inscriptiones Selectae*. Edited by Wilhelm Dittenberger. 2 vols. Leipzig: Hirzel, 1903–1905
PGM	*Papyri Graecae Magicae: Die griechischen Zauberpapyri*. Edited by Karl Preisendanz. 2nd ed. Stuttgart: Teubner, 1973–1974

Philippi II — *Philippi. Band II Katalog der Inschriften von Philippi 2 Auflage*. Edited by Peter Pilhofer. WUNT 119. Tübingen: Mohr Siebeck, 2009

P.Oxy — *The Oxyrhynchus Papyri*. Edited by Bernard Grenfell et al. London: Egypt Exploration Fund, 1898–

RDGE — *Roman Documents from the Greek East: Senatus Consulta and Epistulae to the Age of Augustus*. Edited by Robert K. Sherk. Baltimore: Johns Hopkins University Press, 1969

RIB — *The Roman Inscriptions of Britain*. Vol. 1, *Inscriptions on Stone*. Edited by R. G. Collingwood and R. P. Wright. Oxford: Clarendon, 1965.

RPC — *Roman Provincial Coinage*. Edited by Michael Amandry et al. 10 vols. London: British Museum Press, 1992–

Sardis 7.1 — *Sardis VII, Part 1: Greek and Latin Inscriptions*. Edited by W. H. Buckler and David Robinson. Publications of the American Society of the Excavation of Sardis. Leiden: Brill, 1932

SGDI II — *Sammlung der griechischen Dialekt-Inschriften II*. Edited by Johannes Baunack et al. Göttingen: Vandenhoeck & Ruprecht, 1885–1899

SEG — *Supplementum Epigraphicum Graecum*. Edited by Jacob E. Hondius et al. Leiden: Brill, 1923–

Sel. Pap. — *Select Papyri*. Edited by A. S. Hunt, C. C. Edgar, and D. L. Page. 3 vols. Cambridge: Harvard University Press, 1932, 1942

SIG^3 — *Sylloge Inscriptionum Graecarum*. Edited by Wilhelm Dittenberger. 4 vols. 3rd ed. Leipzig: Hirzel, 1915–1924

TNSI — *Text-book of North-Semitic Inscriptions*. Edited by G. A. Cooke. Oxford: Clarendon, 1903

TSSI — *Textbook of Syrian Semitic Inscriptions*. Edited by C. L. Gibson and John F. Healey. Oxford: Oxford University Press, 1971–2009

TAM 5 — *Tituli Asiae Minoris, V. Tituli Lydiae linguis Graeca et Latina conscripti*. Edited by Georg Petzl. Vienna: Verlag der Österreichischen Akademie der Wissenschaften, 2007

Journals, Series, and Reference Works

A(Y)B — Anchor (Yale) Bible

ABD	*Anchor Bible Dictionary.* Edited by David Noel Freedman. 6 vols. New York: Doubleday, 1992
A(Y)BRL	Anchor (Yale) Bible Reference Library
AJA	*American Journal of Archaeology*
AJP	*American Journal of Philology*
ANRW	*Aufstieg und Niedergang der römischen Welt: Geschichte und Kultur Roms im Spiegel der neueren Forschung.* Part 2, *Principat.* Edited by Hildegard Temporini and Wolfgang Haase. Berlin: de Gruyter, 1972–
ANTC	Abingdon New Testament Commentaries
BBS	*Bulletin of Biblical Studies*
BCH	*Bulletin de correspondance hellénique*
BCHSup	Bulletin de correspondance hellénique Supplements
BDAG	Danker, Frederick W., Walter Bauer, William F. Arndt, and F. Wilbur Gingrich. *Greek-English Lexicon of the New Testament and Other Early Christian Literature.* 3rd ed. Chicago: University of Chicago Press, 2000
BDB	Brown, Francis, S. R. Driver, and Charles A. Briggs. *A Hebrew and English Lexicon of the Old Testament.* Oxford: Clarendon, 1952
BECNT	Baker Exegetical Commentary on the New Testament
BNTC	Black's New Testament Commentaries
BTB	*Biblical Theology Bulletin*
BZNW	Beihefte zur Zeitschrift für die neutestamentliche Wissenschaft
CAH	Cambridge Ancient History
CBQ	*Catholic Biblical Quarterly*
ClQ	*Classical Quarterly*
CTR	*Criswell Theological Review*
DJD	Discoveries in the Judaean Desert
ECL	Early Christianity and Its Literature
EDNT	*Exegetical Dictionary of the New Testament.* Edited by Horst Balz and Gerhard Schneider. ET. 3 vols. Grand Rapids: Eerdmans, 1990–1993
ExpTim	*Expository Times*
GNS	*Good News Studies*
HNTC	Harper's New Testament Commentaries
HTR	*Harvard Theological Review*
HTS	Harvard Theological Studies

IBC	Interpretation: A Bible Commentary for Teaching and Preaching
ICC	International Critical Commentary
Int	*Interpretation*
JDS	Judean Desert Studies
JFSR	*Journal of Feminist Studies in Religion*
JÖAI	*Jahreshefte des Österreichischen archäologischen Instituts*
JRS	*Journal of Roman Studies*
JSNT	*Journal for the Study of the New Testament*
JSNTSup	Journal for the Study of the New Testament Supplement Series
JSOT	*Journal for the Study of the Old Testament*
JSSSup	Journal of Semitic Studies Supplement
JTS	*Journal of Theological Studies*
KEK	Kritisch-exegetischer Kommentar über das Neue Testament (Meyer-Kommentar)
LCL	Loeb Classical Library
LSJ	Liddell, Henry George, Robert Scott, Henry Stuart Jones. *A Greek-English Lexicon*. 9th ed. with revised supplement. Oxford: Clarendon, 1996
LSTS	The Library of Second Temple Studies
MDAI(A)	*Mitteilungen des Deutschen archäologischen Instituts, Athenische Abteilung*
MM	Moulton, James H., and George Milligan. *The Vocabulary of the Greek Testament Illustrated from the Papyri and Other Non-Literary Sources*. London: Hodder & Stoughton, 1914–1929
NICNT	New International Commentary on the New Testament
NIGTC	New International Greek Testament Commentary
NTD	Das Neue Testament Deutsch
NTS	*New Testament Studies*
RAC	*Reallexikon für Antike und Christentum*. Edited by Theodor Klauser et al. Stuttgart: Hiersemann, 1950–
REG	*Revue des études grecques*
RNT	Regensburger Neues Testament
RTR	*Reformed Theological Review*
SBLDS	Society of Biblical Literature Dissertation Series
SNTSMS	Society for New Testament Studies Monograph Series

SP	Sacra Pagina
SPhiloA	Studia Philonica Annual
TBT	*The Bible Today*
TDNT	*Theological Dictionary of the New Testament*. Edited by Gerhard Kittel and Gerhard Friedrich. Translated by Geoffrey W. Bromiley. 10 vols. Grand Rapids: Eerdmans, 1964–1976
TDOT	*Theological Dictionary of the Old Testament*. Edited by G. Johannes Botterweck and Helmer Ringgren. Translated by John T. Willis et al. 8 vols. Grand Rapids: Eerdmans, 1974–2006
TS	*Theological Studies*
TSAJ	Texte und Studien zum antiken Judentum
WBC	Word Biblical Commentary
WUNT	Wissenschaftliche Untersuchungen zum Neuen Testament
ZNW	*Zeitschrift für die neutestamentliche Wissenschaft und die Kunde der älteren Kirche*
ZPE	*Zeitschrift für Papyrologie und Epigraphik*

Introduction

Inscriptions play an important but underappreciated role in the NT from beginning to end. Each of the Gospels note that an inscription was placed on Jesus' cross advertising the reason for his execution: "The King of the Jews" (Matt 27:37; Mark 15:26; Luke 23:38; John 19:19).[1] The author of Acts of the Apostles, Luke, records that Paul the apostle used an inscription on an altar in Athens that said "to an unknown god" as an illustration that provided the impetus for a sermon (Acts 17:23) about the nature of the one true God and the day of judgment (Acts 17:24–31). Paul references an inscription in his letters. To highlight the greater glory of the new covenant of which he was a minister, Paul equates the old covenant with the ministry "engraved on stones." He says that if that ministry had glory, then how much more glory must the new covenant infused with God's Spirit have (2 Cor 3:7–11)?[2] In the last book of our canonical NT, the author of Revelation, John the prophet, uses inscriptions in his description of the new age and the new Jerusalem. The risen Jesus promises the faithful in the church in Pergamum that they will receive a white stone on which "a new name is written that no one knows except the one who receives it" (Rev 2:17). Jesus will make the resilient in the church in Philadelphia pillars in the temple of God, and the name of God and the new Jerusalem will be written on them

1. Mark and Luke call the sign placed above Jesus' head an ἐπιγραφή (Mark 15:26; Luke 23:38). John uses a transliteration of a Latin term for inscription τίτλος (John 19:19; cf. *ILS* 7679; Petronius, *Satyricon* 30, 71; Livy 28.46.16; Suetonius, *Dom.* 5). Matthew notes that a sign was placed above Jesus' head, but focuses on its content rather than its function. Therefore, Matthew notes that the sign contained the αἰτία for Jesus' crucifixion (Matt 27:37). The Evangelists disagree about the exact wording of the inscription on Jesus' cross, but they all agree that it declared Jesus "King of the Jews": "This is Jesus the King of the Jews" (οὗτός ἐστιν Ἰησοῦς ὁ βασιλεὺς τῶν Ἰουδαίων; Matt 27:37); "The King of the Jews" (ὁ βασιλεὺς τῶν Ἰουδαίων; Mark 15:26); "This is the King of the Jews" (ὁ βασιλεὺς τῶν Ἰουδαίων οὗτος; Luke 23:38); "Jesus the Nazarene: The King of the Jews" (Ἰησοῦς ὁ Ναζωραῖος ὁ βασιλεὺς τῶν Ἰουδαίων; John 19:19).

2. For a discussion of 2 Cor 3:7–11 see Victor Paul Furnish, *II Corinthians: Translated with Introduction, Notes, and Commentary*, AB 32A (Garden City: Doubleday, 1984), 201–26.

(Rev 3:12). John concludes his prophecy with a description of this new Jerusalem. He says that it has twelve gates and twelve foundation stones. The names of the twelve tribes of Israel are inscribed on the twelve gates (Rev 21:12) and the names of the twelve apostles of the Lamb are engraved on the foundation stones (Rev 21:14).[3]

In none of these references to inscriptions does an author of the NT take the time to explain what they are. The Evangelists, Paul, and John the prophet assume that their readers and auditors know that inscriptions are messages written on surfaces of some kind. Paul and John the prophet in particular take for granted that their audiences are aware of the function of inscriptions in Greco-Roman culture as publicizing messages for future generations to read. In short, some of our NT authors demand that we as readers have a rudimentary understanding of inscriptions and their function in the early Roman Empire. However, we do not live in the early Roman Empire, but in a world separated by two thousand years, thousands of miles, and huge cultural differences, one of which is the use of inscriptions. Our various distances from the early Roman Empire mean that we have to work to understand inscriptions.

The main purpose of this book is to bridge this chronological and cultural gap by making inscriptions accessible for the seminarian, graduate student, or pastor who is interested in adding another dataset with which to approach the interpretation of the NT (I suspect that some of my NT colleagues may benefit from this book as well). This book is the one that I wish that I had when I began my study of inscriptions. The situation that I faced in graduate school still exists for today's student (until now!). For those interested in using inscriptions to interpret the NT, there are three options for learning more about them: (1) technical introductions to inscriptions geared toward aspiring epigraphers and historians of Greco-Roman history such as B. H. McLean's magisterial *Introduction to Greek Epigraphy* (2002); (2) the works of Adolf Deissmann, most significantly *Light from the Ancient East* (the second German edition was translated into English in 1910); and (3) entries on inscriptions in Bible and NT dictionaries and encyclopedias.[4]

3. John also notes that "names" are written, engraved, and inscribed on numerous objects throughout Revelation: 13:1; 14:1, 11; 17:3, 5; 19:12, 16; 22:4.

4. B. H. McLean, *An Introduction to Greek Epigraphy of the Hellenistic and Roman Periods from Alexander the Great down to the Reign of Constantine (323 B.C.–A.D. 337)* (Ann Arbor: University of Michigan Press, 2002); Adolf Deissmann, *Light from the Ancient East: The New Testament Illustrated by Recently Discovered Texts of the Graeco-Roman World*, trans. Lionel R. M. Strachan, 4th ed. (New York: Hodder & Stoughton,

These three options, however, have their limitations. Technical introductions are not written with the student of the NT in mind and can seem overwhelming. Deissmann provides little background information about inscriptions, directing the reader to a German introduction to inscriptions published in 1906.[5] And, entries on inscriptions in Bible and NT dictionaries and encyclopedias, by their nature, are cursory and undetailed.[6]

Therefore, this book's first goal is to introduce inscriptions by making them accessible to the seminarian, graduate student, and pastor. In the process, I tackle what inscriptions are, why they were set up, how they were made, how they are classified, who could read them, how they are dated, and how to use collections of inscriptions (or corpora), which can

---

1910; repr. Grand Rapids: Baker Books, 1978). For a list of Deissmann's works see Albrecht Gerber, *Deissmann the Philologist*, BZNW 171 (Berlin: de Gruyter, 2009), 591–98.

5. Inscriptions were not Deissmann's ancient source of choice. He calls papyri "the most important" source for studying the NT because he was convinced that the authors of extant papyri and early Christians were both from the lower social classes of the Roman world. Deissmann (*Light from the Ancient East*, 24) concludes: "There is one circumstance which sometimes makes the inscriptions less productive than might have been expected, especially those that are more or less of the official kind. This style has often been polished up, and then they are formal, artificial, cold as the marble that bears them, and stiff as the characters incised upon the unyielding stone. As a whole the inscriptions are not so fresh and natural as the papyri . . . [which] is therefore, linguistically at any rate, the most important." Deissmann does not consider that most of Paul's letters are polished and are not the work of one mind, but are the process of a collaborative effort among Paul and his apostolic colleagues. See Jerome Murphy-O'Connor, *Paul the Letter-Writer: His World, His Options, His Skills, GNS* 41 (Collegeville, MN: Liturgical Press, 1995); E. Randolph Richards, *Paul and First-Century Letter Writing: Secretaries, Composition and Collection* (Downers Grove, IL: InterVarsity Press, 2004).

6. E.g., Stanley E. Porter, "Inscriptions and Papyri: Greco-Roman," in *The Dictionary of New Testament Background*, ed. Craig A. Evans and Stanley E. Porter (Downers Grove, IL: InterVarsity Press, 2000), 529–39; David Noy, "Inscriptions and Papyri: Jewish," in *Dictionary of New Testament Background*, ed. Craig A. Evans and Stanley E. Porter, 539–41. While *ABD* contains entries on Semitic inscriptions (*ABD* 2:561–68; 3:418–23), it does not have one on Greek or Latin inscriptions. In a recent collection of essays on the NT and inscriptions, the editors address the state of the use of inscriptions in NT scholarship, concluding that most NT scholars "keep away from" inscriptions for three reasons. First, NT exegetes find it difficult to access and to handle inscriptions. Second, they believe the payoff of working with inscriptions will not be worth the time and effort that they put into using inscriptions to interpret the NT. And, third, NT scholars think that the most relevant inscriptions have already been discovered. The editors may have overstated the bleakness of the use of inscriptions by NT scholars, but their comment highlights the problem rather well. Joseph Verheyden, Markus Öhler, and Thomas Corsten, "Introduction," in *Epigraphik und Neues Testament*, ed. Thomas Corsten, Markus Öhler, and Joseph Verheyden, WUNT 365 (Tübingen: Mohr Siebeck, 2016), 1–4.

seem complicated for the novice. (Because of the internet, using corpora of inscriptions has never been easier. To aid the reader in their work with inscriptions, I have placed two appendices at this book's conclusion: an appendix containing the most important printed corpora of inscriptions and another containing online databases of inscriptions.) This introduction is not exhaustive, and while I focus mainly on introductory issues related to Greek inscriptions, my desire is to acquaint the reader with a rudimentary knowledge of Semitic and Latin inscriptions as well. I address Semitic and Latin inscriptions because early Christianity began in the trilingual environment of ancient Palestine, where Aramaic and Hebrew were spoken in addition to Greek, and some of our earliest Christian churches were established in Roman colonies where Latin was the dominant language, such as Corinth.

Knowing what inscriptions are, how they were made, and other introductory issues related to them is not enough, however. As Laura Nasrallah points out in her book *Archaeology and the Letters of Paul*, inscriptions (as well as other archaeological materials) do not speak for themselves, but are "*in need of interpretation*" (emphasis hers).[7] Therefore, the second goal of this book is to introduce the proper methodological approach to inscriptions, which consists of treating them as what they are: archaeological artifacts. Approaching inscriptions in this manner means that they are more than just words. The material on which inscriptions were written, where they were set up in Greco-Roman cities, when they were taken down, and the circumstances surrounding their discovery in the modern period often provide information about inscriptions as important as their content.[8] Such information determines how one should interpret an inscription.

I begin to address this approach to inscriptions in the final section of my first chapter, which introduces the concept of inscriptions as archaeologi-

7. Laura S. Nasrallah, *Archaeology and the Letters of Paul* (Oxford: Oxford University Press, 2019), 30.

8. This approach to inscriptions is not found in most interactions with inscriptions by NT scholars. The main reason is that most NT scholars are interested in inscriptions for their content. In the process, they treat them as disembodied texts. For example, Deissmann's main interest in inscriptions (and papyri) is philological; mining them to better understand the syntax and meaning of Greek words found in the NT (due to this scholarly focus, a recent biography of Deissmann by Albrecht Gerber is called *Deissmann the Philologist*). His second stated interest in inscriptions (and papyri) is finding points of contact between Greco-Roman culture and early Christianity. In the search for philological data and points of contact with the larger pagan world, Deissmann fails to consider the archaeological and/or cultural contexts of inscriptions. The case is similar for most entries on inscriptions in Bible and NT dictionaries and encyclopedias: e.g., Porter, "Inscriptions and Papyri," 529–34.

cal artifacts. The rest of the book is made of up intuitive case studies demonstrating this approach to inscriptions and the benefits that this method offers. In the second chapter, I show how inscriptions help to reconstruct some theological developments of early Christianity. Greek and Semitic inscriptions from the southern Levant (ancient Palestine, Syria, and their environs) indicate that "lord" was a royal title particular to the region from the Hellenistic period to the mid-first century CE and that this distinctive custom is not found outside that region until the latter half of the first century CE. These southern Levantine inscriptions that call the reigning sovereign lord and their similarity to the use of *kyrios* for Jesus in our earliest Christian texts, Paul's letters, suggest that Jesus was first called *kyrios* in the southern Levant and that this title was royal, messianic, and not exclusively divine.

In the third chapter, I demonstrate the philological benefit of inscriptions. My test case focuses on the meaning of προλαμβάνω in inscriptions. This verb is critical to Paul's discussion of the Lord's Banquet in Corinth (1 Cor 11:17–34) because its translation in 1 Cor 11:21 affects how one reconstructs the problem that Paul addresses and his solution to it. Some scholars conclude that προλαμβάνω has a temporal meaning and the problem that Paul addresses in 1 Cor 11:17–34 is that richer Corinthians are arriving earlier to the Lord's Banquet and "going ahead with" their own. Paul attempts to solve this problem by telling them to wait for their fellow Christians (1 Cor 11:33). Other scholars, pointing to one inscription, argue that προλαμβάνω means "devour," and that the problem with the Lord's Banquet is that the richer Corinthians are "devouring" (1 Cor 11:21) it. Paul's solution is that these wealthier Christians should share their food (1 Cor 11:33) with the rest of their brothers and sisters in Christ. I show that the case for translating προλαμβάνω as "devour" is not as clear as these scholars propose. The inscription to which they point has one use of προλαμβάνω that is temporal, and other inscriptions closer to the time of the composition of 1 Corinthians (56 CE) testify that the verb probably has a temporal meaning in 1 Cor 11:21. Therefore, the most appropriate reconstruction of the problem that Paul faces with the Lord's Banquet in Corinth is that the richer Corinthians are "going ahead with" their own banquet and not waiting for their fellow Christians.

In the fourth chapter, I demonstrate the limitations and possibilities of contextualizing inscriptions. Taking as my test case one of the charges that Luke says caused early Christians affliction in Thessalonica, "opposing Caesar's decrees," I examine the validity of the widespread proposal that "opposing Caesar's decrees" refers to oaths of loyalty that provincials swore to the reigning emperor. These oaths are found in six inscriptions and some of them call for the pursuit and death of those disloyal to the emperor. In the first part of this chapter, detailed analyses of these imperial loyalty oaths reveal that they are not imperial decrees, but decisions that local communities passed because of transitions of political power in Rome or to show appreciation for imperial benefaction, both of which curried favor with the new or current regime. Therefore, "Caesar's decrees" cannot be imperial loyalty oaths. In the second part of this chapter, I use the historical context of Thessalonica and inscriptions from the city to demonstrate that Thessalonica owed its prominence, prosperity, and status as a "free city" in the empire to Rome. I suggest that Thessalonica's status as a "free city" forms the background for Luke's "Caesar's decrees." Being a "free city" in the Roman Empire was a status that emperors gave sparingly, one that they also could and did take away. Emperors communicated these decisions to communities via letters containing their decrees. Therefore, "Caesar's decrees" probably refers to letters and edicts from Augustus and successive emperors affirming and reaffirming Thessalonica's status as a "free city."

In the fifth chapter, I show the value of inscriptions in illuminating the lives of people in the Roman world who were not elite males and how this information helps us better understand the more egalitarian nature of early Christianity. I demonstrate through a survey of Latin inscriptions from Philippi that certain women of higher social standing were able to gain prominence in the city by becoming benefactresses of Philippi and by acquiring leadership positions in Philippian public and private cults. Provided that the church in Philippi looked to its environment to organize itself, these inscriptions suggest that Lydia, Syntyche, Euodia, and other women of higher social standing had similar roles in the church. Therefore, certain women in the church in Philippi were probably benefactresses and deacons and possibly overseers.

In my final case study, the sixth chapter, I show how inscriptions illuminate certain difficult NT texts by generating more data to interpret them. I use as my test case the number of the beast in Rev 13:18, which has long been a thorn in the side of scholars. Some exegetes point to one or two graffiti from Pompeii to argue that John the prophet's use of calculating the number of the beast resembles a common Greco-Roman practice. Other scholars propose that calculating a person's Greek name is impossible unless one knows how many letters are in it and that the name of the beast does not refer to a person, but is symbolic, highlighting that it is thrice evil.

I collect a total of twenty-three cases of the calculation of a person's Greek name with numbers in the Roman Empire, most of which are unknown to NT scholars. The archaeological contexts of some of these inscriptions indicate that the calculation of a person's Greek name is not impossible and that the practice was geared toward a group of insiders: the one who made the calculation, sometimes the one about whom the calculation is made, and their associates. John the prophet's use of name calculation for the beast functions similarly. He provides all the information that his audience needs to calculate the beast's name as Nero Caesar.

My conclusion, along with providing summaries of each chapter, presents my third and final purpose of this book: to encourage the reader to begin their work with inscriptions and the NT. My hope is that after reading this book they can add inscriptions to their interpretive toolbox, thereby becoming a more complete student of the NT. One of the greatest epigraphers of the last century, Louis Robert, once characterized the historian of the Greco-Roman world as a one-person orchestra whose instruments are the sources that they use: literature, inscriptions, coins, and archaeology. The duty of the historian, Robert says, is to play every instrument in the orchestra themselves to create the symphony that is the reconstruction of the ancient world.[9] My wish for the reader is that after reading this book they will pick up the instrument of inscriptions along with the proper method of interpreting them to play the complex, sweet symphony that is interpreting the NT.

Finally, I have three words of encouragement for the reader that are related to my use of inscriptions throughout this book. First and foremost, every source that I quote, including the NT, is my own translation. I hope that my translations of inscriptions will aid the reader in their progress of reading and interpreting them. Most inscriptions that I discuss in this book are in Greek, the *lingua franca* of the NT world. If the reader works through the Greek of these inscriptions, they will see quickly that this Greek does not always follow the spelling and grammatical rules that students are taught in beginning and intermediate Koine Greek courses. This difficulty is easily overcome with practice, patience, and perseverance. To aid the reader, I have translated all inscriptions as literally as possible, but as free as necessary.

Second, since Jesus and his earliest disciples lived in Palestine and spoke Aramaic (and possibly Hebrew), I consider some Semitic inscriptions in this book, mostly in my second chapter. To facilitate my discussion of Semitic

9. Louis Robert, "Les épigraphies et L'épigraphie grecque et romaine," in *Opera minora selecta. Epigraphie et antiquités grecque* (Amsterdam: AM Hakkert, 1990), 5:87.

inscriptions, I quote only the portions of these inscriptions pertinent to my argument and I transliterate them. My third and final word of encouragement relates to my use of Latin inscriptions. Because Paul established churches in Roman colonies and sent letters to these churches (such as Corinth and Philippi), I consider Latin inscriptions in this book. Most of these inscriptions are found in chapter 5, where I examine the roles of women in the Philippian church. Translating Latin inscriptions is not as difficult as the reader may think. Due to their formulaic nature and the numerous abbreviations that they contain, Latin inscriptions are easily decipherable with some practice even to those who do not know Latin. (To aid the reader in their future work with Latin inscriptions and because some conventions of Latin inscriptions influenced Greek inscriptions, I have included an appendix containing the most frequent Latin and Greek abbreviations that the reader will come across in their work with inscriptions.)

CHAPTER 1

Engraved for All Time: An Introduction to Inscriptions

Inscriptions are critical for any reconstruction of the Greco-Roman world. Christer Bruun, a Roman historian and leading epigrapher, notes, "No one who seriously engages with the Roman world can afford to neglect the contribution made by epigraphy to our understanding of ancient culture and society."[1] Inscriptions are important for four reasons. First, they are direct sources from antiquity. Unlike Greco-Roman literature, including the NT, inscriptions have not passed through the hands of scribes.[2] This means that when we look at an inscription we are looking at a piece of the ancient world that, depending on where and when it was set up, Jesus, Peter, and Paul may have seen. One such inscription that Jesus, Peter, and Paul probably noticed was set up on the boundary between the Court of Nations and the Court of Women in the temple complex of the God of Israel in Jerusalem. It warns that any gentile who crossed the barrier will face certain death (see Figure 1.1).

1. Christer Bruun, "Latin Inscriptions," in *The Oxford Encyclopedia of Ancient Greece and Rome*, ed. Michael Gagarin (Oxford: Oxford University Press, 2010), 4:79. For introductions to inscriptions see Louis Robert, "Les épigraphies et L'épigraphie grecque et romaine," in *Opera minora selecta. Epigraphie et antiquités grecque* (Amsterdam: AM Hakkert, 1990), 5:65–109; B. F. Cook, *Greek Inscriptions* (Berkeley: University of California Press, 1987); Lawrence Keppie, *Understanding Roman Inscriptions* (Baltimore: Johns Hopkins University Press, 1991); A. Geoffrey Woodhead, *The Study of Greek Inscriptions*, 2nd ed. (London: Bristol Classical Press, 1992); John Bodel, ed., *Epigraphic Evidence: Ancient History from Inscriptions* (London: Routledge, 2001); B. H. McLean, *An Introduction to Greek Epigraphy of the Hellenistic and Roman Periods from Alexander the Great down to the Reign of Constantine (323 B.C.–A.D. 337)* (Ann Arbor: University of Michigan Press, 2002); Alison E. Cooley, *The Cambridge Manual of Latin Epigraphy* (Cambridge: Cambridge University Press, 2012); Christer Bruun and Jonathan Edmondson, eds., *The Oxford Handbook of Roman Epigraphy* (Oxford: Oxford University Press, 2015).

2. Robert, "épigraphies," 5:72.

Figure 1.1. One of the warning inscriptions from the temple complex in Jerusalem from the Istanbul Archaeology Museum, Turkey (© D. Clint Burnett): "No foreigner should enter inside of the partition and precinct around the temple complex. Whoever is seized will be responsible for his own (life) resulting in his death" (μηθένα ἀλλογενῆ εἰσπο|ρεύεσθαι ἐντὸς τοῦ πε|ρὶ τὸ ἱερὸν τρυφάκτου καὶ| περιβόλου. ὃς δ' ἂν λη|φθῇ ἑαυτῶι αἴτιος ἔσ|ται διὰ τὸ ἐξακολου|θεῖν θάνατον) (*CIIP* 2).

Second, inscriptions are prized because they provide evidence for local practices, customs, and religion—what is known as social history. Almost all Greco-Roman literature, especially histories and biographies, focuses on major players and major events that changed the course of history, such as Alexander the Great, Julius Caesar, and Augustus Caesar. Ancient historians and biographers tended to ignore the daily goings-on and customs in most Greco-Roman cities around the Mediterranean unless they affected the larger history of the region. To reconstruct social history, especially of cities in which early Christian churches were established, we have to rely on inscriptions (as well as archaeology and coins). As the great French epigrapher Louis Robert concludes, "Social history is the privilege domain of inscriptions."[3]

Third, inscriptions are vital because so many have survived from antiquity. There are over half a million surviving Greek, Latin, and Semitic inscriptions from the Greco-Roman world known today, and more are dis-

3. Ibid., 5:78–79, *L'histoire sociale est le domaine privilégié des inscriptions.*

covered every year.[4] However, this number is only a fraction of what actually existed in the Greco-Roman world, which means that by the time of early Christianity, inscriptions were almost everywhere around cities: on roadsides leading into and out of cities, on streets corners, agoras and forums, temples, temple complexes, shrines, and the sides of buildings. In short, the Greco-Roman world was a "civilization of epigraphy."[5]

Finally, because of the vast number of surviving inscriptions, there is much variety among them, from love messages scratched on walls of buildings known as graffiti to official government documents inlaid into cityscapes, and just about everything in between. B. H. McLean notes there is not an "aspect of ancient life on which epigraphy does not bear."[6] Therefore, inscriptions can provide evidence of the beliefs and values of individuals who are not elite males, such as artisans, shopkeepers, women, and slaves.[7] For all these reasons, inscriptions are an important resource for interpreting the NT. But to use them properly, the reader must be introduced to them.

I. What Are Inscriptions?

An inscription is a message written on a durable material, a definition that the meaning of the synonym epigraph captures nicely. The English word epigraph is a transliteration of the Greek term that is made up of the noun γραφή meaning "writing" and the preposition ἐπί meaning "on": literarily, an epigraph and thus an inscription is "writing on something."[8] The study of inscriptions is called epigraphy and the person who studies inscriptions is an epigrapher. Inscriptions can be found on numerous materials, but the most common are stone blocks (e.g., marble), metal tablets (often bronze), floors, walls, pottery, bricks, tiles, and lead sheets. The length of epigraphs varies. Some are small and consist of one or two words, like the altar from Philippi dedicated to "the subterranean god" (*SEG* 35.761 = *Philippi II* 092) (see Figure 1.2).

4. John Bodel, "Epigraphy and the Ancient Historian," in Bodel, *Epigraphic Evidence*, 2, 8.

5. Robert, "épigraphies," 5:65–66.

6. McLean, *Introduction to Greek Epigraphy*, 1.

7. Adolf Deissmann, *Light from the Ancient East: The New Testament Illustrated by Recently Discovered Texts of the Graeco-Roman World*, trans. Lionel R. M. Strachan, 4th ed. (New York: Hodder & Stoughton, 1910; repr. Grand Rapids: Baker Books, 1978), 7–9.

8. The English word "inscription" derives from the Latin noun *inscriptio* and the verb *inscribere*, which means "to inscribe." Ancient Latin speakers referred to an inscription as a *titulis*, whence our English word "title" comes: Petronius, *Satyricon* 30, 71; Livy 28.46.16; Suetonius, *Dom.* 5; *Res Gestae* 20.1; *ILS* 5466.

Figure 1.2. Altar dedicated to "the subterranean god" (θεῷ Ὑπογαιῷ) from the Archaeological Museum of Philippi, Greece (© D. Clint Burnett).

Other inscriptions are massive. A rich Roman citizen who lived in Ephesus named Caius Vibius Salutaris had a bequest that he set up for the city inscribed on a wall of the entrance of the theater in Ephesus in 103/104

CE. The inscription totals 568 lines, spans five columns, and takes up 4.94 m of space (*GIBM* 3.481 = *IEph* 27).[9]

In addition to length, inscriptions differ in quality. The letters of some inscriptions, like Salutaris's bequest, were of the highest quality, engraved with uniform letters in straight lines. The letters of other epigraphs show no uniformity, are not composed in straight lines, and even contain grammatical errors. The famous Greek graffito from the Palatine Hill in Rome (one of the city's famous seven hills) shows a Christian worshiping Jesus drawn as a crucified donkey (see Figure 1.3). The inscription comments on the action of the worshiper, but does so with a grammatical error: "Alexamenos worships (his) god" (Ἀλεξαμενὸς σέβετε θεόν).[10] The graffitist misspelled the Greek verb worship (σέβομαι) using a second person plural form "you all worship" (σέβετε) instead of the correct third person singular form "he worships" (σέβεται).

Figure 1.3. Sketch of a Greek graffito from Rome's Palatine Hill depicting a Christian worshiping Jesus, who is drawn as a crucified donkey (© Wikimedia Commons: Public Domain).

9. Guy MacLean Rogers, *The Sacred Identity of Ephesos: Foundation Myths of a Roman City* (London: Routledge, 1991), 19–24, 152–85.

10. Heikki Solin and Marja Itkonen, *Graffiti del Palatino, I Paedagogium* (Helsinki: Institutum Romanum Finlandiae, 1966), 209–12, no. 246.

II. Why Were Inscriptions Set Up?

The large number of surviving inscriptions from the Greco-Roman period raises the question of why so many were set up. The answer is that many epigraphs were erected to advertise messages for future generations to read.[11] One of the best examples highlighting this stated purpose comes from an epigraph that was set up in modern-day southeast Turkey in the mid-first century BCE. During that time, this region of Turkey belonged to a small kingdom allied to Rome called Commagene. One of the kings of Commagene, Antiochus the Great (r. 64–34 BCE), had a tomb constructed for himself on top of a mountain known as Mount Nemrut and decorated it with a group of statues of his gods and himself, each of which is eight to nine m tall (see Figure 1.4).

Figure 1.4. Statues on top of the east terrace of Mount Nemrut that Antiochus the Great of Commagene set up. He placed the inscription in question on the backs of these statues (© Wikimedia Commons: Klearchos Kapoutsis).

Antiochus had an inscription boasting of his accomplishments (and a calendar regulating a post-mortem cult dedicated to the gods, his ancestors, and himself) placed on the backs of these statues. In this epigraph,

11. Robert, "épigraphies," 5:71. For more examples of inscriptions directly stating this function see *OGIS* 332 = *IPergamon* 246; *OGIS* 309; *GIBM* 4.893.

Antiochus states clearly that he set up this tomb complex and its inscription so that his accomplishments would remain "for all time" (*OGIS* 383.7–10). Given that these statues and the epigraph on their backs have lasted over two thousand years, so far Antiochus's dream has come true.

There are, however, two exceptions to epigraphs being durable advertisements.[12] First, individuals living in the Greco-Roman period set up inscriptions inside their homes, which were more decorative and functional than semi-permanent. Second, graffiti were part of ongoing dialogues among those who could read and write such messages. It is clear that graffiti were not meant to last for all time because the plastered walls on which many were composed were often re-plastered, recovered, and repainted in antiquity. Therefore, graffitists knew that their messages would soon be covered over.

Inscriptions were set up as semi-permanent advertisements, but that does not explain why individuals living in the Roman Empire produced more inscriptions than people living in any era of history before or after them. The historian Ramsay MacMullan was the first to draw attention to this distinctive widespread use of epigraphs in the Roman Empire. He notes that inscriptions increase in number in the late first century BCE, peak in the second century CE, and decline in the third century CE. He terms the proclivity for people in the early Roman Empire to set up inscriptions "the Roman epigraphic habit" or, as other historians prefer, "Roman epigraphic culture." Ramsay traces the epigraphic habit to the prosperity of the Roman Empire. Individuals living in the Roman Empire from the late first century BCE to the second century CE believed that their empire would survive and so they produced inscriptions because there was a sense of audience, that is, that later generations would read them. However, the third-century crises—barbarian invasions, civil wars, plagues, and economic recessions—shattered that belief, which caused a decline in the production of inscriptions.[13]

Other historians have tried to single out specific factors to explain the Roman epigraphic habit, such as the spread of Roman citizenship among provincials.[14] But the most probable explanation is that several

12. I am indebted to Robert ("épigraphies," 5:71) for this description of inscriptions.

13. Ramsay MacMullen, "The Epigraphic Habit in the Roman Empire," *AJP* 103 (1982): 233–46.

14. Elizabeth Meyer ("Explaining the Epigraphic Habit in the Roman Empire: The Evidence of Epitaphs," *JRS* 80 [1990]: 74–96) uses epitaphs from the western Roman Empire to propose that the epigraphic culture corresponds to Romanization, specifically the spread of Roman citizenship among provincials and the desire to publicize their newly acquired status. The emperor Caracalla's grant of Roman citizenship to every free denizen of the empire explains the third-century-CE epigraphic decline. Roman

interconnected factors—social, political, and economic—contributed to the epigraphic "big bang" of the Roman universe.[15] One often overlooked factor is the role that Octavian (later known as the emperor Augustus) played in contributing to Roman epigraphic culture. His victory over Marc Antony at the battle of Actium (31 BCE) provided peace and stability to a war-torn empire. To aid in recovery, Octavian funded numerous construction projects all over the Mediterranean basin and commemorated them with inscriptions.[16] Wealthy provincials aped Octavian's philanthropy, which contributed to the Roman epigraphic habit.[17]

III. How Were Inscriptions Made?

Given that so many people set up inscriptions in the Roman Empire and that they were part and parcel of Greco-Roman culture, anyone studying epigraphs should have a basic knowledge of how they were produced. The individuals responsible for producing most inscriptions were stonecutters (Greek: λιθουργοί/Latin: *lapidarii*). These were artisans who crafted stone monuments and inscribed epigraphs on them. We know that stonecutters advertised their services, probably near their shops. One of the only sur-

---

citizenship was no longer prized so people no longer set up inscriptions. Greg Woolf ("Monumental Writing and the Expansion of Roman Society in the Early Empire," *JRS* 86 [1996]: 22–39), using data from the western Roman Empire, posits that rapid changes occurring during the Roman Empire motivated its epigraphic culture. The empire's denizens wished to stave off oblivion so they engraved their identities on stone, which mollified their troubled psyches. For a recent discussion of the empire's epigraphic culture see Francisco Beltán Lloris, "The 'Epigraphic Habit' in the Roman World," in Bruun and Edmondson, *Oxford Handbook*, 131–48.

15. I am indebted to Bodel ("Epigraphy and the Ancient Historian," 7) for the concept of the epigraphic big bang in the Roman universe. The epigraphic habit did not occur uniformly across the Roman Empire. For example, the high point of inscriptional activity in the city of Hierapolis in Asia Minor (Col 4:13) was the second century CE to the first half of the third century CE, which corresponds to the apex of the city's expansion.

16. For a recent and well-balanced discussion of what Roman peace means see Adrian Goldsworthy, *Pax Romana: War, Peace and Conquest in the Roman World* (London: Weidenfeld & Nicolson, 2016). For more information about Augustus, his use of inscriptions, and how this contributed to the Roman epigraphic habit see Géza Alföldy, "Augustus und die Inschriften: Tradition und Innovation Die Geburt der imperialen Epigraphik," *Gymnasium* 98 (1991): 289–324; Bodel, "Epigraphy and the Ancient Historian," 7–8; Lloris, "'Epigraphic Habit,'" 144.

17. In the *Res Gestae* Augustus boasts about his numerous building projects. Suetonius (*Aug.* 28.3) says that Augustus beautified the city, having found it built with mud-bricks and left it built with marble.

viving advertisements is an inscription from Rome. The epigraph tries to grab the attention of passersby by imitating a funerary inscription with its first words, "To the departed spirits" (*D(is) M(anibus)*). This is a stock phrase for Roman tombstones and would have looked out of place near the stonecutter's shop because almost all people were buried outside the limits of Greco-Roman cities (unless they provided some amazing service to the state). When we continue reading the epigraph, we see that the stonecutter is cleverly advertising his services: "Here you can have inscriptions engraved or any work on marble done" (*titulos scri|bendos vel| si quid ope|ris marmor|ari opus fu|erit, hic ha|bes*) (*ILS* 7679).[18]

The engraving of an inscription was a twofold process.[19] The first part of the process was the arrangement of the message on the stone (or *ordinatio*), which consists of the stonecutter receiving the message from his customer and arranging (*ordino*) it on his material. He could receive the message in two ways: either the customer provided the exact message (or *forma*) or the customer dictated the order while the stonecutter took notes.[20] Once the

18. My discussion of how inscriptions were produced has been informed by the following scholars and for extended discussions of the topic see Robert, "épigraphies," 5:72–74; Keppie, *Understanding Roman Inscriptions*, 12–16; McLean, *Introduction to Greek Epigraphy*, 7–18; Giancarlo Susini, *The Roman Stonecutter: An Introduction to Latin Epigraphy*, trans. A. M. Dabrowski (Oxford: Blackwell, 1973); Jonathan Edmondson, "Inscribing Roman Texts: *Officinae*, Layout, and Carving Techniques," in Bruun and Edmondson, *Oxford Handbook*, 111–30. Edmondson (114) discusses a stonecutter's workshop that was excavated at Ostia (one of the main ports for Rome), where archaeologists found unfinished sculpture and fragments of Latin inscriptions. Governmental decrees and laws in Rome, Italy, and Roman colonies were inscribed on bronze tablets, and stonecutters did not produce these. Rather, bronze-smiths engraved inscriptions on bronze tablets while the bronze was still pliable. See Edmondson, 113. Most inscriptions that have survived from the Greco-Roman world are funerary, and marked graves of the deceased. For this reason, stonecutters probably had small monuments on hand to handle the requests of their customers.

19. The main evidence for the twofold inscription producing process is a bilingual Greek and Latin inscription (second century CE) from Palermo (in modern-day Sicily) that says, "Stelae arranged and engraved for sacred buildings and public works here. Inscriptions arranged and engraved for sacred buildings and public works here" (στῆλαι| ἐνθάδε| τυποῦνται καὶ| χαράσσονται| ναοῖς ἱεροῖς| σὺν ἐνεργείαις| δημοσίαις| *tituli| heic| ordinantur et| sculpuntur| aidibus sacreis| cum operum| publicorum* (*IG* XIV 297 = *CIG* 5554 = *ILS* 7680 = *IGRR* II 503). For a discussion of this inscription and the grammatical errors that are in it see Olga Tribulato, "The Stone-Cutter's Bilingual Inscription from Palermo (*IG* XIV 297 = *CIL* X 7296): A New Interpretation," *ZPE* 177 (2011): 131–40.

20. An example of a *forma* is found in Petronius's *Satyricon*, where Trimalchio dictates the exact words and decoration of his funerary monument in his will. His tomb is to be decorated with sailing ships, a symposium scene, and an image of Trimalchio in a toga wearing five gold rings and passing out coins from a bag. Its inscription is to read:

stonecutter had his text, he laid out guidelines on the stone and composed the message first with charcoal, chalk, ink, or a sharp stylus (see Figure 1.5).[21]

Figure 1.5. Greek inscription (*Corinth* 8.3 534) (267–668 CE) with guidelines still visible from the Archaeological Museum of Ancient Corinth, Greece (© D. Clint Burnett).

"Here rests C(aius) Pompeius Trimalchio the freedman of Maecenas. The dignity of a *sexvir* was decreed upon him in absence. He could have been among all the *decurions* in Rome, however he was unwilling. He was pious, strong, and faithful. He started with little money, but he left behind thirty million sesterii. He never listened to a philosopher. Greetings to you!" (*Satyricon* 71). Given that most individuals in the Roman Empire were either illiterate or possessed a low level of writing literacy (see chapter 1.V), the second method of describing the content of inscriptions to a stonecutter probably occurred most.

21. Epigraphers suggest that errors, if there are any in an epigraph, entered an inscription at this first stage. The reason is that the customer's *forma* or the stonecutter's notes were probably written in cursive and this script may have been illegible at times. For a discussion see Susini, *Roman Stonecutter*, 39–49; McLean, *Introduction to Greek Epigraphy*, 14–17.

After drafting the message, the stonecutter began the second part of the process (or *sculptio*) and engraved the text on the stone in capital letters with a mallet (*malleus*), chisel (*scalprum*), and assortment of other tools (see Figure 1.6).

Figure 1.6. Sketch of late first century CE funerary altar of Cossutia Arescusa and Cnaeus Cossutius Cladus depicting the tools that stonecutters used to make inscriptions from the Musei Capitolini, Rome, Italy (used by permission of Robert Singler).

Finally, the stonecutter painted the letters of the inscription with red or black paint to make them more visible (see Figure 1.7).

Figure 1.7. Inscription from the architrave on the Baths of Caracalla (212 CE) in Sardis, Turkey, that has been repainted to demonstrate how the epigraph would have looked in the third century CE when the baths were operative (© D. Clint Burnett).

IV. What Are the Different Types of Inscriptions?

Inscriptions are diverse, so epigraphers have developed categories to facilitate the discussion of this disparate lot. I must stress that these are modern heuristic models and it is unclear if individuals living in the Roman Empire classified inscriptions in these ways. With that warning in mind, epigraphs are broadly classified into two main types: public and private. Public inscriptions were commissioned by civic governments and tend to have a commemorative function. Private inscriptions were commissioned by individuals and do not necessarily have a commemorative function.[22] This classification of epigraphs is not perfect and some inscriptions cross the boundary between public and private. For example, sometimes individuals paid for the construction of public monuments and commemorated them with epigraphs. Nevertheless, the categories of public and private inscriptions are helpful because public inscriptions are official government documents and were made with the best resources available, while the same cannot always be said of private inscriptions.

Epigraphers disagree about subdivisions of public and private inscriptions. Latin and Greek epigraphers tend to approach the classification of epigraphs differently because Greek and Latin inscriptions differ somewhat in content. Take for example two differing classification systems from two recent introductions to Greek and Latin inscriptions:

---

22. For more on private and public inscriptions see McLean, *Introduction to Greek Epigraphy*, 181; Francisco Beltrán Lloris, "Latin Epigraphy: The Main Types of Inscriptions," in Bruun and Edmondson, *Oxford Handbook*, 89–110.

Greek Epigraphy

- Decrees, laws, treaties, and official letters
- Honorific decrees, proxeny decrees, and honorific inscriptions
- Dedications and ex-votos
- Prose and metrical funerary inscriptions
- Legal instruments of common law
- Boundary stones
- Milestones
- Herms
- Sacred laws
- Sacred inscriptions
- Inscriptions on public and private works and buildings
- Accounts and catalogues
- Inscriptions on portable objects
- Quarry and masons' marks
- Graffiti
- Artists' signatures[23]

Latin Epigraphy

- Sacred
- Sepulchral
- Honorific
- Public works
- *Instrumentum domesticum* (or domestic instruments)
- Legal
- Collegial acts
- Calendars and *fasti*
- Wall inscriptions[24]

---

23. McLean, *Introduction to Greek Epigraphy*, 181–214, esp. 182.

24. Ida Calabi Limentani, *Epigrafia Latina*, 4th ed. (Bologna: Cisalpino, 1989), 159–404. Cooley (*Cambridge Manual*, 127–220) acknowledges that these are the traditional categories for Latin inscriptions, but prefers to classify inscriptions based on their function: epitaphs, honorific, building inscriptions, milestones, judicial epigraphy, religious inscriptions, *instrumentum domesticum*, inscriptions within artistic media, graffiti, and rock-cut inscriptions.

My purpose is neither to provide a comprehensive subcategorization of public and private inscriptions nor to discuss every type of epigraph that the reader may encounter. Rather, I wish to introduce the most essential types of public and private inscriptions that the reader will find throughout this book and in their work with epigraphs and the NT. To facilitate my discussion of inscriptions throughout this book, I have opted for a simplified epigraphic subcategorization based on content.[25]

(1) Public Inscriptions
- (1.1) Official Documents
- (1.2) Honorific Inscriptions
- (1.3) Sacred Inscriptions

(2) Private Inscriptions
- (2.1) Epitaphs
- (2.2) Honorific Inscriptions
- (2.3) Sacred Inscriptions
- (2.4) Domestic Inscriptions
- (2.5) Financial Documents
- (2.6) Graffiti
- (2.7) Curse Tablets

(1) Public Inscriptions

Public inscriptions are ones that cities in the Greco-Roman world chose to set up. These epigraphs are not government archives. Cities passed hundreds of pieces of legislation per year and most of these were not engraved as inscriptions. A law that a city passed or a judgment that it rendered was published on a wooden board painted white that was displayed for a set number of days, usually in the agora or forum, and a copy was placed in the city's archives.[26] Any law or decree that a city put in an inscription was essential for civic life and identity and for future citizens to remember. For example, an epigraph found on the Greek island of Astypalaia in the Aegean Sea, originally addressed to the Greek city of Cnidus, consists of a letter that the emperor Augustus sent to the latter's council and citizen body in 6 BCE. An embassy from Cnidus had approached Augustus because of a judgment

25. For more introduction on epigraphic categories and subcategories see McLean, *Introduction to Greek Epigraphy*; Cooley, *Cambridge Manual*.

26. Robert, "épigraphies," 5:70–71.

of the city. A couple from Cnidus had been attacked in their home for three successive nights, and on the third night they ordered one of their slaves to go upstairs and empty excrement from one of their chamber pots on the head of their attackers. The slave did so, but accidentally let go of the chamber pot, which fell onto one of the attackers, killing him. The council and the citizen body of Cnidus had found the couple guilty of murder. Augustus wrote to encourage Cnidus to overturn this verdict, to find the attackers guilty, and then "to make the records in your public archive agree" (τὰ ἐν τοῖς δημ[οσίοις] ὑμῶν ὁμολογεῖν γράμματα) with this decision (*IG* XII.3 174 = *SIG*[3] 780 = *IGRR* IV 1031 = *RDGE* 67). Presumably, the council and body of citizens of Cnidus obliged Augustus's request and altered their public records because an inscription was set up chronicling the entire affair.

(1.1) Official Documents

Official documents cover a wide range of topics, the most important of which are decrees, letters, inventories, treaties, and law codes. Although cities were under the authority of the Roman Empire, for the most part they governed themselves. Councils (βουλαί) and citizen bodies (δῆμοι) passed legislation in Greek cities. Some Greek cities joined a federation or league (called a κοινόν in Greek), such as the league of Asia, and these federations occasionally passed legislation that applied to all the Greek cities in the league. In Rome, Italian municipalities, and Roman colonies, local magistrates (*duumviri*, *aediles*, and *decurions*) and senates (*senatus*) passed legislation.

Decrees

Engraved decrees in Greco-Roman cities were often placed in highly trafficked areas such as temple complexes, theaters, and agoras or forums so that people might see them.[27] Greek and Latin decrees differ in their structure and the type of material they were inscribed on, but both types of decrees are formulaic. Greek decrees were generally inscribed on marble or limestone. They usually begin with some kind of preamble. The gods were typically consulted in the decision-making process and sometimes Greek cities wished to showcase this by adding the words "gods" (θεοί) or "to good fortune" (ἀγαθῆι τύχηι) at the beginning of the preamble.[28] Afterward, there

27. E.g., *SIG*[3] 609, 630, 664, 694; *OGIS* 762. For a discussion of the displaying of inscriptions see John Ma, "Epigraphy and the Display of Authority," in *Epigraphy and the Historical Sciences*, Proceedings of the British Academy 177, ed. John Davies and John Wilkes (Oxford: Oxford University Press, 2012), 133–58.

28. E.g., *IG* II[2] 1140; *IG* X.2.1 259.

is a reference to the approval of the city's council, body of citizens, or both. The stock phrase is, "It seemed good to the council and the body of citizens" (ἔδοξεν τῆι βουλῆι καὶ τῶι δήμωι).[29] The last portion of a preamble is the date. A Greek decree is dated by the tenure of civic eponymous magistrates, which differed from city to city. For example, the eponymous magistrates from Thessalonica were called *politarchs*, which is a fact about the city that Luke correctly notes.[30] Following the preamble, a decree can mention the person who sponsored the legislation and then provide the decree itself.[31] To provide a famous example also discussed in chapter 3, the league of Asia decreed that the New Year of the calendars of the Greek cities of Asia should be changed to correspond to Augustus's birthday (September 23). The preamble begins with a reference to the league of Asia (the Greeks of Asia) and the person who sponsored the bill (the imperial high priest Apollonius), which also serves to date the decree, and then the decree itself follows (*OGIS* 458 = *IPriene* 105).

Latin decrees were engraved on bronze tablets instead of stone (see Figure 1.8).[32] This choice of material means that fewer Latin decrees survive because bronze tablets were melted down and reused in the Greco-Roman world, late antiquity, and up to the modern period. Like Greek decrees, Latin decrees begin with a preamble, the first portion of which names the person who summoned the senate's meeting. Afterward, the preamble provides the date of the meeting and even where it occurred. The final portion of the preamble gives a list of witnesses present at the senatorial meeting. The decree itself is found next and ends with a reference to the senate's approval (*censuere*).[33]

---

29. E.g., *GIBM* 3.418, 420, 449; *SIG*³ 278.

30. E.g., *IG* X.2.1 31, 37, etc.; Acts 17:6.

31. My discussion of Greek decrees has been informed by Woodhead, *Study of Greek Inscriptions*, 37–39; McLean, *Introduction to Greek Epigraphy*, 215–25.

32. Pliny says that public constitutions were inscribed (*publicae constitutions inciduntur*) on bronze tablets (*tabulis aereis*) to ensure their durability (*ad perpetuitatem monumentorum*) (*Nat.* 34.99). Suetonius says that after fire damaged the temple of Captioline Jupiter in Rome Vespasian had three thousand bronze tablets re-engraved (*Vesp.* 8). The text of the *Res Gesetae* and the discovery of copies of it highlight the differences in material used in Roman and Greek epigraphic culture. The document was engraved on bronze tablets in Rome in front of Augustus's mausoleum, but the surviving copies of the *Res Gestae* from Greek cities and territories such as Pisidia Antioch in Galatia were inscribed on stone. For information on the *Res Gestae* and the inscriptions that attest to it see Alison E. Cooley, *Res Gestae Divi Augusti: Text, Translation and Commentary* (Cambridge: Cambridge University Press, 2009).

33. My discussion on Latin decrees draws on the work of Cooley, *Cambridge Manual*, 5–15, 168–77; Gregory Rowe, "The Roman State: Laws, Lawmaking, and Legal Documents," in Bruun and Edmondson, *Oxford Handbook*, 299–310. For actual Latin

Figure 1.8. Copy of Table Number 9 from the bronze tablet containing the municipal law of Taranto (89–62 BCE) from Museo Nazionale Archeologico, Taranto, Italy. The original is in the Museo Archeologico Nazionale di Napoli, Naples, Italy (© D. Clint Burnett).

For example, the senate in Rome passed a decree curtailing the worship of Bacchus (also known as Dionysus among the Greeks) in Italy (186 BCE). At that time, Bacchus's cult was not part of official state religion in Rome. Evidently, the cult had a well-defined leadership structure, encouraging the comingling of men and women from various social classes in secret meetings, the collection of a common fund, and the swearing of oaths. The

decrees see Robert K. Sherk, ed., *The Municipal Decrees of the Roman West* (Buffalo: State University of New York at Buffalo, 1970). For examples of Latin decrees translated into Greek see *SIG*^{3} 646, 664, 747; *IGRR* IV 262.

senate considered these aspects seditious and limited the worship of Bacchus in Italy.[34] The decree's preamble lists the persons who summoned the senatorial meeting (Quintus Marcius and Spurius Postumius), when (Oct 7, 186 BCE) and where (Bellonae's temple in Rome) the meeting occurred, and the meeting's witnesses (Lucius Valerius and Quintus Minucius). After the preamble, the decree proscribes certain aspects of the cult and ends by noting that the senate in Rome has approved it and that the decree must be published in public assembles of the cities of Italy for no less than three market days (*ILS* 18).

Letters

Letters are found mostly in cities of the Greek East and are missives written in Greek that Hellenistic kings, Roman generals, Roman consuls, the senate in Rome, and Roman emperors sent to cities and that these cities in turn inscribed on stone. Most letters are responses to requests of embassies and almost all the letters found in epigraphs are favorable decisions.[35] In one case, however, the city of Aphrodisias (in modern-day Turkey) set up an inscription containing a letter to another city, Samos (an island off the western coast of modern-day Turkey), because said letter mentioned Aphrodisias in a favorable light. Aphrodisias engraved a letter that Augustus sent to Samos because the letter noted that the emperor considered Aphrodisias to be special. Augustus had granted Aphrodisias the status of a "free city" in the Roman Empire after the emperor's civil war with Marc Antony ended in 31 BCE. Being a "free city" meant that Aphrodisias was politically autonomous and did not have to pay tribute to Rome. In 27 BCE, Samos petitioned Augustus for the right to be a "free city" like Aphrodisias. In the letter to Samos, the emperor declined the request, stating that being a "free city" is the greatest honor that he can bestow and that he does not do it lightly. Somehow Aphrodisias found out about the letter, acquired a copy of it, and in the second or third century CE carved it on the archive wall located in its theater (*IAph2007* 8.32) (see Figure 1.9).

---

34. For a discussion of the suppression of the Bacchanalia in Italy see Mary Beard, John North, and Simon Price, *Religions of Rome* (Cambridge: Cambridge University Press, 1998), 1:91–96.

35. For letters sent to Greek cities in the Hellenistic period see C. Bradford Welles, ed., *Royal Correspondence in the Hellenistic World: A Study in Greek Epigraphy*, Studia Historica 28 (Rome: L'erma di Bretschneider, 1966). For letters sent to Greek cities in the Roman period see James H. Oliver, ed., *Greek Constitutions of Early Roman Emperors from Inscriptions and Papyri* (Philadelphia: American Philological Society, 1989).

Figure 1.9. The archive wall from the theater at Aphrodisias, Turkey, where Augustus's letter to Samos is engraved (© D. Clint Burnett).

Inventories

Inventories are inscriptions that are lists of any kind, sometimes with accounting purposes. For instance, inventories for Greek temples were commonly engraved either on the temple walls or on stelae in temple complexes to provide checks and balances for how the money of the gods was being used.[36] A marble stele from Delphi contains a list of contributors who paid for the rebuilding of Pythian Apollo's temple in 360 BCE (*CID* 2.4), and another list (197 BCE) contains the persons on whom Delphi had bestowed the honor of not having to wait in line for its famous oracle (or the honor of proxeny) (*SIG*[3] 585). In chapter 3, I discuss an inscription that contains a law regulating a grain fund of Samos that paid for monthly distributions of grain to its citizens. More than two-thirds of the text is a list of contributors to the grain fund and how much they donated.

Treaties

Treaties are diplomatic agreements made between cities, rulers, or even monarchs and their subjects. Treaties tend to stipulate the terms of peace,

36. For more on inventories in Greek inscriptions see Woodhead, *Study of Greek Inscriptions*, 40.

how long the peace should last, and include a provision that both parties have the same friends and enemies.[37] Greek treaties usually end with the parties swearing by the gods and invocating a divine curse on the party who breaks the peace.[38] In chapter 4, I discuss six inscriptions that are technically treaties (although they are one-sided): imperial loyalty oaths or oaths of fealty that provincials swore to reigning emperors. These imperial loyalty vows can be divided into two types: Greek and Latin. Greek loyalty oaths tend to be communal in nature (the verbs and pronouns are first-person plural) and the oath-takers promise to be well-disposed (εὐνοέω) to the reigning emperor and to be a friend or an enemy to whomever the emperor desires. Latin imperial fealty vows are taken individually (the verbs and pronouns are in the first-person singular) and focus on stamping out seditious behavior on land and sea.

Law Codes

Each Greco-Roman city had its own law code, which is a fact that the Jewish philosopher Philo acknowledges. He notes that although cities of his day are under the power of the Roman Empire, they each have their own constitutions, laws, and customs, which are not identical (πολιτείαις χρῶνται διαφερούσαις καὶ νόμοις οὐχὶ τοῖς αὐτοῖς, ἄλλα γὰρ παρ' ἄλλοις ἔθη καὶ νόμιμα παρεξευρημένα καὶ προστεθειμένα) (Philo, *Joseph* 29). Many of these law codes to which Philo refers were published in the form of inscriptions.[39] Some of the earliest ones come from Athens. In 409/408 BCE, the city voted to re-publish one of the famous seventh-century-BCE Athenian lawgiver Draco's laws on homicide (*IG* I³ 104). The most famous set of laws from the Roman world are the Twelve Tables, which are said to be a collection of laws made in Rome in 450/449 BCE inscribed on twelve bronze tablets and displayed in Rome for anyone to see (Livy 3.57).[40]

37. E.g., *OGIS* 762; *SIG*³ 588; *IG* XII.2 510 = *IGRR* IV 2 = *SIG*³ 693; 1 Macc 8:22–32.

38. E.g., *OGIS* 762; *IG* XII.2 510 = *IGRR* IV 2 = *SIG*³ 693; *IG* XII.3 173 = *IGRR* IV 1028.

39. For more on Greek laws and inscriptions see Rosalind Thomas, "Writing, Law, and Written Law," in *The Cambridge Companion to Ancient Greek Law*, ed. Michael Gagarin and David Cohen (Cambridge: Cambridge University Press, 2005), 41–60.

40. For more on Roman laws see M. H. Crawford, ed., *Roman Statutes*, 2 vols. (London: Institute of Classical Studies, 1996).

(1.2) Honorific Inscriptions

Honorific inscriptions are honorary decrees, building inscriptions, and boundary markers that cities set up to honor benefactors.[41] The reason that such inscriptions were set up relates to the infrastructure of Greco-Roman cities. Taxes that cities collected did not typically fund building works or the repair of civic infrastructure. Those tasks fell to wealthy men and sometimes women who bettered their cities.[42] Benefactors were willing to spend their personal funds in such ways to advance their political and religious careers and status within their communities. In the Greco-Roman political system, elites vied against each other for political and religious posts, which created a competitive atmosphere with wealthy members of communities trying to outdo one another to gain the attention, respect, and the vote of the larger populace. Greeks and Romans had a name for this struggle: the love of honor/rivalry (φιλοτιμία/*ambitio*), which Pliny the Elder (23–79 CE) calls "the most civilized form of rivalry" (*humanissima ambitione*) (*Nat.* 34.9).[43]

The reason that such beneficent actions aided elites in their political and religious careers was that cities publicized their benefactions in epigraphs, which occurred in three ways. First, cities passed honorific decrees lauding benefactors for their munificent deeds and bestowing honors on them such as crowns, privileged access to oracles (or proxeny decrees), citizenship, etc. Such decrees resembled the ones that I have already discussed. Heralds often read these honorific decrees aloud at festivals or games to ensure that the populace was aware of the benefactor and why the city honored them.[44] Second, cities allowed benefactors to engrave their name on the building

41. For more on Greek honorary decrees see Woodhead, *Study of Greek Inscriptions*, 42–43; McLean, *Introduction to Greek Epigraphy*, 196–97, 228–44. For more on Latin honorary decrees see Cooley, *Cambridge Manual*, 145–52.

42. For more on benefaction in Greek cities see Philippe Gauthier, *Les cites grecques et leurs bienfaiteurs*, BCHSup 12 (Paris: École française d'Athènes, 1985). For more on the importance of benefactors in the upkeep of cities in the Roman Empire see Marietta Horster, "Urban Infrastructure and Euergetism outside the City of Rome," in Bruun and Edmondson, *Oxford Handbook*, 515–36.

43. Pliny says that this "most civilized desire for honors" "preserves the memory of persons as their honors are inscribed and read for eternity" (*propagarique memoria hominum et honores legend aevo basibus inscribi*) (*Nat.* 34.9). For more on the love of honor among elites in the Roman Empire see Lloris, "'Epigraphic Habit,'" 132.

44. According to Aristotle, a properly functioning city honors its benefactors with "sacrifices, memorials in meters and verses, gifts, sanctuaries, privileged seating, public burial, statues, and food that belongs to the people" (*Rhet.* 1361A). The most common rewards for benefactors were public praise, a crown, and some form of precedence, either at a local oracle or games: e.g., *Sardis* 7.1 4; *SIG*³ 624, 630, 656, 700.

that they financed. For example, Marcus Agrippa, Augustus's son-in-law and the friend of Herod the Great, built the Pantheon in Rome in 25 BCE and commemorated its construction with a Latin inscription on the horizontal beam atop the columns in the front of the Pantheon or its architrave (see Figure 1.10). The name of the building, the Pantheon, is missing from the epigraph because it was obvious which building Agrippa had built: "Marcus Agrippa, the son of Lucius, consul three times built (this temple)" (*M · Agrippa · L · F · Co(n)s(ul) · tertium · fecit*) (*CIL* 6.896 = *ILS* 129).

Figure 1.10. Pantheon, Rome, Italy (© D. Clint Burnett).

If the construction project was a restoration, epigraphs tend to acknowledge this fact by noting that the benefactor restored the building in question.[45] However, this is not always the case. The emperor Hadrian (r. 117–138 CE) restored the Pantheon in Rome, but did not alter the inscription that Agrippa had placed on it.

Third, cities encouraged benefactors to fund civic projects by erecting their statues in either agoras or forums in and near the buildings that they constructed.[46] In such cases, inscriptions were placed on the bases of statues. These epigraphs tend to be short. Most such inscriptions provide the name

45. McLean, *Introduction to Greek Epigraphy*, 196–97, 228–44.

46. E.g., *SIG*³ 616.

of the benefactor, the reason that they are honored, and who is honoring them. Some of them describe the political and religious career (or *cursus honorum*) of the benefactor.[47] For example, a wealthy benefactress from Pompeii named Eumachia paid for the construction of a building with a porch, covered passage, and colonnade in the city's forum between 9 BCE and 22 CE. An inscription was set up commemorating the construction project (*ILS* 3785) and then an association of Pompeian wool-workers honored Eumachia for her benefaction by setting up a statue of her in a niche inside the building (see Figure 1.11).

Figure 1.11. Statue of the Pompeian benefactress Eumachia from a niche in Eumachia's building, Pompeii, Italy (© D. Clint Burnett).

47. Cooley, *Cambridge Manual*, 145–52.

The base of the statue contains an inscription identifying Euchamia, listing her *cursus honorum* (she is a public priestess), and providing who it was that honored her (the wool-workers): "The wool-workers (set up this statue of) Eumachia, Lucius's daughter, public priestess" (*Eumachiae · L(uci)· F(ilia) | sacerd(oti) · publ(icae)| fullones*) (*ILS* 6368) (see Figure 1.12).[48]

Figure 1.12. Latin inscription from Eumachia's statue base, Pompeii, Italy (© D. Clint Burnett).

Greco-Roman cities were defined by space and filled with boundary markers (*termini/cippi*). These inscriptions are considered honorific because they tend to name a governmental official or an emperor, thereby honoring them. There were boundary markers delimiting when one city's territory ended and another's began. For example, in 54/55 CE, the city of Sagalassus in the province of Galatia (in modern-day Turkey) had a border dispute with the nearby village Tymbrianassus, which belonged to the future emperor Nero. A local governor, Quintus Petronius Umber, and an imperial legate, Lucius Pupius Prassens, were forced to solve the dispute with the blessing of the emperor Claudius before he died in 54 CE. They decided where Sagalassus's territory began and erected boundary markers to demarcate it. The land to the right of these boundary markers belonged to Sagalassus and the land to the left belonged to Tymbrianassus (*SEG* 19.765).

48. August Mau, *Pompeii: Its Life and Art*, trans. Francis W. Kelsey (London, 1899), 110–18.

To date a total of seven boundary markers attesting to this dispute have been found (see Figure 1.13).[49]

Figure 1.13. One of seven extant boundary markers that were set up to solve a territory dispute between the city of Sagalassus and the village of Tymbrianassus from the Burdur Museum, Burdur, Turkey (© D. Clint Burnett).

49. For a discussion of this boundary marker from Galatia see Tom Elliott, "Epigraphic Evidence for Boundary Disputes in the Roman Empire" (PhD diss., University of North Carolina at Chapel Hill, 2004), 204–6.

Within cities themselves, there were boundary markers demarcating public versus private space. Archaeologists have found several of these markers in their excavations at Pompeii and some are simple, containing three Latin letters: "Public space of the Pompeians" (*L(ocus) P(ublicus) P(ompeianorum)*) (*AE* [2006]: 290). There were boundary markers inside cities delineating sacred space from profane. The example that opened this chapter, the warning sign to gentiles from the temple complex in Jerusalem, is one such case. It cautions that no gentile may pass by it, or they will forfeit their life. Space was particularly important for religion in Rome, in Italian cities, and in colonies of Rome. The reason is that certain Roman religious practices could not occur outside the formal boundary of the city, called the *pomerium*. For example, augurs were Roman priests who interpreted omens (most often from the flight of birds) to determine the auspices or the will of the gods. The auspices could be taken only inside the *pomerium*. Roman priests established a location's *pomerium* by plowing a line in the ground with two oxen and marking it with boundary markers.[50] An example of such a boundary marker comes from Capua, Italy, where Octavian extended the colony's *pomerium* in 36 BCE: "By the command of the victorious general Caesar, the plow was drawn here" (*Iussu Imp. Caesaris | qua aratrum ductum est*) (*CIL* 10.3825.4) (see Figure 1.14).[51]

Finally, there were even boundary markers on the sides of Roman roads. These were milestones (*milliaria*), which were some of the most ubiquitous boundary markers in the Roman Empire. Augustus set up the so-called "golden milestone" (*milliarium aureum*) in the forum of Rome near Saturn's temple in 20 BCE, cataloguing the major cities of the empire and their distances from the capital. Every Roman road in the Roman Empire was said to begin at the golden milestone (Suetonius, *Otho* 6.2; Dio Cassius 54.8.3–5).[52] Milestones (1.8 m in height) were set up at every Roman mile (1,481 m) informing travelers of the distance coming and going to the nearest city. Some of these contained the name of the person responsible for the construction and/or repair of the road. In the Roman Empire, this

50. Beard, North, and Price, *Religions of Rome*, 1:21–23.

51. Laura Chioffi, "[---] *Capys* [---] *cum moenia sulco signaret* [---]. Un nuovo termine di pomerium da Capua," in *Se déplacer dans l'Empire romain Approches épigraphiques. XVIIIe rencontre franco-italienne d'épigraphie du monde romain, Bordeaux 7–8 octobre 2011*, ed. Ségolène Demougin and Milagros Navarro Caballero (Paris: de Boccard, 2014), 237–39.

52. For more on the "golden milestone" in Rome see Adriano la Regina, *Archaeological Guide to Rome*, trans. Richard Sadleir (Milan: Electa, 2017), 25–26.

Figure 1.14. Boundary marker establishing the extension of Capua's *pomerium* from Museo Archeologico Nazionale di Napoli, Naples, Italy (© D. Clint Burnett).

person was most often the emperor.[53] An example of a Roman milestone is a bilingual Latin and Greek one from the famous road on which Paul travelled from Neapolis to Philippi and thence to Thessalonica, the Via Egnatia (Acts 16:11–12; 17:1). This boundary marker was found near Thessalonica and

53. For more on Roman milestones see Keppie, *Understanding Roman Inscriptions*, 60–69; McLean, *Introduction to Greek Epigraphy*, 187–88; Cooley, *Cambridge Manual*, 159–68.

tells travelers that they are: "260 miles [from Dyrrachium]. Gnaeus Egnatius, son of Gaius; Gnaeus Egnatius, son of Gaius proconsul of the Romans: 260 miles [from Dyrrachium]." (*CC | X| Cn(aeus) · Egnati(us) · C(ai) · f(ilius)|* Γναῖος Ἐγνάτιος Γαίου| ἀνθύπατος|Ῥωμαίων| σξ´.)[54]

(1.3) Sacred Inscriptions

The final type of public inscriptions is sacred epigraphs, which consist of religious laws, calendars, lists of priests, and dedications. Religious laws resemble public decrees in their form, and are legislation regarding cults that cities supported financially and religious associations that they allowed to exist.[55] These epigraphs are more common in Greek epigraphy than Latin, once again, due to the fact that Latin inscriptional decrees were engraved on bronze, which was melted down and later reused. Often sacred laws were deposited in temple complexes or placed on the front porches of temples so that those who entered these spaces could read them (if they knew how). For example, the inscription that changed the calendars of the Greek cities of Asia's New Year to correspond to Augustus's birthday (September 23) is a sacred law because it deals with time, which affects when one worships the gods, and copies of the decree were set up in the temples of Augustus in Asia (*OGIS* 458 = *IPriene* 105).

Every Greco-Roman city (and in rarer cases provinces in the Roman Empire) had its own calendar. These calendars prescribed when the festivals of the gods occurred, when courts could be convened, and even the most effective days for planting and harvesting crops.[56] To return the previous example, the decree of the league of Asia changing the New Year so that it occurred on Augustus's birthday was very unusual because it demanded that the Greek cities in the league of Asia standardize their calendars, thereby altering their centuries-old practices and even requiring that the election of civic magistrates take place on the same month in every city in the Asian federation (*OGIS* 458 = *IPriene* 105).

Another type of religious calendar was agricultural. In the Roman Empire, the gods were the ultimate source of rain and favorable growing conditions, so people performed certain rites to ensure good harvests.[57] One of the ways that

---

54. Catherine Romiopoulou, "Un nouveau milliaire de la Via Egnatia," *BCH* 98 (1974): 813–16. For more examples of such milestones see *IGRR* IV 880, 1659.

55. For a discussion of sacred laws see Woodhead, *Study of Greek Inscriptions*, 41; McLean, *Introduction to Greek Epigraphy*, 189–92.

56. For more on calendars in Greek cities see McLean, *Introduction to Greek Epigraphy*, 169–77. For more on the calendars in Rome, Italian cities, and colonies see Lloris, "Latin Epigraphy," 101–3.

57. Beard, North, and Price, *Religions of Rome*, 1:45.

individuals facilitated farming and the religious rites associated with it was by producing agricultural calendars. These calendars give the days of each month and their length, the corresponding zodiac sign and the patron god for that month, and the agricultural chores and festivals that must be performed. There are two such calendars that have survived from Rome. One of them is engraved on a marble block, dates to the first century CE, and has three months on each side along with the above information (*CIL* 6.2305) (see Figure 1.15).

Figure 1.15. Agricultural calendar from Rome (first century CE) depicting the months of July, August, and September from the Museo Archeologico Nazionale di Napoli, Naples, Italy (© D. Clint Burnett).

Sometimes cities and temples compiled lists of priests to honor those who served the gods in their cults. These lists were occasionally inscribed either on the walls of the temples or on stelae set up in the temple complexes. For instance, one of our best pieces of evidence for imperial cultic activity in the province of Galatia comes from an inscription on the wall of the front porch of the temple of Augustus and Roma in Ancyra (the modern-day capital of Turkey). The epigraph provides the names of high priests of the cult of Augustus and Roma, when they served (from 5 BCE to 17 CE), and what benefactions they provided in cities in the province, including dedications that facilitated the worship of Augustus, Livia, and Tiberius, such as the construction of the temple of Augustus and Roma (*CIG* 4039 = *OGIS* 533 = *IGRR* III 157 = *GLIA* 2).

The final subcategory of sacred inscriptions is public dedications, which covers any object dedicated to gods or rulers. These objects could be as big as temples or as little as small altars. The inscriptions on these dedications tend to be standardized. The epigraphs contain the name of the dedicator (the governing body), the god or ruler to whom the object is dedicated, and sometimes the reason for the dedication. Often public dedications omit the Greek or Latin verb "to dedicate" and do not mention what is being dedicated because that was typically apparent.[58] For example, between 27 BCE and 14 CE the city of Priene (in modern-day Turkey) rededicated the temple of its patron goddess, Athena, to include the emperor Augustus because of some imperial benefaction. The city re-inscribed the architrave of the temple with the following inscription: "The citizen-body dedicated (this temple) to Athena Polias and to the victorious general Caesar God Augustu[s], son of god" (Ὁ δῆμος Ἀθηναῖ [Π]ολιάδι καὶ [Αὐτ]οκράτορι Καίσαρι θεοῦ υἱῶι θεῶι Σεβαστῶ[ι καθιέρωσεν]) (*IPriene* 157) (see Figure 1.16).

(2) Private Inscriptions

The second major category of inscriptions is private epigraphs. They are classified as such because they were set up by individuals, not local or imperial governments. These inscriptions can be divided into seven subcategories based on their content: (2.1) epitaphs, (2.2) honorific inscriptions,

58. For more on Greek public dedications see Woodhead, *Study of Greek Inscriptions*, 41–42; McLean, *Introduction to Greek Epigraphy*, 246–59. For more on Latin public dedications see Cooley, *Cambridge Manual*, 156–59.

(2.3) sacred inscriptions (2.4) domestic inscriptions, (2.5) financial documents, (2.6) graffiti, and (2.7) curse tablets.

Figure 1.16. Architrave inscription from the temple of Athena and Augustus, Priene, Turkey (© D. Clint Burnett).

(2.1) Epitaphs

Epitaphs, or funerary inscriptions, make up most of our extant inscriptions from the Greco-Roman world.[59] People from all social classes appear to have set up epitaphs, so they vary in size, quality, and content. It is important to remember that although many epitaphs have survived, they were originally part of funerary monuments that no longer exist. This situation places us at a disadvantage in interpreting such inscriptions, because it is preferable to study these monuments and their inscriptions together to ensure proper interpretation of both. Therefore, most of our interpretations of funerary inscriptions will be somewhat incomplete. This limitation notwithstanding, some epitaphs contain the deceased's name only, others display messages encouraging passersby to read them, and still others boast of the deceased's accomplishments.[60] For example, one funerary inscription (70–96 CE) from Hierapolis (Turkey) (cf. Col 4:13) found in situ on a large tomb notes that a certain Titus Flavius Zeuxis (see Figure 1.17) sailed to Italy over seventy times during his life:

59. Bodel ("Epigraphy and the Ancient Historian," 30) estimates that epitaphs make up almost two-thirds of all surviving Greek and Latin epigraphy from the Roman world.

60. For more on Greek epitaphs see Woodhead, *Study of Greek Inscriptions*, 43–46; McLean, *Introduction to Greek Epigraphy*, 260–88. For more on Latin epitaphs see Cooley, *Cambridge Manual*, 128–45.

Figure 1.17. Tomb of Titus Flavius Zeuxis, Hierapolis, Turkey (© D. Clint Burnett).

"[T]itus [Fla]vius Zeuxis, worker who s[a]iled around Cape Maleon to I[t]aly during seventy-two sailings, built this memorial for himself and his children, Flavius Theodorus and Flavius Theudas, and to whomever they make room for with them" ([T]ίτος| [Φλά]ουι{ι}ος Ζεῦξις ἐργαστὴς,| [πλ]-εύσας ὑπὲρ Μαλέαν εἰς Ἰ|[τ]αλίαν πλόας ἑβδομήκοντα| δύο κατεσκεύασεν τὸ μνημεῖ|ον ἑαυτῷ καὶ τοῖς τέκνοις Φλα|ουίῳ Θεοδώρῳ καὶ Φλαουίῳ| Θευδᾷ καὶ ᾧ ἂν ἐκεῖνοι| συνχωρήσωσιν) (*IHierapJ* 51) (see Figure 1.18).[61]

61. Tullia Ritti, *An Epigraphic Guide to Hierapolis of Phrygia (Pamukkale): An Archaeological Guide*, trans. Paul Arthur (Istanbul: Ege Yayinlari, 2006), 67–70, no. 9.

Figure 1.18. Inscription from the tomb of Titus Flavius Zeuxis, Hierapolis, Turkey (© D. Clint Burnett).

Latin epitaphs differ from their Greek counterparts in that they are formulaic and include abbreviations and sometimes important biographic details about the deceased. The three most common abbreviations are D · M/D · M · S, H · S · E, and VIX · ANN. The first stands for the Latin phrase *Dis Manibus* or *Dis Manibus Sacrum*, which means "To the departed spirits/to the departed sacred spirits." The second abbreviation stands for the sentence *hic situs est*, which means "so-and-so is buried here." The third and final abbreviation stands for the Latin sentence *vixit annos*, which means "she or he lived . . ." The length of the deceased's life in an epitaph is a Latin epigraphic convention; if a Greek funerary inscription recounts the age of the deceased it evidences Latin influence. Such information can help to establish important demographic information about life expectancy in certain cities and regions of the Roman Empire.[62] Latin epitaphs of elite men and women usually contain their *cursus honorum*, and some Latin funerary inscriptions of non-elites list the deceased's profession. One such epitaph, which may have implications about the gender of Paul the apostle's secretaries, is from Rome, and says that the deceased is a female strenographer or secretary who wrote in Greek: "To the sacred deceased spirits. For Hapate, stenographer of Greek, who lived twenty-five years. Pittosus set up (this tomb) for his sweetest wife"

62. Latin epitaphs do not contain information that we consider important such as the date of birth and the date of death. See Cooley, *Cambridge Manual*, 128–45.

([D(is)] · M(anibus · S(acrum)| Hapateni| notariae | Gr(a)ec(a)e · qu(a)e| vix · ann · xxv| Pittosus · fe|cit · coniugi| dulcissim(a)e) (*ILS* 7760).

(2.2) Honorific Inscriptions

Individuals and associations set up honorary inscriptions to show appreciation for their patrons. Such epigraphs follow the same form as public honorary inscriptions discussed above (1.2) with the exception that individuals or associations, and not governing bodies, dedicated the monument to their benefactors. Private dedications often cross the boundary between private and public inscriptions because they were set up in public places, which required official permission. For example, between 4 and 2 BCE two freedmen of Marcus Agrippa, Mazaeus and Mithridates, erected a monumental gateway to Ephesus's southern agora to honor their patron, Agrippa. This gateway was massive and originally included statues of members of the imperial family.[63] Mazaeus and Mithridates commemorated their building activity with inscriptions, one of which says: "Mithridates (set up this monumental gate) for his patrons Marcus Agrippa, son of Lucius, three times consul, victorious general, six times tribunican power, Julia, Caesar Augusti, and their children" (*M(arco) · Agrippae · L(ucii) · f(ilio) · co(n)s(uli) · tert(ium) · Imp(eratori) · tribunic(iae)| potest(atis) · VI · et| Iuliae · Caesaris · Augusti · fil(iae)| Mithridates patronis*) (*IEph* 3006) (see Figure 1.19).

Figure 1.19. Gate of Mazaeus and Mithradates at Ephesus, Turkey, with a dedicatory inscription to the imperial family (© D. Clint Burnett).

63. Peter Scherrer, "The City of Ephesos: From the Roman Period to Late Antiquity," in *Ephesos: Metropolis of Asia; An Interdisciplinary Approach to its Archaeology, Religion, and Culture*, ed. Helmut Koester, HTS 41 (Cambridge: Harvard University Press, 1995), 6.

(2.3) Sacred Inscriptions

Like many religious individuals throughout history, people who lived in the Roman Empire made vows to their gods. Many of these vows were made in exchange for safety during travel, childbirth, and battle, or healing of a disease. In such cases, persons promised to dedicate something to the gods provided that they answered their prayers. The objects that people dedicated are called votives or ex-votos and the inscriptions on them varied.[64] Some contain the vower's name, a description of the object that they dedicated, and the name of the god to whom it is dedicated. Other ex-votos are much simpler and have only the name of the relevant god. Take, for example, Figure 1.2 at the beginning of this chapter, which is an ex-voto that is an altar dedicated to a subterranean god worshiped at Philippi.

(2.4) Domestic Inscriptions

The excavations of houses at Pompeii and Ephesus in particular have demonstrated that many objects inside ancient homes had inscriptions on them. Domestic inscriptions encompass any item within a house that has been written on, which means that these epigraphs are numerous and varied. For example, the satirical novel that Petronius wrote between 54 and 68 CE about the pretentious rich freedman, Trimalchio, who shows off his wealth at every opportunity, mentions several domestic inscriptions on Trimalchio's walls, doorposts, glassware, and pottery (*Satyricon* 29–34).[65] One notable epigraph is the one in the atrium of Trimalchio's house that greets guests as they enter. It is the picture of a dog with the caption "Beware of the dog!" (*Satyricon* 19). Interestingly, archaeologists have found a similar inscription in a mosaic in Pompeii in the vestibule of the House of the Tragic Poet (see Figure 1.20).

(2.5) Financial Documents

Sometimes individuals chose to engrave important financial documents in stone, such as wills and the manumission of slaves, to ensure the validity of their transactions. It was common in the Greco-Roman period for slaves to buy or earn their freedom from their masters. We have already seen that one of Marcus Agrippa's freedmen, Mithridates, moved to Ephesus and

64. For a discussion of Greek ex-votos see McLean, *Introduction to Greek Epigraphy*, 246–57. For a discussion of Latin ex-votos see Cooley, *Cambridge Manual*, 178–85.

65. For more on the epigraphic habit of Petronius's *Satyricon* see Jocelyne Nelis-Clément and Damien Nelis, "Petronius' Epigraphic Habit," *Dictynna* 2 (2005): 1–16.

Figure 1.20. Mosaic from the vestibule of the House of the Tragic Poet in Pompeii, Italy, with a dog and the message "Beware of the dog!" (*cave canem*) (*CIL* 10.877) (© Wikimedia Commons: Public Domain).

(along with a colleague) paid for a monumental gate at the city's southern agora. Sometimes inscriptions were set up commemorating the emancipation of slaves. One such epigraph has particular import for the NT and for Paul's references to Christians as slaves of God (Rom 6:16–20; cf.1 Cor 6:20; 7:23).[66] It is called sacred manumission and is mainly attested in Delphi at the temple of Pythian Apollo. Adolf Deissmann summarizes the process well. The slave would pay their ransom price to Apollo's treasury. The owner would bring them to the temple, sell the slave to the deity by collecting the funds that the slave deposited previously, and then the slave would become the god's property.[67] One such manumission epigraph (200/199 BCE) says:

66. For more on sacred manumission and its connections to freedpersons in 1 Corinthians see Laura S. Nasrallah, "'You Were Bought with a Price': Freedpersons and Things in 1 Corinthians," in *Corinth in Contrast: Studies in Inequality*, ed. Steven J. Friesen, Sarah A. James, and Daniel N. Schowalter (Leiden: Brill, 2014), 54–73.

67. Deissmann, *Light from the Ancient East*, 318–27. For more on sacred manumission see Woodhead, *Study of Greek Inscriptions*, 46; McLean, *Introduction to Greek Epigraphy*, 289–99.

"Pythian Apollo purchased for freedom a female slave whose name is Nicaia, a Roman, from Sosibius of Amphissus for a price of three and a half silver minae. Eumnastus was the original owner (of Nicaia) according to the law. He [i.e., Sosibus] paid the entire price, but Nicaia had entrusted the entire purchase price to Apollo for freedom. Witness . . . [there are a total of 27 of them]" (ἐπρίατο ὁ Ἀπόλλων ὁ Πύθιος παρὰ Σωσιβίου Ἀμφισσέος ἐπ' ἐλευθερίαι| σῶ[μα] γυναικεῖον ἆι ὄνομα Νίκαια τὸ γένος Ῥωμαίαν, τιμᾶς ἀργυρίου| μνᾶν τριῶν καὶ ἡμιμναίου. προαποδότας κατὰ τὸν νόμον· Εὔμναστος| Ἀμφισσεύς. τὰν τιμὰν ἀπέχει, τὰν δὲ ὠνὰν ἐπίστευσε Νίκαια τῶι Ἀπόλλωνι| ἐπ' ἐλευθερίαι. μάρτυροι) (*SGDI* II.2116).

(2.6) Graffiti

Excavations at Pompeii, Herculaneum, Ephesus, and most recently in the basilica in the agora of Smyrna (in modern-day Turkey) showcase the prominent place of graffiti in Greco-Roman life. Graffiti are messages incised or written on walls in public and private spaces. Unlike inscriptions, they were not typically intended for future generations to read (because walls in antiquity were re-plastered) but were created for varied reasons. Some of these messages boast about sexual encounters, others about the graffitist's civic pride or favorite gladiator, and still others are word puzzles.[68] Such messages could be numerous. In fact, one graffitist from Pompeii remarks on the number of people who have written on a wall: "Since you support the tedious works of so many writers, I am astonished that you, wall, have not fallen down" (*admiror te, paries, non cecidisse| qui tot scriptorum taedia sustineas*) (*CIL* 4.2487). Some graffiti are warnings. One individual from Ephesus threatens divine retribution on the person who urinates in a niche in the Gate of Mazaeus and Mithridates (see Figure 1.21): "If anyone pisses here, then Hecate will be angry at him" (ε̣ἴ| τις ἂν ὧδε| οὐρήσι, ἡ Ἑκά|τη αὐτῷ κε|χώλωται) (*IEph* 567).

68. J. A. Baird and Claire Taylor, "Ancient Graffiti in Context: Introduction," in *Ancient Graffiti in Context*, ed. J. A. Baird and Claire Taylor (New York: Routledge, 2011), 1–19; Peter Keegan, *Graffiti in Antiquity* (London: Routledge, 2014); Rebecca R. Benefiel, "Dialogues of Ancient Graffiti in the House of Maius Castricius in Pompeii," *AJA* 114 (2010): 59–101.

Figure 1.21. Scratched graffito from Ephesus, Turkey, warning against public urination (© D. Clint Burnett).

Older scholarship tended to interpret graffiti as products of the lower classes. The following comment on graffiti by August Mau, a prominent German archaeologist of the nineteenth and early twentieth century, is representative:

> Cultivated men and women of the ancient city, were not accustomed to scratch their names upon stucco or to confide their reflections and experiences to the surface of a wall. . . . We may assume that the writers were as little representative of the best elements of society as are the tourists who scratch or carve their names upon ancient monuments to-day.[69]

Historians, however, now consider this view incorrect. Individuals living in the Roman Empire did not work with modern conceptions of graffiti and seem to have tolerated them. Peter Keegan notes, "Tolerance towards graffiti in public *and* private contexts is a pan-Mediterranean phenomenon across all chronological, geo-political and socio-cultural boundaries in antiquity" (emphasis his).[70] For example, graffiti in the form of thank you notes are found scratched or written on painted frescoes inside elite houses, which

69. Mau, *Pompeii*, 481–82.
70. Keegan, *Graffiti in Antiquity*, 6.

were not the products of the lower members of society. In fact, the emperor Titus's doctor may have memorialized one of his bowel movements in the latrine in the House of the Gem in Herculaneum: "Apollinaris the doctor of victorious general Titus defecated well here!" (*Apollinaris · medicus · Titi · Imp| hic cacavit bene*) (*CIL* 4.10619). Finally, graffiti are most often clustered, not appearing in isolation but next to other graffiti (and drawings called dipinti). Consequently, graffiti were part of ongoing dialogues among individuals who could read and write them.[71]

(2.7) Curse Tablets

"Magic" played a large role in Greco-Roman religion. While historians disagree about its precise definition, broadly speaking magic is the attempt to solicit power outside the established religious order.[72] One popular magical act was the curse tablet (*defixio*, after the Latin word *deficio*, "I curse"), which is found all over the Roman Empire (e.g., Corinth and Cyprus), even as far north as the province of Britannia (modern-day England). These were typically lead sheets on which a curse was scratched. The lead was then folded, pierced with a nail, and either buried or tossed into a well.[73] The following Latin *defixio* was found in London (1934). The creator used lead stripped from part of a building and then pierced it with a nail seven times (see Figure 1.22):

> "I curse Tretia Maria, her life, her mind, her memory, her liver, her lungs, her fate and thoughts intermixed, and her memory. In this way, she will neither be able to speak about what things are hidden nor will she be able to SINITA MERE [. . . .] CL VDO" (*Tretia(m) Maria(m) defico et| illeus uita(m) et me(n)tem| et memoriam [e]t iocine|ra pulmones interm<x>ix<i>|ta fata cogitata memor|iam sci(=sic) no(n) possitt loqui| (quae) sicreta si(n)t neque SINITA| MERE possit neque [.| . . .] CL VDO*) (*RIB* 1.7).[74]

71. For a discussion see Benefiel, "Dialogues of Ancient Graffiti," 59–101.

72. For a discussion of "magic" in the Roman world see Beard, North, and Price, *Religions of Rome*, 1:220–21.

73. See John G. Gager, ed., *Curse Tablets and Binding Spells from the Ancient World* (Oxford: Oxford University Press, 1992). For magical spells see Hans Dieter Betz, ed., *The Greek Magical Papyri in Translation: Including the Demotic Spells*, 2nd ed. (Chicago: University of Chicago Press, 1992).

74. The meaning of SINITA MERE remains unclear.

Figure 1.22. Curse tablet from London, England (Wikimedia Commons: Marie-Lan Nguyen).

V. Who Could Read Inscriptions?

Now that the reader is familiar with the content of inscriptions, we can move to other introductory topics, beginning with who could read them. Given the Roman epigraphic habit and the sheer number of inscriptions that have survived from the Greco-Roman world, it seems clear that epigraphs were set up so that people could read them. But who? In a seminal work in 1989, William V. Harris, relying on UNESCO's 1958 definition of literacy, defined literacy as the ability to read and to write a sentence. He concludes that no more than twenty percent of the population of the Roman world was literate and that the number is probably more like ten.[75] Historians, however, point out a significant limitation of Harris's work: his definition of literacy is a modern and not an ancient one.[76] Greg Woolf proposes that the act of

75. William V. Harris, *Ancient Literacy* (Cambridge: Harvard University Press, 1989), esp. 323–37.

76. Greg Woolf, "Literacy," in CAH 11:875; John Bodel, "Inscriptions and Literacy," in Bruun and Edmondson, *Oxford Handbook*, 745–47.

reading in the Roman world was communal and that those who could read inscriptions probably aided those who could not.[77]

Woolf's observation may explain a remark that Trimalchio's slave, Hermerus, makes in *Satyricon*. Hermerus boasts that while he does not have a formal Greco-Roman education, "I know my letters cut in stone" (*sed lapidarias litteras scio*) (*Satyricon* 58). This comment suggests that some people could read the large block letters of epigraphs, which differed from everyday cursive writing. In addition, public declarations of decrees were read aloud at community gatherings. Given the ubiquity of inscriptions, that public reading accompanied some of them, that inscriptions are filled with formulaic phrases, and that people probably asked those who could read them to decipher the epigraphs for them, there were likely people in the Roman Empire who, like the fictious Hermerus, were epigraphically literate.[78] While putting a number on the percentage of the population that could read inscriptions is impossible, it is probably higher than Harris's ten to twenty percent. One final note about epigraphic literacy: it seems most appropriate that we view it on a sliding scale of proficiency. That is to say, if someone could read a simple inscription like an epitaph—so-and-so lived X number of years—that does not mean they could read every inscription that they encountered in a given city.

VI. How Are Inscriptions Dated?

To use inscriptions in the reconstruction of the Greco-Roman world and in the interpretation of the NT, we must be able to date them. The Roman Empire was made up of countless communities that were constantly changing and evolving. Therefore, what is true of one city at one time is not necessarily the case at a different time. For example, in the first century BCE and CE Latin was the dominant language in the Roman colony of Corinth. However, by the second century CE that began to change and Greek became the dominant language by the third century.[79] To use epigraphs to interpret the NT, we need to be able to confidently date them to the first century CE (and possibly the second, depending on the dating of certain NT books).

77. Woolf, "Literacy," 11:881–91.

78. Bodel, "Inscriptions and Literacy," 750–51.

79. See D. Clint Burnett, "Divine Titles for Julio-Claudian Imperials in Corinth: Neglected Factors in Reconstructions of Corinthian Imperial Worship and Its Connections to the Corinthian Church," *CBQ* 82 (2020), forthcoming.

Epigraphers have developed four criteria for dating inscriptions. The first and easiest way is when dates are provided in the actual epigraphs. When this is the case, inscriptions provide the year of a city's magistrates, the reign of a king or emperor, or of an epoch in which the inhabitants of a city are living, such as the following inscription from Philadelphia in Lydia (modern-day Turkey) that is dated to "the twentieth year of [Augustus] Caesar's victory (at Actium)" (ἔτους κʹ τῆς Καίσαρος νίκης) or 12/11 BCE (*TAM* 5.3 1430). Second, inscriptions can be dated by their content. They may mention a historical event or a historical figure whose date is secure, thereby allowing them to be dated.[80] Third, archaeologists can sometimes date epigraphs discovered during an excavation even if they lack internal dating formulae. For example, excavators found the famous Theodotus inscription, which contains the only reference to a Second Temple synagogue in Jerusalem, in a cistern south of the temple complex in Jerusalem. Even though the epigraph has no internal date, its archaeological context, a stratum where all evidence dates to the late Second Temple period, means that the inscription must date before 70 CE (*CIIP* 9). Finally, the least accurate method of dating inscriptions is the last resort: dating by the letterforms, or a practice known as paleography. The problem with paleographic dating is that different letterforms circulated concurrently in different parts of the Roman Empire. The only sound way to use paleographic dating is for the epigrapher to focus on the history of letterforms in a given city or region, thereby providing criteria by which to judge the shape of letters.[81]

VII. Where Does One Find Inscriptions?

Unless the reader visits the places where the Roman Empire used to exist or a good museum, they will only encounter inscriptions in a 2D form: either printed (books and articles) or digital (i.e., online). Epigraphers

---

80. The reconstruction of the lives of prominent ancient Greeks and Romans is known as prosopography. Olli Salomies defines it as "a listing, in alphabetical order, of persons of a certain rank or occupation and belonging to a certain period, in which each entry contains a full enumeration of the person's offices and other accomplishments and of all the relevant sources." "Names and Identities: Onomastics and Prosopography," in Bodel, *Epigraphic Evidence*, 74.

81. For more on dating Greek inscriptions see Cook, *Greek Inscriptions*, 12–14, 18; Woodhead, *Study of Greek Inscriptions*, 52–66; Bodel, "Epigraphy and the Ancient Historian," 49–51. For more on dating Latin inscriptions see Cooley, *Cambridge Manual*, 398–434.

call such collections of epigraphs corpora, deriving from the Latin word *corpus* meaning body of literature.[82] Most corpora of inscriptions arrange epigraphs by date, beginning with the earliest and moving to the later ones. Corpora differ, however, in their content. Some are categorized by location (e.g., *IG* X.2.1: Thessalonica). Others gather similar types of epigraphs (e.g., epitaphs or associational inscriptions).[83] There are corpora that collect inscriptions around themes such as women, slaves, Jews, and Christians in the Roman world, around time periods like the Hellenistic or Roman period, or a combination of any of these.[84]

The form epigraphic corpora have today took its shape in the nineteenth century.[85] Augustus Boeckh edited the first modern epigraphic corpus, *Corpus Inscriptionum Graecarum* (*CIG*) (six volumes from 1828 to 1877), in which he tried to gather all published Greek inscriptions into one collection and to organize them geographically. Theodor Mommsen followed Boeckh's method for Latin epigraphs, founding *Corpus Inscriptionum Latinarum* (*CIL*) in 1853 (it is still being produced). He arranged inscriptions geographically (e.g., Britannia: volume 7) as well as thematically (e.g., domestic instruments: volume 15). To account for discoveries of Greek epigraphy of the later nineteenth century, which were legion, a

---

82. The earliest recorded epigraphic corpus is the Anonymus Einsidlensis, which dates to the eighth/ninth century CE. A traveler compiled it and then copied the corpus into a manuscript: P. Gabriel Meier, ed., *Catalogus codium manu scriptorum qui in Bibliotheca Monasterii Einsidlensis O.S.B. servantur: Tomus I complectens centurias quinque priores* (Einsidlensium: Eberle & Rickenbach, 1899), no. 326. The father of modern epigraphy is Cyriac of Ancona (1391–1452 CE), who travelled throughout Ottoman-controlled Greece and Turkey recording inscriptions. Cyriac of Ancona, *Life and Early Travels*, The I Tatti Renaissance Library, ed. and trans. Charles Mitchell, Edward W. Bodnar, and Clive Foss (Cambridge: Harvard University Press, 2015); Cyriac of Ancona, *Later Travels*, The I Tatti Renaissance Library, ed. and trans. Edward W. Bodnar with Clive Foss (Cambridge: Harvard University Press, 2003).

83. Richmond Lattimore, ed., *Themes in Greek and Latin Epitaphs* (Urbana, IL: University of Illinois Press, 1962); Philip A. Harland, ed., *Greco-Roman Associations: Texts, Translations, and Commentary*, vol. 2, *North Coast of the Black Sea, Asia Minor*, BZNW 204 (Berlin: de Gruyter, 2014).

84. Jean-Baptiste Frey, ed., *Corpus of Jewish Inscriptions: Jewish Inscriptions from the Third Century B.C. to the Seventh Century A.D.*, Sussidi allo studio delle antichità cristiane 1 (New York: Ktav, 1975); Russell Meiggs and David M. Lewis, eds., *A Selection of Greek Historical Inscriptions to the end of the Fifth Century B.C.*, rev. ed. (Oxford: Clarendon, 1988).

85. My discussion on epigraphic collections was informed by John Bodel, "Appendix: A Brief Guide to Some Standard Collections," in Bodel, *Epigraphic Evidence*, 153–74; Christer Bruun, "The Major Corpora and Epigraphic Publications," in Bruun and Edmondson, *Oxford Handbook*, 66–77.

companion corpus to *CIG* was launched called *Inscriptiones Graecae* (*IG*) (which began in 1903 and is still being produced), following the same format as *CIG* and *CIL*.

Given that I discuss Semitic inscriptions in the second chapter, I must mention four corpora of Semitic inscriptions. The first is *Corpus Inscriptionum Semiticarum* (*CIS*), which is in five parts that date from 1881 to 1962. Two volumes of this corpus, *CIS* 2 (Aramaic and Nabataean inscriptions) and *CIS* 3 (Jewish inscriptions), contain Semitic epigraphs dating to the Hellenistic and Roman periods and are still widely used by scholars. The second corpus, *Corpus Inscriptionum Iudaeae/Palaestinae* (*CIIP*), consists of a projected six volumes that began to be produced in 2010 and contain all known Latin, Greek, and Aramaic inscriptions from ancient Palestine dating from the fourth century BCE to the seventh century CE. The third corpus is a four-volume series entitled *Textbook of Syrian Semitic Inscriptions* (*TSSI*) (1971–2009), which is not meant to be exhaustive, but to present select inscriptions in Semitic dialects with limited commentary on them. The discussions of Aramaic inscriptions from Palestine and its environs in these two newer corpora, *CIIP* and *TSSI*, have superseded those in *CIS*. The final Semitic corpus is G. A. Cooke's *Text-book of North-Semitic Inscriptions* (*TNSI*) (1903), which contains select Semitic epigraphy from the tenth century BCE to the Roman period. While this volume is dated, it is still used by scholars.

From 1892 to 1916, Henry Dessau produced a corpus of select Latin inscriptions, *Inscriptiones Latinae Selectae* (*ILS*), providing an overview of the breadth of Latin epigraphy. Wilhelm Dittenberger and René Cagnat produced their own corpora of select Greek inscriptions for a similar purpose. The former edited two such collections. The first, *Sylloge Inscriptionum Graecarum* (*Syll* or *SIG*), is a four-volume work that underwent three editions (1883–1924). The second, *Orientis Graeci Inscriptiones Selectae* (*OGIS*) (1903–1905), is a two-volume collection of Greek inscriptions from the eastern Mediterranean from Alexander the Great to the Roman Empire. Cagnat's work, *Inscriptiones graecae ad res romanas pertinentes* (*IGRR*) (1901–1927), is a four-volume selection of Greek inscriptions from the entire Mediterranean with a fourth volume produced after Cagnat's death. The above corpora, *CIG*, *CIL*, *CIS*, *IGRR*, *ILS*, *OGIS*, *SIG*^{3}, and *TNSI* are available for free download on the internet through archive.org and books.google.com, which means that the reader does not have to leave the comfort of their own home or office to use them. For more information about these corpora see this book's appendices.

To account for newly discovered inscriptions, there are several annually published journals. *L'Année épigraphique* (*AE*) (which began in 1888) supplements *CIL* and publishes newly discovered Latin inscriptions, while *Supplementum Epigraphicum Graecum* (*SEG*) (which began in 1923) serves the same function for Greek inscriptions for *IG*. *Bulletin épigraphique* (*BE*) (which began in 1888) reviews newly found Greek inscriptions and the *Epigraphic Bulletin for Greek Religion* (*EBGR*) focuses on newly published Greek epigraphs associated with Greek religion and is found in the online journal *Kernos* for free and in English (http://journals.openedition.org/kernos/605?lang=en.). In addition to the above standard corpora of Greek and Latin epigraphy, many individual sites have published inscriptional corpora (e.g., *Philippi II*; *CIPh*; *Corinth* 8.1; *Corinth* 8.2; *Corinth* 8.3). These corpora are too many to list, but a growing number of these are published online, such as Sardis (http://sardisexpedition.org) and Aphrodisias (http://insaph.kcl.ac.uk). Finally, work with inscriptions has become easier with the rise of online searchable databases. One of the best sites for Greek inscriptions is *Greek Searchable Inscriptions* that the Packard Humanities Institute has produced (https://epigraphy.packhum.org) and one of the most extensive websites for Latin epigraphy is the *Epigraphik-Datenbank Clauss/Slaby* (http://www.manfredclauss.de).[86] For a list and discussion of online inscriptional databases see this book's appendices.

VIII. How Does One Use Corpora?

Once the reader has located a print edition or a digital copy of a corpus, they must familiarize themselves with its layout. Corpora are organized around entries for inscriptions and a single entry can span several pages or there can be multiple entries on the same page. Often the entry will contain a concise title of the epigraph, usually related to how the editor how categorized it, such as decree, honorary inscription, etc. Underneath this entry number and title comes a small discussion of the object on which the epigraph is found listing such information as its material, size, shape, where it was discovered, the measurement of its letters, and where it can be found physically as of publication. The transcription of the epigraph, sometimes its translation, and a commentary on the inscription follow. Finally, pictures

86. For more information on digital collections of inscriptions see Tom Elliott, "Epigraphy and Digital Resources," in Bruun and Edmondson, *Oxford Handbook*, 78–85.

or drawings of the actual epigraphs can usually be found either next to the entry or in the plate section of the corpus after the indices.

One thing that the reader will notice is that corpora contain numerous symbols. These symbols are called *sigla* and are found in every epigraphic corpus because they facilitate the presentation and discussion of epigraphs. After 1932, epigraphers use a standardized set of *sigla* called the Leiden System. *Sigla* in corpora that predate 1932 do not necessarily follow this system, and readers should acquaint themselves with the *sigla* of every corpus that they use. Corpora vary in their presentations of inscriptions. They can be written as they appear on their original material or in continuous script, which is how I have chosen to present inscriptions in this book to save paper. When an inscription is written in continuous script, the *siglum* of a vertical line | is placed to demarcate line divisions in the inscription and double vertical lines || to mark (most often) every fifth line, which is how I use them in this book.

Few inscriptions have survived intact due to war (both ancient and modern), weathering, or reuse in later construction projects, so most epigraphs are damaged in some way and have lost some of their content.[87] Epigraphers call the areas that no longer exist lacunae (lacuna in the singular) and they attempt, if possible, to restore these lost letters. These restorations are placed in square brackets [ ] to let readers know that what is found inside is an editor's proposal. Many restorations are neither fanciful nor as difficult as they may seem and there are three criteria for making them. First, the lines of an inscription and the size of its letters are measured to determine the size of the lacuna and how many letters must be restored. Second, the inscription in question is read closely to acquire the content of the restoration because epigraphs, especially decrees, are repetitive. What is said in one part of the inscription tends to be repeated in another part. Often that part can be in the lacuna. Third, parallel inscriptions, especially those from the same location, are consulted because epigraphs are formulaic and these formulae have local characteristics. The scientific method of restoring lacunae notwithstanding, it is unwise to build any arguments on what is found in them. The epigrapher Ernst Badian famously calls such hypotheses "history from 'square brackets.' "[88]

---

87. My discussion of restorations of inscriptions was informed by Robert, "épigraphies," 5:89–93; Woodhead, *Study of Greek Inscriptions*, 67–75.

88. E. Badian, "History from 'Square Brackets,' " *ZPE* 79 (1989): 59–70. For example, Douglas Campbell ("Possible Inscriptional Attestation to Sergius Paul[l]us [Acts 13:6–12], and the Implications for Pauline Chronology," *JTS* 56 [2005]: 1–29) argues that

Sometimes an inscription has been damaged after its initial publication, with the result that letters that one editor recorded are no longer visible. In such cases, a line is placed underneath letters that a previous editor saw, but that are no longer visible, like so: αβγ. Epigraphers use parentheses ( ) to mark letters that do not appear in the actual inscription because they have been abbreviated. Such abbreviations are common in Latin epigraphy, especially with names, titles, familial relations, and governmental offices. Editors employ angular brackets < > to insert letters that engravers omitted from inscriptions or to demarcate correct letters that editors have inserted. Sometimes an ancient stone worker made a mistake by engraving too many letters and repeating whole words, syllables, or letters. In such cases, epigraphers place hooked brackets { } around these letters.

Occasionally, a stonemason noticed a mistake or cities and empires damned a person's memory, at which time the stonecutter erased his mistake or, in the case of a damned memory, a name from the inscription. Editors use double brackets [[ ]] to mark this. If the letters inside the double brackets are illegible, then editors insert dashes: [[- - - -]]. If the editor knows how many letters once existed, then one dot marks each erased letter: [[. . . .]]. Editors use dots for one other purpose. If a letter, often at the edge of a fracture on the stone, is partial but its identity is known, then editors place a dot, not inside brackets, but underneath it. The final *siglum* that the reader needs to know is *v*. Sometimes an engraver left a space intentionally on a stone. When this occurs, editors place an italic v, *v*., in their corpora, which stands for the Latin verb *vacat* ("it is missing"). Typically, editors place as many *v*'s as there are intentional vacant spaces, i.e., *vvv*. marks three vacant spots.[89]

---

a fragmentary inscription found at Chytri, Cyprus probably mentions the proconsul Sergius Paullus (cf. Acts 13:7–12) in line 10: Κοίντου Σερ[. . .]. The epigraph mentions the last three letters of an emperor's name in line 9: [. . .]ίου Καίσαρος Σεβαστοῦ. Most epigraphers restore the letters Κλαυδ and conclude that the inscription refers to [Κλαυδ]ίου Καίσαρος Σεβαστοῦ and they date it to 46–48 CE (*SEG* 20.302; *IGRR* III 935). Campbell, however, proposes that the emperor is Tiberius and restores his name in the square brackets: [Τιβερ]ίου Καίσαρος Σεβαστοῦ. Campbell uses this restoration to re-date Paul's missionary journey to Cyprus before 37 CE, a full decade earlier than what most scholars accept. Such history from square brackets is methodologically unsound and should be avoided.

89. For more on *sigla* see Woodhead, *Study of Greek Inscriptions*, 6–11; McLean, *Introduction to Greek Epigraphy*, 27–39; Cooley, *Cambridge Manual*, 350–55.

<table>
<tr><th>Sigla</th><th>Explanation</th></tr>
<tr><td>[ ]</td><td>Restored letters</td></tr>
<tr><td>( )</td><td>Abbreviated letters</td></tr>
<tr><td>< ></td><td>Letters that have been omitted or substituted by the engraver</td></tr>
<tr><td>[[ ]]</td><td>Letters that have been erased in antiquity</td></tr>
<tr><td>{ }</td><td>Letters that are superfluous</td></tr>
<tr><td>[. . .]</td><td>Number of missing letters are known</td></tr>
<tr><td>[- - -]</td><td>Number of missing letters are unknown</td></tr>
<tr><td>α̣</td><td>Letter partially preserved</td></tr>
<tr><td>α̲</td><td>Letter seen by an older editor but now missing</td></tr>
<tr><td>v.</td><td>Intentional space left by the engraver</td></tr>
<tr><td>|</td><td>Marks a new line</td></tr>
<tr><td>||</td><td>Marks (most often) every fifth line</td></tr>
</table>

IX. Interpretation of Inscriptions

The final aspect of inscriptions that I must address is how I approach them in this book. Adolf Deissmann was an early pioneer of using inscriptions to interpret the NT, but his interest in inscriptions was in what they said, which he used for two reasons: either to establish that the Greek of the NT was common or Koine Greek, or to demonstrate a relationship between facets of early Christianity and the larger Greco-Roman world.[90] Deissmann was little concerned with the archaeological context of inscriptions and what this information can tell us about them. We must remember always that the inscriptions that we encounter in this book and that the reader will find in their own studies were never meant to be read as texts or pictures on pages. Rather, they were intended as messages embedded in specific contexts and these contexts determine their interpretation. As Robin Osborne notes, “Inscriptions are never just texts. . . . The writing assumes that the reader is looking not just at the text but at the object.”[91] In short, my

90. Deissmann, *Light from the Ancient East*, 1–145, 252–392.

91. Robin Osborne, “Greek Epigraphy and Archaeology,” in *The Diversity of Classical Archaeology*, ed. Achim Lichtenberger and Rubina Raja (Turnhout, Belgium: Brepols, 2017), 127. For similar comments see Cooley, *Cambridge Manual*, 222–27; McLean, *Introduction to Greek Epigraphy*, 65–67.

approach to epigraphs is to interpret them for what they are: archaeological artifacts. Objects found on archaeological excavations are most helpful when they can be placed within their archaeological contexts: specific places and times, which affect and determine their meaning, function, and interpretation. While some older corpora (e.g., *ILS*) and even some current NT scholars are not interested in treating inscriptions like artifacts, all modern epigraphers are. To ensure the most accurate epigraphic reconstruction, I encourage readers to find the latest discussions of them by epigraphers: either in articles or newer corpora where the epigrapher has done an autopsy (or examination of the inscription itself).

X. Conclusion

This introductory chapter on inscriptions has attempted to lay a solid foundation for readers. While there is a lot of information, some of which is probably new, I hope that you are not overwhelmed but instead challenged to use inscriptions in the interpretation of the NT. In particular, I hope you take up the gauntlet to treat inscriptions as archaeological artifacts so that they can illuminate the text of the NT and the history of early Christianity. For the rest of this book, I demonstrate this method of interpreting the NT with five case studies. Throughout the following chapters, I refer back to this chapter to give you an opportunity to solidify your understanding of what you've read.

CHAPTER 2

Jesus, the Royal Lord: Inscriptions and Local Customs

Inscriptions provide evidence for local customs because they are products of local communities. We can use inscriptions to reconstruct the culture and beliefs of people living in certain places of the Roman Empire for which there is little to no literary evidence. Such information can illuminate the NT. To showcase this benefit of epigraphs, I demonstrate how inscriptions can shed light on a facet of Christology of the early church; namely, the development of the early Christian belief in Jesus' Lord-ship or *kyrios*-ship and its theological implications. For most of the twentieth century, scholars debated when, where, and how Jesus' *kyrios*-ship developed among early Christians. In this discussion, most scholars overlooked Greek and Semitic (Aramaic and Hebrew) inscriptions from the southern Levant (southern Syria, ancient Palestine, and their immediate environs), which provide evidence that "lord" was a royal title particular to the region during the formation of early Christianity. These epigraphs support the proposal that Jesus' *kyrios*-ship developed in the southern Levant, and early Jewish Christians connected to this region viewed Jesus' *kyrios*-ship as royal, messianic, and not exclusively divine.

I. Jesus Is Lord, but When and for Whom?

What we know as Christianity formed in the trilingual environment of Judea and Galilee where Aramaic, Hebrew, and Greek were spoken.[1] When considering the matter of Jesus' *kyrios*-ship, historians must take each of these languages into account. Aramaic, Hebrew, and Greek have various words

1. Michael Owen Wise (*Language and Literary in Roman Judaea: A Study of the Bar Kokhba Documents*, AYBRL [New Haven: Yale University Press, 2015]) demonstrates that Roman Judea was trilingual, that Aramaic was the most common vernacular, followed by Hebrew and Greek, and that these last two languages were not used exclusively for religious purposes.

for "lord," but the ones that concern me are those that early Christians could and did use for Jesus: the Aramaic term *mr'*, the Hebrew word *adon*, and the Greek term κύριος. In each of these languages, lord is a relational term stressing that someone or something possessed higher authority than the speaker. Therefore, lord is a common honorary address for someone of higher rank, resembling our English "sir" or "madam" (cf. Gen 23:6 MT and LXX; 1QapGen ar 2:24; 22:18; Matt 8:2). The master of a slave is known as lord (cf. Gen 24:10 MT and LXX; Col 3:22). Certain gods were called lord (1 Cor 8:5–6). Finally, emperors are addressed as lord (Acts 25:26) (but as I discuss later in this chapter this observation must be nuanced).[2]

The adoption of Lord for Jesus by early Aramaic, Hebrew, and Greek speaking Jewish Christians differed from the above common uses of the term, however. For early Christians, Jesus was not "sir" or a "lord," but *the* unquestionable and only Lord of the cosmos (when the English Lord refers to the exalted and enthroned Jesus, it is capitalized). He had been resurrected and exalted to God's right hand (Acts 2:34–36; Phil 2:9–11) and he would return soon to establish God's kingdom on earth (1 Thess 4:13–18). In our earliest agreed-upon Christian sources, Paul's undisputed letters (Romans, 1–2 Corinthians, Galatians, Philippians, 1 Thessalonians, and Philemon), *kyrios* is one of the most used titles for Jesus, occurring about 180 times.[3] If we focus on Paul's use of *kyrios* in his earliest letter, 1 Thessalonians (written about 49 CE), we see that Paul uses *kyrios* for Jesus twenty-five times in five chapters and takes for granted that his converts are aware

2. Otto Eissfeldt, "אדון," *TDOT* 1:59–72; "אדון," BDB 10–11, 1101; Werner Foerster, "κύριος," *TDNT* 3:1039–58, 1081–98; Werner Foerster and Gottfried Quell, *Lord*, Bible Key Words, trans. H. P. Kingdon (London: Black, 1933); "κύριος," BDAG 576–79; "κύριος,"*LSJ* 1013; "κύριος," *MM* 365–66; Larry W. Hurtado, "Lord," in *Dictionary of Paul and His Letters*, ed. Gerald F. Hawthorne, Ralph P. Martin, and Daniel G. Reid (Downers Grove, IL: InterVarsity Press, 1993), 560–69; Hurtado, *Lord Jesus Christ: Devotion to Jesus in Earliest Christianity* (Grand Rapids: Eerdmans, 2003), 108–18; Marco Frenschkowski, "Kyrios in Context: Q 6:46, the Emperor as 'Lord', and the Political Implications of Christology in Q," in *Zwischen den Reichen: Neues Testament und Römische Herrschaft*, TANZ 36, ed. Michael Labahn and Jürgen Zangenberg (Tübingen: Francke, 2002), 95–114; Frenschkowski, "Kyrios," *RAC* 22:754–94.

3. This number is provided by Hurtado, *Lord Jesus Christ*, 108. If 2 Thessalonians and Colossians are considered as Pauline, then the number of times that Paul calls Jesus Lord is about two hundred. See James D. G. Dunn, *The Theology of Paul the Apostle* (Grand Rapids: Eerdmans, 1998), 244n47. I have counted twenty-four occurrences of *kyrios* in Ephesians and twenty in the Pastorals, which would put the number of times Jesus is call Lord in letters attributed to Paul at 244. The difficulty with an exact number is the number of textual variants of *kyrios* within the Pauline corpus.

of what Jesus' *kyrios*-ship means.[4] Paul even assumes that churches he did not establish knew the finer points of Jesus' *kyrios*-ship. He opens his letter to the Romans by referencing the resurrection from the dead of "our Lord Jesus Christ" (Rom 1:4) and Paul assumes that the Roman Christians had confessed Jesus as *kyrios*, presumably at their baptism (Rom 10:9, 12–13).

If we use Paul's undisputed letters to reconstruct his understanding of Jesus' *kyrios*-ship, then Paul's kerygma centered on God's work through *kyrios* Jesus Christ (2 Cor 4:5). He believed that God bestowed the title Lord onto Jesus when he raised him from the dead and exalted him to the heavenly throne (Phil 2:9–11). Paul defined Christians as those who call on the name of *kyrios* Jesus Christ (1 Cor 1:2) and he considered that Christians belong to *kyrios* Jesus whether dead or alive (Rom 14:8). Early Christian worship services included a declaration of Jesus as *kyrios* (1 Cor 12:3), which may have been a call for Jesus to return to establish God's kingdom on earth (1 Cor 16:22). And, Paul describes the Second Coming as some form of the day of *kyrios* Jesus.[5] In short, Jesus' *kyrios*-ship is a cardinal tenet of early Christianity from our earliest sources.

The difficulty with Jesus' *kyrios*-ship in Paul's letters is when it developed. According to our earliest canonical gospel, Mark (written about 69 CE), Jesus' followers did not have to acknowledge him as *kyrios* during his earthly ministry. Jesus' disciples rarely addressed him as *kyrios* and when they did they were not calling Jesus *kyrios* of the cosmos, but "sir" (Mark 7:28).[6] This change in the word's meaning is a massive theological development that

---

4. Hurtado ("Lord," 562) notes of Paul's use of *kyrios* that the apostle calls "Jesus [Lord] without explanation or justification, suggesting that his readers already were familiar with the term and its connotation." For a discussion of Paul's tenure in Thessalonica and the date and composition of 1 Thessalonians see Abraham J. Malherbe, *The Letters to the Thessalonians: A New Translation with Introduction and Commentary*, AB 32B (New York: Doubleday, 2000), 54–92.

5. Day of *kyrios*: 1 Cor 5:5; 1 Thess 5:2. Day of *kyrios* Jesus: 2 Cor 1:14. Day of *kyrios* Jesus Christ: 1 Cor 1:8. Cf. 1 Cor 11:26; Phil 3:20; 4:5; 1 Thess 2:19; 3:13; 4:15–5:2; 5:9, 23; 2 Thess 2:8.

6. For a discussion of the dating of Mark see Adela Yarbro Collins, *Mark: A Commentary*, Hermeneia (Minneapolis: Fortress, 2007), 11–14. *Kyrios* appears sixteen times in Mark: 1:3; 2:28; 5:19; 7:28; 11:3, 9; 12:9, 11, 29 [2x], 30, 36 [2x], 37; 13:20, 35, and twice in the later addition to the gospel, 16:19, 20. Of these sixteen occurrences, seven are from quotations of the Greek OT and refer to God (1:3; 11:9; 12:11, 29 [2x], 30, 36), another use refers to God (13:20), one use of *kyrios* refers to Jesus as the "master" of the Sabbath (2:28), two occurrences are found in parables (12:9; 13:35), two appearances of *kyrios* refer to the coming messiah (12:36, 37), two occurrences could be Jesus or God (5:19; 11:3), and one is a polite address to Jesus (7:28).

must be explained. Larry Hurtado captures the problem well: "The central questions [of Paul's and early Christian use of *kyrios* for Jesus] have to do with the historical background and influences upon the application of *kyrios* to Christ, the origin of this use of the term in early Christianity, and its use and significance as a christological title."[7]

The most obvious, relevant place to look for a historical background to Jesus' *kyrios*-ship is Jewish literature of Jesus' and Paul's day. However, there are no clear analogies to Jesus' *kyrios*-ship in those sources. The first verse of the preexilic royal psalm, Psalm 110, calls the Israelite and/or Judahite king "lord" (*adon*).[8] When the psalms were translated into Greek (probably in the second century BCE in Alexandria, Egypt), *adon* was rendered as *kyrios*.[9] The problem with using Ps 110:1 as a historical background to Jesus' *kyrios*-ship is that there is no hard evidence that Second Temple Jews interpreted the verse as referring to a messianic figure.[10] The Psalms of Solomon (written in Palestine and probably dating to the late first century BCE) appear to call a messianic figure *kyrios* twice—ἔτι τοῦ χριστοῦ κυρίου (Psalms of Solomon 18 [superscription]); ῥάβδον παιδείας χριστοῦ κυρίου (Psalms of Solomon 18:7)—but some propose that *kyrios* refers to God or that it is an interpolation of a later Christian scribe.[11]

7. Hurtado, "Lord," 561.

8. See Hans-Joachim Kraus, *Psalms 60–150*, trans. Hilton Osward (Minneapolis: Augsburg Fortress, 1989), 343–54. Frank-Lothar Hossfeld and Erich Zenger (*Psalms 3: A Commentary on Psalms 101–150*, Hermeneia, trans. Linda M. Maloney [Minneapolis: Fortress, 2011], 139–54) consider a late preexilic date of Ps 110 possible, but propose that the divine oath of Ps 110:4 favors a postexilic setting.

9. See Henry Barclay Swete, ed., *The Psalms in Greek According to the Septuagint with the Canticles*, 2nd ed. (Cambridge, 1896); Swete, *An Introduction to the Old Testament in Greek* (Cambridge: Cambridge University Press, 1900), 250–53; James K. Aitken, "Psalms," in *T&T Clark Companion to the Septuagint*, ed. James K. Aitken (London: Bloomsbury T&T Clark, 2015), 320–34.

10. There is only one agreed upon allusion to Ps 110:1 in the Second Temple period (Testament of Job 33:3). This text, however, does not refer to a messianic enthronement but to the reward of a righteous sufferer. See David Hay, *Glory at the Right Hand: Psalm 110 in Early Christianity* (Nashville: Abingdon, 1973); D. Clint Burnett, *Christ's Enthronement at God's Right Hand and Its Greco-Roman Cultural Context*, BZNW (Berlin: de Gruyter, forthcoming).

11. For a discussion of dating of the Psalms of Solomon see Robert B. Wright, *Psalms of Solomon: A Critical Edition of the Greek Text* (London: T&T Clark, 2007), 1–7. Wilhelm Bousset (*Kyrios Christos: A History of the Belief in Christ from the Beginnings of Christianity to Irenaeus*, trans. John E. Staley [Nashville: Abingdon, 1970], 124) attributes these occurrences to a mistake of a later Christian editor, concluding that it should be translated the Lord's (i.e., Yahweh's) Messiah. Wright (*Psalms of Solomon*, 48–49) notes that several scholars amend the Greek text similarly, but that there is

Throughout the last century, scholars looked elsewhere for historical backgrounds to Jesus' *kyrios*-ship. One of the oldest proposals is that Jesus' *kyrios*-ship evolved from the address of Jesus as "sir" (Matt 8:2, 6, 8, 21, 25; 9:28; 14:28, 30; 15:25, 27; etc). For example, Gustaf Dalman points to the use of *adon* and *mr'* in the Hebrew Bible, Palestinian Semitic inscriptions, and the Talmuds, noting that most uses of the terms refer to humans, not to God, and when *adon* and *mr'* occur pronominal suffixes are almost always attached to them. Therefore, he concludes, "To speak of 'the Lord' [for an esteemed human being] with no suffix is contrary to Palestinian usage."[12] During Jesus' earthly ministry, his Semitic-speaking followers called him *mrî*, which was a respectful designation acknowledging Jesus' status as their teacher. After these same disciples experienced Jesus' resurrection, they no longer considered him to be their teacher but their sovereign Lord. Thus, they hailed him as *mr'n'*. Given that Semitic-speaking Jews, Dalman proposes, rarely used this term for God, Semitic-speaking Jewish Christians easily distinguished between God and Jesus; the latter being *mr'n'*. On the other hand, Greek-speaking Jews frequently referred to God as *kyrios*. When these Jews became followers of Jesus, they continued this practice and began to call Jesus by the same title. Given that suffixes are not attached directly to nouns in Greek, Greek-speaking Jewish Christians called Jesus and God *kyrios* or *ho kyrios*. The result was the loss of the Semitic-speaking Jewish Christian distinction between Jesus and God among Greek-speaking Jewish and eventually gentile Christians. Henceforth, this led to the theological development of the exalted *kyrios* Jesus that we find in Paul's letters, which were written to Greek-speaking Christians.[13]

Soon after Dalman's work, Wilhelm Bousset, who is part of a scholarly movement known as the History of Religions School, used Greco-Roman pagan literature and inscriptions to argue that Jesus' *kyrios*-ship developed under the influence of pagan cults among gentile Hellenistic Christians in

no manuscript tradition that supports this amendment. The assumption that χριστὸς κύριος was an impossible combination to flow from the pen of a devout Judean Jew is to read χριστὸς in terms of its meaning for later Christology and not in terms of its use as a political title in its own time.

12. Gustaf Dalman, *The Words of Jesus: Considered in the Light of Post-Biblical Jewish Writings and the Aramaic Language*, trans. D. M. Kay (Edinburgh: T&T Clark, 1902), 326.

13. Ibid., 325–30. For similar theses with various nuances see Foerster and Quell, *Lord*, 105–10; Oscar Cullmann, *The Christology of the New Testament*, trans. Shirley Guthrie and Charles A. M. Hall, rev. ed. (Philadelphia: Westminster, 1963), 199–234, esp. 200–207.

the more Hellenized cities of the Greek East. Bousset articulated a division between conservative Aramaic-speaking Jewish Christianity based in Palestine and a more liberal gentile Greek-speaking Christianity found in Antioch, Damascus, and Cilicia. The former espoused a rigid monotheism, only referred to God as "our Lord," and knew Jesus only as the coming eschatological Son of Man.[14] Therefore, Jesus' *kyrios*-ship could not have developed among Aramaic-speaking Jewish Christians. Given that hero and mystery cults of the Greek East had exalted lords at the center of their cults, the most probable historical background for Jesus' *kyrios*-ship is that gentile Christians in Antioch, Damascus, and Cilicia were influenced by such cults.[15]

Today most scholars reject both Dalman's and Bousset's proposals for the development of Jesus' *kyrios*-ship because of newer evidence that was unavailable to them and the refinement of the methods of historical investigation of early Christianity. Bousset's work suffers from an oversimplification.[16] Because of the diversity of early Christianity, the movement cannot be reduced to two groups: a conservative Aramaic Jewish version and a liberal gentile Greek one.[17] Martin Hengel demonstrated that all Second Temple Jews, even Aramaic speaking ones living in Palestine, were Hellenized to some extent.[18] And, many scholars pointed out that our earliest

---

14. Bousset, *Kyrios Christos*, 31–152. See also Rudolf Bultmann, *Theology of the New Testament*, trans. Kendrick Grobel (New York: Scribner's Sons, 1951, 1955), 1:121–29; Ferdinand Hahn, *The Titles of Jesus in Christology: Their History in Early Christianity*, trans. Harold Knight and George Ogg (Cleveland, OH: World Publishing Company, 1969), 12, 68–135; Reginald Fuller, *Foundations of New Testament Christology* (New York: Scribner's Sons, 1965), 111, 185. Hahn (*Titles*) nuanced the History of Religions School's scheme by adding Hellenistic Jewish Christianity between Palestinian Christianity and gentile Christianity to soften the distinction.

15. Bousset, *Kyrios Christos*, 119–52. Bousset (151) concludes, "In an age in which people honored the ruler with the solemn religious title of κύριος and prayed to him in the cult as κύριος, in a time in which there were many 'lords' in heaven and on earth, the Hellenistic Christian communities also had to set this crown upon the head of their Lord and address him as 'our Lord.'"

16. See Hurtado, *Lord Jesus Christ*, 20–23; Hurtado, "New Testament Christology: A Critique of Bousset's Influence," *TS* 40 (1979): 312–16.

17. See I. Howard Marshall, "Palestinian and Hellenistic Christianity: Some Critical Comments," *NTS* 19 (1973): 271–87.

18. Martin Hengel, *Judaism and Hellenism: Studies in Their Encounter in Palestine during the Early Hellenistic Period*, trans. John Bowden, 2 vols. (Philadelphia: Fortress, 1974); Hengel, *The "Hellenization" of Judaea in the First Century After Christ*, trans. John Bowdon (London: SCM, 1989).

reference to Jesus' *kyrios*-ship in Paul's letters is a transliteration of the Aramaic prayer "our Lord come!" (1 Cor 16:22).[19]

In 1979, Joseph A. Fitzmyer showed from newly published Dead Sea Scrolls the incorrectness of Dalman's proposal that Aramaic-speaking Jews rarely called God Lord and when they did so they always attached a suffix to the title. He demonstrates conclusively that Aramaic speaking Jews addressed God as *mr'* without suffixes on a number of occasions.[20] One such occurrence is in the Aramaic version of 1 Enoch and calls God *mry'* (4Q202 4:5). What is important about this specific usage of *mr'* for God is that we know how the Second Temple Greek translation of 1 Enoch rendered this occurrence of *mry'*, *ho kyrios* (1 Enoch 10:9). Given that Aramaic speaking Jews in Palestine referred to God as *mr'*, Fitzmyer concludes that Jesus' *kyrios*-ship developed in the Jerusalem church. There, Aramaic and Hebrew speaking Jewish Christians called God and Jesus *mr'* and *adon*, while their Greek speaking Jewish brothers and sisters called both God and Jesus *kyrios*.[21] Today, Fitzmyer's conclusion forms the scholarly consensus.[22]

I agree with this consensus about the location of the development of Jesus' *kyrios*-ship, but there are two difficulties with the discussion of the historical background for Jesus' *kyrios*-ship of the last century. First, most scholars have focused exclusively on the divine connotations of *kyrios*. For example, Hurtado notes at the outset of his discussion of the background of *kyrios* in Paul, "It is this use of *kyrios* as a title for deities that seems most relevant for appreciating Paul's application of the term to Christ."[23] To justify this focus on the divine connotation of *kyrios*, a number of historians point to two uses of *kyrios* for the God of Israel among Second Temple Jews. The first is the use of *kyrios* to translate God's covenant name, Yahweh, or the

---

19. Bousset (*Kyrios Christos*, 129) tries to trace this Aramaic prayer to the churches of Antioch, Damascus, and Cilicia. Bultmann (*Theology*, 1:51–52) argues that the Lord in question is God and not Jesus.

20. 1QapGen ar 20:12–13; 11Q10 24:5–6; 26:8. To Fitzmyer's evidence from the Dead Sea Scrolls, we can add a first-century-CE Aramaic graffito from Herodium that calls God *'lh'* (*CIIP* 3351).

21. Joseph A. Fitzmyer, "The Semitic Background of the New Testament *Kyrios*-Title," in *A Wandering Aramean: Collected Aramaic Essays* (Missoula, MT: Scholars Press, 1979), 115–42; Fitzmyer, "κύριος," *EDNT* 2:329–31. See also Hurtado, *Lord Jesus Christ*, 108–18, 179–84.

22. Hurtado, *Lord Jesus Christ*, 11–18, 108–18. See also Richard Bauckham, *Jesus and the God of Israel: God Crucified and Other Studies on the New Testament's Christology of Divine Identity* (Grand Rapids: Eerdmans, 2008); N. T. Wright, *Paul and the Faithfulness of God* (Minneapolis: Fortress, 2013), 2:619–773.

23. Hurtado, "Lord," 561.

Tetragrammaton (called such because it consists of four Hebrew letters) (Exod 3:13–15), in the Greek OT. The second is that some form of Lord in Aramaic, Hebrew, or Greek was spoken for God's covenant name when it was read aloud in Second Temple synagogue services.[24] Therefore, calling Jesus *mr,' adon*, or *kyrios* means at the least he is divine.[25] For some scholars, calling Jesus by this title means that he is in some sense Yahweh. For example, Richard Bauckham concludes that when Paul calls Jesus *kyrios* in Phil 2:9–11 he is identifying Jesus "with and as Yahweh."[26]

This conclusion, however, needs to be nuanced. Even though Fitzmyer demonstrated that Semitic speaking Jews of Jesus' day called God *mr'* and *adon*, he notes that there is no evidence that Jewish scribes used *mr'* to translate God's covenant name. So, *mr'* was used to call God Lord, but not to address God as Yahweh.[27] The same reticence to translate God's covenant name with *kyrios* is found in Greek manuscripts of Second Temple Jewish documents. Throughout the nineteenth and early twentieth centuries, the evidence that scholars had for how Second Temple Jews translated God's covenant name in Greek were Christian manuscripts of the Greek OT that translated the Tetragrammaton with *kyrios*. Since that time, pre-Christian papyrus fragments of the Greek OT have been discovered and these evidence that Jewish scribes either left God's covenant name in Hebrew or they rendered it with the Greek letters ΙΑΩ.[28]

This lack of Second Temple Jewish manuscripts with *mr'*, *adon*, or *kyrios* translating God's covenant name is probably due to survival of evidence, however. Some of Philo's, Paul's, and Luke's theological arguments indicate that they and their auditors knew of manuscripts of the Greek OT where *kyrios* rendered God's covenant name (Philo, *Abraham* 121; Letter of Aristeas 155; Josephus, *Ant.* 13.68; 20.90; 1 Cor 8:5–6; Acts 2:34–35). It does

24. Hurtado, *Lord Jesus Christ*, 108–18. W. G. Baudissin's (*Kyrios als Gottesname im Judentum und seine Stelle in der Religionsgeschichte*, 4 vols. [Giessen: Töpelmann, 1926–1929]) multivolume survey of *kyrios* in ancient Judaism concluded that the Greek OT used *kyrios* for the divine name.

25. Hurtado, *Lord Jesus Christ*, 11–18, 108–18.

26. Bauckham, *Jesus and the God of Israel*, 197–210; Wright, *Paul and the Faithfulness of God*, 2:619–773.

27. Fitzmyer, "Semitic Background," 125.

28. Ibid., 120–23. The situation has not changed since the publication of Fitzmyer's article. For a recent discussion see Martin Rösel, "The Reading and Translation of the Divine Name in the Masoretic Tradition and the Greek Pentateuch," *JSOT* 31 (2007): 411–28, although I disagree with Rösel that *kyrios* was the original rendering of God's covenant name in the Second Temple period. Emanuel Tov (*Hebrew Bible, Greek Bible, and Qumran*, TSAJ 121 [Tübingen: Mohr Siebeck, 2008], 339–64) proposes that ΙΑΩ reflects the "original text" of the Greek OT.

seem probable that *kyrios*, *adon*, or *mr'* was read in place of God's covenant name in Second Temple synagogue services. In short, I contend that the conclusion about whether or not Jews used *kyrios*, *adon*, or *mr'* to translate God's covenant name is not an "either/or" solution, but a "both/and" one. I propose that there was diversity in the rendering of God's covenant name in Second Temple Judaism. Philo's use of the divine name captures this diversity well. He says that God's covenant name consists of four letters, which means he cannot be referring to *kyrios* and *IAŌ*, but the Tetragrammaton in Hebrew (*Moses* 2.115, 132).[29] On the other hand, some of Philo's philosophical discussions presuppose that God's covenant name is *kyrios* (*Abraham* 121). If we take the evidence seriously, *kyrios*, *mr'*, and *adon* can, but do not always, refer to God's covenant name in the Second Temple period, including early Christianity. Therefore, we cannot conclude or assume without good reason that every Second Temple Jew, including early Christians, associated *kyrios* with Yahweh.

The second difficulty with most of the discussion of Jesus' *kyrios*-ship is that scholars have paid little attention to inscriptions from the southern Levant and Palestine and how these texts can illuminate early Christian usage of *mr'/adon/kyrios* for Jesus. Dalman, writing in 1902, did not have access to many inscriptions that we now have, but even so he points out that *mr'* is used for kings in three Aramaic inscriptions (one from Nabatea, one from Palmyra, and one from Egypt). Given this evidence, Dalman concludes that Palestinian Jewish Christians considered Jesus' resurrection as him entering "into His state of kingly majesty."[30] He extrapolates no further on what he means by this, but Dalman seems to suggest that this royal state was subsumed by Jesus' divinity among Greek speaking Jewish Christians who used *kyrios* with divine connotations because it referred to God as well.[31]

Bousset bases his conclusion that Jesus' *kyrios*-ship developed from influence of pagan cults from non-Jewish Greek inscriptions. He does not consider Semitic and Greek epigraphs from the southern Levant presumably because of their "profane" and not "religious" character.[32] Finally, Fitzmyer

29. For a discussion see James R. Royse, "Philo, ΚΥΡΙΟΣ, and the Tetragrammaton," SPhiloA 3 (1991): 167–83.

30. Dalman, *Words of Jesus*, 329.

31. Ibid., 326–30.

32. Bousset (*Kyrios Christos*, 121–29, quote from 122n12) concludes that the early Christian community in Palestine called Jesus *adoni* because of the influence of the Hebrew of Ps 110:1 ("the Lord said to my lord, 'Sit at my right hand . . .'"). However, this use of *adoni* for Jesus "still has an explicit profane character and not a religious one."

does not focus on inscriptions, but acknowledges that *mr'* is a royal title in Semitic papyri, the Dead Sea Scrolls, and some passages from our canonical gospels (cf. Mark 12:35–37; etc.). However, he concludes that early Christian use of *kyrios* extends beyond a royal connotation because Christians considered themselves slaves of *kyrios* Jesus.[33] Therefore, as late as 1998 the German NT scholar Helmut Merklein lamented that inscriptions "have barely played a role in the previous discussion of the NT problem [of Jesus as *kyrios*]."[34] Merklein's assessment still rings true today. In what follows, I show that Greek and Semitic inscriptions from the southern Levant support the proposal that Jesus' *kyrios*-ship developed in the region and that Jesus' lordship had a royal, messianic, and not exclusively divine background.

II. The Semitic Royal Nuance of "Lord"

Inscriptions from the southern Levant composed in Greek and in Semitic dialects demonstrate that lord was a royal title particular to the region prior to, during, and after the development of Jesus' *kyrios*-ship.[35] This localized meaning and use of lord stems from an ancient Near Eastern tradition of addressing kings as such, which dates back to the third millennium BCE and is attested in the OT.[36] Therefore, calling a ruler lord is not a Greek or

33. Fitzmyer, "Semitic Background," 131–32.

34. Helmut Merklein, "*Marānā* (»unser Herr«) als Bezeichnung des nabatäischen Königs: Eine Analogie zur neutestamentlichen Kyrios-Bezeichnung?," in *Von Jesus zum Christus: Christologische Studien*, ed. Erich Gräßer, BZNW 93 (Berlin: de Gruyter, 1998), 27.

35. In an underappreciated article first published in 1922–1923, Lucien Cerfaux ("Le titre Kyrios et la dignité royale de Jésus," in *Recueil Lucien Cerfaux: Études d'Exégèse et d'Histoire Religieuse de Monseigneur Cerfaux* [Gembloux: Duculot, 1954], 1:3–63) gathered Greek and Semitic inscriptions and a few literary sources from the southern Levant, concluding that lord was a royal title. He traces Jesus' *kyrios*-ship to this royal tradition, proposing that when early Christians referred to Jesus as Lord they stressed his celestial enthronement at God's right hand. In 1998, Helmut Merklein ("*Marānā*," 25–41) gathered newly published Nabatean inscriptions, concluding that Lord may be a royal title for Jesus and there may be a connection between Lord and Paul's scenario of Jesus returning as a triumphant king (1 Thess 4:13–18). More recently (2002), Frenschkowski ("Kyrios in Context," 95–114, esp. 97, 109–10) reviewed published Nabatean inscriptions and concluded that given the use of lord in them, the early Christian use of Lord for Jesus in the Q tradition is royal.

36. Surviving inscriptions, treaties, cuneiform tablets, and letters from the ancient Near East and the OT testify that the inhabitants of the ancient Near East referred to kings as lords, especially in direct speech: *ANESTP* 46, 48, 49, 52, 199, 234, 483–90 (= *COS* 3:92), 534–41, 606, 623–32, 662, 664, 670; *COS* 3:54; 1 Kgs 1:2, 17, 18, 20, 21, 24, 27, 31, 33, 36, 37, 43, 47; 2:38; etc.

Roman custom. It is not until the mid-first century CE, roughly twenty years after Jesus' crucifixion and a few years after the earliest use of *kyrios* for Jesus in the NT (1 Thessalonians) that this custom spread outside the southern Levant. Most of the major scholarly word studies of *kyrios* that incorporate inscriptions agree that the use of the title for a sovereign by Greeks outside the southern Levant is evidence of the influence of this regional tradition on the larger Greco-Roman world.[37]

The regional custom of calling the reigning monarch lord is found mostly in private inscriptions, epitaphs and dedications, but it also appears in some public epigraphs. This evidence suggests that the designation of a sovereign as lord was an institutional practice that monarchs' subjects accepted. An example of a public inscription is a sacred inscription (see chapter 1.IV.1.3) that was found in modern-day Hammon, Lebanon (south of Tyre), dating to 222 BCE. It was written in a dialect of Aramaic known as Phoenician, and it commemorates the dedication of part of a portico of the temple complex of the Phoenician god Milkashtart to Astarte, a Phoenician goddess. What is important about this inscription is the date of the dedication: the twenty-sixth year of Ptolemy, who is "lord of kings" (*adn mlkm*).[38] To provide an example of a private inscription, there is a boundary marker (*msgd'*) (see chapter 1.IV.1.2) written in Nabatean and dating to 93 CE that was found in modern-day Bostra (in southern Syria). The epigraph is a dedication (see chapter 1.IV.1.3) to the Nabatean gods Dushara and Ara that thanks them for bringing "life and victory to [the Nabatean king Rabel's] people" (*'ḥyy wš yzb 'mh*). In this inscription, the gods are identified as those of "our lord . . . the king Rabel" (*'lh mr'n' . . . lrb'l mlk'*).[39]

---

37. Foerster, "κύριος," *TDNT* 3:1046, 1051–55; Cerfaux, "titre Kyrios," 7–14; Frenschkowski, "Kyrios," 755–56; Frenschkowski, "Kyrios in Context," 98–99. There are a few references to Augustus, Tiberius, Caligula, and Claudius as lord in Greek papyri and inscriptions from Egypt, but there is an explosion of sources from Egypt calling Nero lord during his reign (54–68 CE). See Paul Bureth, *Les Titulatures imperiales dans les papyrus, les ostraca et les inscriptoins d'Égypte (30 a.C. – 284 p.C.)* (Brussells: Foundation égyptologique reine Elisabeth, 1964), 21–35. This conclusion contradicts the common assertation found among some scholars (e.g., Wright, *Paul and the Faithfulness of God*, 2:1285) that "lord" always meant the emperor in the early first century CE. Frenschkowski ("Kyrios in Context," 99) aptly notes, "[Lord] is never formally bestowed or awarded [on an emperor], and it never becomes part of imperial or senatorial decrees. In 1st century imperial ideology it never is part of the official way of addressing the emperor, which means it is also never used on coins, in official correspondence or in State inscriptions."

38. *TSSI* 3:118–21, no. 31 lines 5–6. Cf. *CIS* 1.7 line 5.

39. *TNSI* 254–55, no. 101.

There are a number of epitaphs (see chapter 1.IV.2.1) from the southern Levant that refer to the reigning king as *adon/mr'/kyrios*. John Healey has collected forty-three Nabatean funerary inscriptions (mostly from the ancient city of Hegra, but some from other locations that were once a part of the Nabatean kingdom, such as Petra). All of these funerary inscriptions were part of tomb complexes that were carved into rock. Of these forty-three epitaphs, thirteen or 30 percent refer to a reigning Nabatean monarch as *mr'*.[40] Most of these references are found in instructions regarding fines for people caught violating the tombs. These epitaphs prescribe that the fines should be paid to the king of Nabatea who is: "our lord the king Harethath" (*vlmr'n' ḥrttt mlk'*),[41] "our lord Harethath, king of the Nabateans" (*vl'mr'n' ḥrtt mlk' nḅtw*),[42] or "our lord" (*vl'mr'n'*).[43] The king in question for most of these epitaphs, Harethath, is none other than Aretas IV (9 BCE–40 CE) whom students of Paul know (2 Cor 11:32). Given the prevalence of references to the Nabatean king as *mr'n'* in these inscriptions, Lucien Cerfaux, Helmut Merklein, and Marco Frenschkowski conclude in three separate treatments that it is a Nabatean royal title.[44]

These Nabatean inscriptions are important because we know for certain that Jews and Nabateans interacted (both positively and negatively) during the Second Temple period. First Maccabees reports that Nabateans were hospitable to Judas Maccabeus on his military expedition into the territory where they lived (5:24–25a) and that the Nabateans provided intelligence to Judas about the ill-treatment of Jews in Gilead (5:25b–27). According to Josephus, the Hasmonean king Alexander Jannaeus waged an unsuccessful war against the Nabatean king Obodas I around 90 BCE, after which Obodas took control of Moab and Gilead (*Ant.* 13.375, 382). Josephus testifies that in 31 BCE Herod the Great defeated the Nabatean king Malichus in a battle near Philadelphia (modern-day Amman, Jordan) (*J.W.* 1.360–364) and exacted tribute from Malichus. The Nabatean king, however, was slow in paying, which led Herod to go to war with him again (*Ant.* 15.107). Herod took his army to Philadelphia for a second time and was victorious (*Ant.* 15.111). Afterward, Herod engaged the Nabateans in

---

40. *H* 1, 5, 9, 11, 12, 19, 28, 29, 30, 34, 36, 38, and (i) Petra.

41. *H* 1 line 8 (= *CIS* 2.199 line 8); *H* 12 line 10 (= *CIS* 2.205 line 10). Cf. *CIS* 2.206 lines 7–8.

42. *H* 29 lines 4–5 (= *CIS* 2.201 lines 4–5).

43. *H* 9 line 8 (= *CIS* 2.212 line 8). Cf. *CIS* 2.209 line 9.

44. Cerfaux, "titre Kyrios," 19; Merklein, "*Marānā*," 37; Frenschkowski, "Kyrios in Context," 97, 109–10.

another battle near Cana, but was defeated (*Ant.* 15.112–120). Herod mustered his troops a third time, crossed the Jordan, and defeated the Nabateans (*Ant.* 15.147–154), after which he became their "defender" (προστάτης) (*Ant.* 15.155–160).[45]

Later, Herod the Great's son, Herod Antipas, married the daughter of the Nabatean king Aretas IV (Josephus, *Ant.* 18.109). The marriage did not last because Antipas divorced her to marry Herodias, his brother Aristobulus's wife (*Ant.* 18.109–112; cf. Mark 6:17–29).[46] Josephus says that Aretas used a border dispute as an opportunity to go to war against Antipas to avenge his daughter. Aretas was victorious against Antipas (*Ant.* 18.111–115). The only reference to the Nabateans in the NT comes from Paul, who says that after his call/conversion he "immediately departed into Arabia," which is the kingdom of Nabatea, and that after some time he returned to Damascus, where he stayed for three years (Gal 1:17–18a).[47] During Paul's tenure in Damascus, the ethnarch of the city, under the authority of Aretas, attempted to arrest Paul, forcing him to escape by being let down in a basket from the city's wall (2 Cor 11:32).[48] Finally, we know from a first-century-CE inscription from Hegra and from the Babatha archive from the Cave of Letters in the Judean wilderness (dating to 130s CE) that Jews and Nabateans lived together peaceably and interacted with each other.[49]

There are a number of inscriptions related to Herod the Great and his dynasty that showcase the southern Levantine custom of calling the reigning sovereign *kyrios*. To date, there are five Greek epigraphs from the southern Levant that call Herod the Great or one of the members of his dynasty *kyrios* (*OGIS* 415, 418, 423, 425, 426). For instance, a man named Obaisatus set up a statue of Herod the Great at the right-hand entrance of the temple of Baal Shamim in Palymra (in modern-day Syria). He paid for the statue's construction with his own money and memorialized it with a

---

45. See David F. Graf, "Nabateans," *ABD* 4:970–73.

46. For a discussion of Herod Antipas's marriages and their association with the Synoptic tradition found in Mark 6:17–29 see Yarbro Collins, *Mark*, 303–14.

47. Hans Dieter Betz, *Galatians: A Commentary on Paul's Letter to the Churches in Galatia*, Hermeneia (Philadelphia: Fortress, 1979), 73–74.

48. For a discussion see Victor Paul Furnish, *II Corinthians Translated with Introduction, Notes, and Commentary*, AB 32A (Garden City: Doubleday, 1984), 521–22.

49. For the tomb of Jewish man in Herga see *H* 4 (= *CIS* 2.219). Babatha was a Jewish woman who owned property in Nabatean territory and whose archive has been discovered. See Yigael Yadin et al, *The Documents from the Bar Kokhba Period in the Cave of Letters: Hebrew, Aramaic, and Nabatean-Aramaic Papyri*, JDS 3 (Jerusalem: Israel Exploration Society, 2002).

private, honorary inscription (see chapter 1.IV.2.2) on the statue's base that says "to *kyrios* King Herod" ([Βα]σιλεῖ Ἡρώδει κυρίῳ) (*OGIS* 415). What is important about this inscription and the other four from the southern Levant that call a Herodian lord is that we can compare them with epigraphs outside the southern Levant that mention Herod the Great and members of his dynasty. This comparison is possible because the Herodians patronized building projects and pagan religious rites in Greco-Roman cities, and these cities set up inscriptions commemorating their benefactions.[50] To date, there are five such epigraphs known from Athens, Cos, Ephesus, and Delos, and none of these call a Herodian monarch *kyrios*.[51] Therefore, the practice of referring to the reigning sovereign as *kyrios* is particular to the southern Levant in the early Roman Empire.[52]

Finally, I appeal to Philo, an ancient Jewish source predating the development of early Christianity that acknowledges the royal nuance of *kyrios* in the southern Levant. He records that Agrippa I sojourned in Alexandria on a return trip from Rome and when he arrived anti-Jewish riots ensued.[53] The Alexandrians accused Agrippa of trying to make himself a king (*Flaccus* 25–35). In their fervor, the Alexandrians grabbed an insane person named Carabbas, adorned him with fake royal trappings—a scroll for a crown, some kind of cloth for a robe, and a small papyrus reed for a scepter—to imitate a king (βασιλεύς). The Alexandrians then pretended that Carabbas was adjudicating justice for them (*Flaccus* 36–38). Philo says that they hailed him as μάρις, which is a Greek translation of the Aramaic *mr'*, because "it is said to be the name for 'lord' (κύριος) among the Syrians because they knew that Agrippa was a native Syrian and that he had a large Syrian district over which he reigned" (βασιλεύω) (*Flaccus* 39). What is noteworthy about Philo's discussion is that he testifies that the populace of Alexandria was aware of the royal meaning of lord in Syria/Palestine. Philo, who was well educated, well versed in the Greco-Roman world, and had at least traveled to Jerusalem and Rome (Philo, *Embassy*), seems to agree with their

50. For a list of Herod the Great's building projects see Peter Richardson, *Herod the Great: King of the Jews and Friend of the Romans* (Columbia: University of South Carolina Press, 1996), 197–202.

51. *OGIS* 414, 427, 428 (Athens), 416 (Cos), 417 (Delos), and 429 (Ephesus).

52. Not all inscriptions from the southern Levant mentioning members of the Herodian dynasty call a Herodian monarch lord (*OGIS* 419, 420, 421, 422, 424), but those that do are ones from the southern Levant.

53. Agrippa I was called lord in an inscription from southern Syria (*OGIS* 418).

assessment. Thus, both inscriptions and literary sources attest that *adon*/*mr'*/*kyrios* is a royal title particular to the southern Levant.

III. The Significance of Jesus' Royal Lordship

When we compare the data above with our earliest evidence from the NT, Paul's letters, there are striking similarities between the use of lord in inscriptions from the southern Levant and in Paul's letters. It is generally agreed that Paul's prayer μαράνα θά in 1 Cor 16:22 means "our Lord come!" and that this petition is a Greek translation of an Aramaic prayer, *mrn't'*, which probably originated in Aramaic-speaking churches in Palestine.[54] Evidently, this petition was part of the early Christian tradition that was passed on to Paul (Gal 1:18–20), who taught it to the Corinthian Christians when he established their church (about 50/51 CE). It is probable that Paul did likewise with other churches. Provided that this is correct, then μαράνα θά is a tradition common among early Christians both in Paul's predominately gentile churches and in the Jewish churches of Palestine. The Lord of this prayer matches verbatim the above references to Nabatean kings in epitaphs: μαράνα = *mr'n'*.[55] Aramaic-speaking Jewish Christians in Jerusalem and its environs and those Christians whose main language was Greek but who spent time in the southern Levant, like Paul (Gal 1:17–18; 2 Cor 11:32; cf. Acts 22:3), would have known this similarity between their Christian prayer and the address of monarchs in the region.

Paul frequently qualifies the identity of "our *kyrios*," by noting that he is "our *kyrios* Jesus," (Rom 4:24; 16:20; 1 Cor 5:4; 9:1; 1 Thess 2:19; 3:11, 13), "our *kyrios* Christ" (Rom 16:18), or "our *kyrios* Jesus Christ" (Rom 1:4; 5:1, 11, 21; 6:23; 7:25; 8:39; 15:6, 30; 1 Cor 1:2, 3, 7, [8], 9, 10; 15:31, 57; 2 Cor 1:2, 3; 8:9; Gal 6:14, 18; 1 Thess 1:3; 5:9, 23, 28). We have seen that kings in the southern Levant are addressed similarly. The Nabatean boundary marker from Bostra calls the sovereign "our lord . . . the king Rabel" (*'lh mr'n' . . . lrb'l mlk'*).[56] Several of the Nabatean epitaphs qualify Aretas IV's royal name in like manner: "to our lord the king Harethath" (*vlmr'n' ḥrttt mlk'*)[57] and "our

54. Joseph A. Fitzmyer, "Kyrios and Maranatha and Their Aramaic Background," in *To Advance the Gospel: New Testament Studies* (New York: Crossroad, 1981), 218–35.

55. *H* 1 line 8 (= *CIS* 2.199 line 8), 12 line 10 (= *CIS* 2.205 line 10). Cf. *CIS* 2.206 lines 7–8; *H* 29 lines 4–5 (= *CIS* 2.201 lines 4–5), 9 line 8 (= *CIS* 2.212 line 8). Cf. *CIS* 2.209 line 9.

56. *TNSI* 254–55, no. 101; *CIS* 2.323, 337.

57. *H* 1 line 8 (= *CIS* 2.199 line 8), 12 line 10 (= *CIS* 2.205 line 10). Cf. *CIS* 2.206 lines 7–8.

lord Harethath, king of the Nabataeans" (*vl'mr'n' ḥrtt mlk' nḅtw*).[58] Recently, Matthew Novenson has argued that "Christ" in our earliest Christian documents is not Jesus' last name, as many scholars have concluded throughout the twentieth century, but rather an honorific term comparable to Epiphanes and Augustus. Therefore, Paul's use of "Christ language" for Jesus is an example of royal messianism.[59] Provided that Novenson is correct, Paul's qualifications of Jesus' *kyrios*-ship with "Christ" and/or "Jesus" resemble Nabatean royal titles.

The final similarity between the use of lord in inscriptions from the southern Levant and in Paul's letters relates to the special relationship between the deity and the sovereign. Three epigraphs acknowledge that the god in question is somehow in a unique relationship with the king. Two first-century-CE Nabatean epitaphs refer to the kingdom's patron god, Dushara, as "the god of our lord" the king (*'lh mr'n'*);[60] one Aramaic sacred inscription from Salkad (in modern-day southern Syria) that is a stele is dedicated "to Allat, the mother of the gods of our lord Rabel" (*'lt 'm 'lhy' dy mr'n' rb'l*).[61] Similarly, Paul acknowledges that *kyrios* Jesus has a special relationship with the God of Israel by referring to the latter as "the God and Father of our *kyrios* Jesus Christ" (Rom 15:6; 2 Cor 1:3; 11:31).

These similarities between our earliest Christian usage of *kyrios* for Jesus and the use of lord for monarchs in the southern Levant suggest that for Jewish Christians with connections to the region, including Paul, *adon*/*mr'*/*kyrios* is a royal title. Provided that this is the case, this royal connotation of *kyrios* can illuminate the development of Jesus' *kyrios*-ship and certain NT texts in three ways. First, the above southern Levantine inscriptions support the current scholarly consensus that Jesus' *kyrios*-ship developed in Palestine, most probably among early Jewish Christians in Jerusalem. We should remember that contrary to popular scholarly consensus lord was not a widespread title for emperors in the first half of the first century CE and that it is not until Nero's reign that the practice began to be attested outside the southern Levant.[62]

Second, Jewish Christians may not have thought exclusively of Jesus' divinity when they addressed him as *adon*/*mr'*/*kyrios*, even though most scholars conclude otherwise. For example, Fitzmyer argues that because

58. *H* 29 lines 4–5 (= *CIS* 2.201 lines 4–5). Cf. *CIS* 2.184.

59. Matthew V. Novenson, *Christ among the Messiahs: Christ Language in Paul and Messiah Language in Ancient Judaism* (Oxford: Oxford University Press, 2012), 174.

60. *CIS* 2.209 line 8 (31/32 CE) H (i) Petra (first century CE).

61. *CIS* 2.185 (70–106 CE).

62. Foerster, "κύριος," 3:1046, 1051–55; Cerfaux, "titre Kyrios," 7–14; Frenschkowski, "Kyrios," 755–56; Frenschkowski, "Kyrios in Context," 98–99.

Aramaic-speaking Jews addressed God as the Lord, when Jewish Christians called Jesus by the same title this "gives evidence of a veneration of Jesus by early Jewish Christians . . . as a figure associated with Yahweh of the Old Testament, even as one on the same level with him, without saying explicitly that he is divine."[63] Some scholars go beyond Fitzmyer's conclusion proposing that the early Christian use of *kyrios* for Jesus identifies him as Yahweh in some sense. As noted above, Bauckham contends that the early Christian use of *kyrios* for Jesus identifies him as intrinsic to the identity of God.[64] The above Greek and Semitic inscriptions from the southern Levant suggest otherwise. Three more inscriptions showcase that those living in the southern Levant could distinguish between a human, non-divine *kyrios* who is king and a god *kyrios* who is divine.

Two of these epigraphs are private dedications (see chapter 1.IV.2.3) to Zeus that subjects of Agrippa I and II made. Both inscriptions call Zeus and the Agrippas *kyrios* with no hint of divine honors for the latter. The first dedication (37–44 CE) is from Aqraba (in modern-day southern Syria) and is dated "in the sixteenth year of *kyrios* King Agrippa" ("Ετους ιη´ βασιλέως Ἀγρ|ίππα κυρίου). The objects dedicated are doorways and an altar to Zeus because of the dedicator's "piety toward the lord Zeus" (ἕν|[ε]κα Διὶ κυρίῳ) (*OGIS* 423). The second inscription is from Al-Sanamayn (in modern-day southern Syria) and is dated during "the thirty-second year of *kyrios* King Agrippa [II]" (λβ´ βασιλέως Ἀγρίππα κυρίου). The object dedicated is a doorway "to *kyrios* Zeus" (Διὶ κυρίῳ) (*OGIS* 426). The third epigraph is the earliest use of *kyrios* for a Roman emperor in the southern Levant (29–37 CE) and is a dedication from Abila (in modern-day Syria) that a freedman of the tetrarch Lysanias (Luke 3:1) dedicated to "*kyrios* [god] Cronos" ([θεῷ] Κρόνῳ κυρίῳ) "on behalf of the safety of the Au[gusti] *kyrioi*" (ὑπὲρ (τ)ῆ(ς) τῶν κυρίων Σε[βαστῶν]| σωτηρίας), Tiberius and his mother Livia (*OGIS* 606). There is nothing cultic about these references to Agrippa I or II and Tiberius and Livia as *kyrios*, suggesting that the populace of the southern Levant could refer to human sovereigns and gods as lords without attributing divinity to the former.[65]

Let me make two qualifications about the observation that *adon*/*mr'*/*kyrios* is a royal title in the southern Levant. First, I am not suggesting that those Jewish Christians who called Jesus by this title did not think of him

63. Fitzmyer, "Kyrios and Maranatha," 229.

64. See Bauckham, *Jesus and the God of Israel*, 197–210.

65. Foerster, "κύριος," *TDNT* 3:1056; Cerfaux, "titre Kyrios," 16–17, 25.

as divine. It is clear that Paul works with Christian tradition predating his letters that acknowledges Jesus' divinity (Phil 2:6–11; Col 1:15–20). Larry Hurtado has shown that early Christians incorporated Jesus into their devotional practices in unheard of and innovative ways for Second Temple Jews.[66] My contention is that for early Jewish Christians with connections to the southern Levant, *adon/mr'/kyrios* is first and foremost a royal and thus messianic title and not exclusively a divine one (cf. Acts 2:34–36). Second, I am not advocating a position like Bousset's, proposing that early Christians in Palestine "borrowed" the concept of Jesus' *kyrios*-ship from their neighbors or that they were "unconsciously influenced" by them. Rather, I contend that the royal use of *adon/mr'/kyrios* by Jewish Christians in the southern Levant and those with connections to the region belongs to the older ancient Near Eastern tradition of calling monarchs lord, to which the OT attests.[67] It is probable, however, that when Christianity moved outside the southern Levant and as the first generation of Jewish Christians with connections to the region passed away, this royal meaning of Jesus' *kyrios*-ship was lost.[68]

The final way that the royal nuance of *kyrios* illuminates early Christology is that it explains some of the regal aspects of Jesus' *kyrios*-ship in our early Christian sources. It is generally agreed that Paul describes the parousia of Jesus in 1 Thess 4:13–18 in terms of a triumphant monarch visiting a city. One of the first scholars to discuss this point at length was George Milligan in 1908. He notes that Jewish writings provide little evidence for Paul's use of the Greek term παρουσία, but that there are numerous Greek papyri that describe a king's παρουσία to a particular city, detailing preparations for it.[69] Every time that Paul refers to Jesus' parousia he connects it with *kyrios* Jesus (1 Thess 2:19; 3:13; 4:15; 5:23). It seems that Paul's use of this phrase to describe Jesus' regal Second Coming in 1 Thessalonians reflects the royal meaning of *kyrios* in the southern Levant.[70]

In addition to Paul's use of *kyrios*, the royal meaning of the title illuminates Luke's testimony that Jewish Christians in Jerusalem first used *kyrios* for Jesus soon after they experienced his resurrection and exaltation (Acts 2:34–36). Scholarly opinion about the historicity of Luke's testimony about

66. See Hurtado, *Lord Jesus Christ*, 134–53.

67. The tradition of calling the reigning monarch lord is found in 1–2 Kings (1:2, 13, 17, etc.); Ps 110:1; Dan 4:16 = ET 4:19; 4:21 = ET 4:24.

68. Merklein, "*Marānā*," 38–40.

69. George Milligan, *St Paul's Epistles to the Thessalonians: The Greek Text with Introduction and Notes* (London: Macmillan, 1908), 145–46.

70. Merklein, "*Marānā*," 38–39.

the use of Ps 110:1 by early disciples of Jesus in Jerusalem is divided. On the one hand, some scholars contend that the type of exegesis of Ps 110:1 that we find in Acts 2:34–36 is too developed for the earliest days of the Christian movement.[71] On the other hand, some exegetes argue that Luke's picture of the early disciples searching their scriptures to make sense of their experience of Jesus' resurrection and ascension is accurate.[72]

There is no doubt that Luke's handiwork is all over Acts 2 and that he has crafted Peter's speech for his own theological agenda.[73] However, Luke's testimony and use of *kyrios* accurately reflects the royal nuance of *kyrios* in the southern Levant in the early first century CE. What is more, Luke has draped Peter's sermon in Davidic, royal imagery and its climax is Jesus' enthronement at God's right hand. This action, according to Luke, fulfills Ps 110:1. Whereupon, God proclaimed Jesus both *kyrios* and Messiah, which appear to be synonyms (Acts 2:34–36). In short, the royal meaning of *adon/mr'/kyrios* in the southern Levant suggests that Luke's tracing of the *kyrios* title for Jesus to the earliest days of the Christian movement reflects a local, royal custom.[74]

IV. Conclusion

To summarize, inscriptions provide evidence for regional and civic customs and traditions. Epigraphs from the southern Levant illuminate the development of Jesus' *kyrios*-ship. Both public and private inscriptions from the region provide evidence that *adon/mr'/kyrios* was a royal title particular to the southern Levant. Given that the use of this title for sovereigns in the area resembles, verbatim at times, our earliest use of *kyrios* for Jesus in Paul's letters, I contend that these epigraphs support the scholarly consensus of the provenance for the development of Jesus' *kyrios*-ship in Palestine and the idea that Jesus' lordship is royal, messianic, and not exclusively divine.

---

71. Donald Juel, *Messianic Exegesis: Christological Interpretation of the Old Testament in Early Christianity* (Philadelphia: Fortress, 1992), 139–41, 146–50.

72. C. H. Dodd, *According to the Scriptures: The Sub-Structure of New Testament Theology* (London: Nisbet, 1952), 34–35, 120–21; Barnabas Lindars, *New Testament Apologetic: The Doctrinal Significance of the Old Testament Quotations Study Edition* (London: SCM, 1973), 32–51. See also Matt 25:34, 37, 40, 44.

73. See Joseph A. Fitzmyer, *The Acts of the Apostles: A New Translation with Introduction and Commentary*, AB 31 (New York: Doubleday, 1998), 103–14, 247–67.

74. Cerfaux, "titre Kyrios," 43, 48, 62–63.

CHAPTER 3

"Devour" or "Go Ahead with" the Lord's Banquet? Inscriptions and Philology

One of the most important contributions that inscriptions (and papyri) made to the study of the NT in the late nineteenth and early twentieth century was helping to establish the relationship between NT Greek and the common or Koine Greek of the Hellenistic and Roman periods. Until the discovery of inscriptions (and papyri), many scholars, who only read classical Greek like the works of Plato, noted the differences in syntax and style between classical Greek and NT Greek and concluded that the latter was a special form of Greek spoken by Jews of the Second Temple period or even inspired by the Holy Spirit. Today, most scholars acknowledge that NT Greek is part of the Koine dialect of Greek even if they debate the extent to which Aramaic influenced the Greek of the writers of NT.[1]

In addition to the significant role that inscriptions played in establishing the nature of NT Greek, epigraphs still offer benefits to the student of the NT, such as helping to establish the meaning of specific Greek words at a given place and time by providing a snapshot of how individuals living in the Hellenistic or Roman periods used them. The reason that inscriptions can function in this way is that epigraphs are historically contextual documents: products of particular persons or groups, at particular times, and from particular cities and regions. To demonstrate the philological ability of inscriptions, this chapter's epigraphic case study focuses on the meaning of a particular verb, προλαμβάνω (1 Cor 11:21), found in Paul's discussion of the problem with the sacrament of the Lord's Banquet in Corinth (1 Cor 11:17–34). Scholars disagree over the verb's translation, whether it should be rendered "to go ahead with" or "to eat," which affects their reconstruc-

1. For a discussion of NT Greek see Stanley E. Porter, "Language and Translation of the New Testament," in *The Oxford Handbook of Biblical Studies*, ed. J. W. Rogerson and Judith Lieu (Oxford: Oxford University Press, 2006), 184–96; Daniel B. Wallace, *Greek Grammar Beyond the Basics: An Exegetical Syntax of the New Testament* (Grand Rapids: Zondervan, 1996), 12–29.

tion of both the problem that Paul addresses and his solution to it. What is more, some scholars have introduced epigraphy into the discussion, arguing that one particular inscription proves that προλαμβάνω means "to eat" in certain circumstances, such as in 1 Cor 11:21. The purpose of this chapter is to adjudicate this scholarly use of inscriptions and to discover the most probable translation of προλαμβάνω.

I. Προλαμβάνω in 1 Cor 11:21: Scholarly Proposals

The critical issue in reconstructing the problem that Paul addresses with the Lord's Banquet in Corinth (1 Cor 11:17–34) rests on the translation of the verb προλαμβάνω (1 Cor 11:21). There, Paul says, "For each προλαμβάνει their own banquet. Some go hungry and others become drunk." To date, there are two popular translations for the verb. Many scholars point to the preposition πρό attached to προλαμβάνω and translate the verb with the temporal meaning of "go ahead with." If προλαμβάνω means "go ahead with," then Paul is indicting a group of more affluent Corinthians who "*go ahead with* their own banquet."[2] His solution to the problem is that these richer Corinthians must "wait for" their fellow Christians to arrive at the Lord's Banquet (1 Cor 11:33). If they cannot, then they should eat at home (1 Cor 11:34). Gerd Theissen has articulated the most persuasive proposal for this reconstruction, arguing that some elite Corinthians, "the haves," are bringing their own food to the church gathering and consuming it before the poorer Corinthians, "the have-nots," arrive (1 Cor 11:17–34).[3]

---

2. C. K. Barrett, *A Commentary on the First Epistle to the Corinthians*, HNTC (New York: Harper & Row, 1968), 262; Gerd Theissen, *The Social Setting of Pauline Christianity: Essays on Corinth*, ed. and trans. John H. Schütz (Philadelphia: Fortress, 1982), 151; Hans-Josef Klauck, *Herrenmahl und Hellenistischer Kult: Eine religionsgeschichtliche Untersuchung zum ersten Korintherbrief* (Münster: Aschendorff, 1982), 292; Jerome Murphy-O'Connor, "House Churches and the Eucharist," *TBT* 22 (1984): 38; Otfried Hofius, "The Lord's Supper and the Lord's Supper Tradition: Reflections on 1 Corinthians 11:23b–25," in *One Loaf, One Cup: Ecumenical Studies on 1 Cor. 11 and other Eucharistic Texts*, ed. B. F. Meyer (Macon, GA: Mercer University Press, 1993), 90–91; Peter Lampe, "Das korinthische Herrenmahl im Schnittpunkt hellenistisch-römischer Mahlpraxis und paulinischer Theologia Crucis (1Kor 11,17–34)," *ZNW* 82 (1991): 183–213; Lampe, "The Eucharist: Identifying with Christ on the Cross," *Int* 48 (1994): 40; James D. G. Dunn, *The Theology of Paul the Apostle* (Grand Rapids: Eerdmans, 1998), 609–13; Raymond F. Collins, *First Corinthians*, SP 7 (Collegeville, MN: Liturgical Press, 1999), 416, 422; Joseph A. Fitzmyer, *First Corinthians: A New Translation with Introduction and Commentary*, AYB 32 (New Haven: Yale University Press, 2008), 434.

3. Theissen, *Social Setting*, 145–74.

The second translation of προλαμβάνω discounts the temporal meaning of πρό, especially in the context of referring to food, and renders the verb as "devour." In that case, the difficulty with the Lord's Banquet is that the richer Corinthians are "devouring" their food in front of their poorer companions.[4] This translation of προλαμβάνω is found first in James Hope Moulton's and George Milligan's lexicon based on Greek epigraphy and papyri. They point to one inscription (discussed below) in which προλαμβάνω clearly means "consume, eat or drink." More recently, Bruce Winter uses the same epigraph to argue that προλαμβάνω takes the nuanced meaning of "eat" when food is the object of the verb. Accepting this translation of προλαμβάνω and the idea that the richer Corinthians are consuming all the food at the Lord's Banquet, Winter proposes that Paul's solution is that they should "share" with their poorer brothers and sisters (1 Cor 11:33).[5] To date, Hans Conzelmann, Anthony Thiselton, Dennis E. Smith, and Richard B. Hays translate προλαμβάνω as "eat" or "devour" and follow some form of this second reconstruction.[6] Is this philological reconstruction from epigraphy plausible? Does προλαμβάνω mean "eat" in Greek inscriptions, especially when the verb appears with food as its object? To these matters, I now turn.

II. "Devour" or "Go Ahead with": προλαμβάνω in Epigraphy

Uses of προλαμβάνω in Greek inscriptions attest to a semantic range wider than the two options that most exegetes acknowledge in discussions of the

---

4. "προλαμβάνω," *MM* 542.

5. Bruce Winter, "The Lord's Supper at Corinth: An Alternative Reconstruction," *RTR* 37 (1978): 73–82, esp. 74–77; Winter, *After Paul Left Corinth: The Influence of Secular Ethics and Social Change* (Grand Rapids: Eerdmans, 2001), 143–48.

6. Bradley B. Blue, "The House Church at Corinth and the Lord's Supper: Famine, Food Supply, and the *Present Distress*," *CTR* 5 (1991): 229–31; Hans Conzelmann, *1 Corinthians: A Commentary on the First Epistle to the Corinthians*, trans. James W. Leitch, Hermeneia (Philadelphia: Fortress, 1975), 195n22; Anthony C. Thiselton, *The First Epistle to the Corinthians: A Commentary on the Greek Text*, NIGTC (Grand Rapids: Eerdmans, 2000), 848, 863; David E. Garland, *1 Corinthians*, BECNT (Grand Rapids: Baker Academic, 2003), 535, 540–41; Dennis E. Smith, *From Symposium to Eucharist: The Banquet in the Early Christian World* (Minneapolis: Fortress, 2003), 192; Ben Witherington III, *Making a Meal of It: Rethinking the Theology of the Lord's Supper* (Waco, TX: Baylor University Press, 2007), 53; Richard B. Hays, *First Corinthians*, IBC (Louisville: Westminster John Knox, 1997), 197; Gordon D. Fee (*The First Epistle to the Corinthians*, rev. ed., NICNT [Grand Rapids: Eerdmans, 2014], 598–601) appears to be noncommittal.

problem with the Lord's Banquet in Corinth. This is consistent with how προλαμβάνω is used in literary sources.[7] Inscriptions attest that προλαμβάνω can mean "to be taken," "to defeat," and "to be seized," depending on context. The first meaning of προλαμβάνω is found in a private sacred inscription (see chapter 1.IV.2.3) that a Greek man from Phrygia whose name begins with Neik- set up at a Phrygian temple of the god Helius Apollo. The man confesses that he has committed some sin against the god and describes how Apollo threatened in a dream to "seize my slave by the feet" (ποδῶν <π>ρολαβὼν ἐμὸ[ν] δοῦλον).[8] The meaning "defeat" in the inscriptional use of προλαμβάνω is evident in an epitaph (see chapter 1.IV.2.1) of a gladiator named Autolycus from Alexander Troas who says to passersby, "After I had so beaten [my opponent], I wished to spare him" (οὕτως πως προλαβών, σῶσαι δὲ θέλω). The defeated opponent, however, rewarded the gladiator's clemency by striking him with a death blow (νικήσας ἔθανον παρὰ μοῖραν).[9] The meaning "to be taken" for προλαμβάνω appears in Greek epitaphs (see chapter 1.IV.2.1), and can be seen from a second-century-CE funerary epigraph from Antioch of Pisidia that says that the deceased, Anthius, "was taken at fifteen years old" (πέν|πτον καὶ δέκατον| προλαβὼν ἔτος).[10]

The crux of the argument for the translation of προλαμβάνω as "devour" rests on the appearance of the verb with food as its object in one inscription, a private sacred inscription (see chapter 1.IV.2.3) that a certain Apellas set up around 160 CE at Asclepius's temple in Epidaurus, Greece.[11]

---

7. *LSJ*, 1488; BDAG, 872; *MM*, 542; Delling, "προλαμβάνω," *TDNT* 4:14–15.

8. *MAMA* 4:279 = Georg Petzl, *Die Beichtinschriften Westkleinasiens* (Bonn: Habelt, 1994), no. 106, although he questions the reading of προλαβὼν. For a discussion of this enigmatic text and the possible scenarios to which it refers see A. Cameron, "Inscriptions Relating to Sacral Manumission and Confession," *HTR* 32 (1939): 155–78.

9. *IG* XII.2 644 = Marijana Ricl, ed., *The Inscriptions of Alexandreia Troas*, Österreichische Akademie der Wissenschaften Nordrhein-Westfälische Akademie der Wissenschaften 53 (Bonn: Habelt, 1997), no. 104.

10. W. M. Calder, "Colonia Caesareia Antiocheia," *JRS* 2 (1912): 90, no. 10 = Werner Peek, ed., *Griechische Vers-Inschriften I, Grab-Epigramme* (Berlin: Akademie, 1955), no. 1023.

11. Ulrich von Wilamowitz-Moellendorff, *Isyllos von Epidauros* (Berlin, 1886), 116–24; Mary Hamilton, *Incubation or the Cure of Disease in Pagan Temples and Church Christians* (London: Henderson, 1906), 40–43; Emma J. Edelstein and Ludwig Edelstein, *Asclepius: A Collection and Interpretation of the Testimonies* (Baltimore: Johns Hopkins University Press, 1945), 1:247–48, no. 432; Maria Girone, *Ἰάματα: Guarigioni miracolose di Asclepio in testi epigrafici* (Bari, Italy: Levante, 1998), 58–70; George Luck, *Arcana Mundi: Magic and Occult in the Greek and Roman Worlds; A Collection of Ancient Texts*, 2nd ed. (Baltimore: Johns Hopkins University Press, 2006), 191–92, no. 44; Marco Galli, "Pilgrimage as Elite *Habitus*: Educated Pilgrims in Sacred Landscapes during the Sec-

The epigraph was engraved on a limestone block, consists of thirty-three lines, and recounts the miraculous healings that Asclepius provided for Apellas.[12] I provide the entire inscription and a translation of it, but I have left προλαμβάνω untranslated so as not to prejudice the reader's opinion about its meaning.

> ἐπὶ ἱερέως *ν.* Πο(πλίου) *ν.* Αἰλ(ίου) *ν.* Ἀντιόχου| Μ(ᾶρκος) Ἰούλιος Ἀπελλᾶς Ἰδριεὺς Μυλασεὺς μετεπέμφθην| ὑπὸ τοῦ θεοῦ, πολλάκις εἰς νόσους ἐνπίπτων καὶ ἀπεψί|αις χρώμενος. κατὰ δὴ τὸν πλοῦν ἐν Αἰγείνῃ ἐκέλευσέν|| με μὴ πολλὰ ὀργίζεσθαι. ἐπεὶ δὲ ἐγενόμην ἐν τῷ ἱερῷ, ἐ|κέλευσεν ἐπὶ δύο ἡμέρας συνκαλύψασθαι τὴν κεφαλήν,| ἐν αἷς ὄμβροι ἐγένοντο, τυρὸν καὶ ἄρτον προλαβεῖν, σέλει|να μετὰ θρίδακος, αὐτὸν δι' αὑτοῦ λοῦσθαι, δρόμῳ, γυμνάζε|σθαι, κιτρίου προλαμβάνειν τὰ ἄκρα εἰς ὕδωρ ἀποβρέξαι, πρὸς|| ταῖς ἀκοαῖς ἐν βαλανείῳ προστρίβεσθαι τῷ τοίχωι, περιπάτῳ χρῆ|σθαι ὑπερῴῳ, αἰώραις, ἁφῇ πηλώσασθαι, ἀνυπόδητον περι|πατεῖν, πρὶν ἐνβῆναι ἐν τῶι βαλανείῳ εἰς τὸ θερμὸν ὕδωρ| οἶνον περιχέασθαι, μόνον λούσασθαι καὶ Ἀττικὴν δοῦναι| τῶι βαλανεῖ, κοινῇ θῦσαι Ἀσκληπιῷ, Ἠπιόνῃ, Ἐλευσεινίαις,|| γάλα μετὰ μέλιτος προλαβεῖν μιᾷ δὲ ἡμέρᾳ πιόντός μου γά|λα μόνον, εἶπεν· μέλι ἔμβαλλε εἰς τὸ γάλα, ἵνα δύνηται διακό|πτειν ἐπεὶ δὲ ἐδεήθην τοῦ θεοῦ θᾶττόν με ἀπολῦσαι, ᾤμην <ν>ά|πυϊ καὶ ἁλσὶν κεχρειμένος ὅλος ἐξιέναι κατὰ τὰς ἀκοὰς ἐκ τοῦ| ἀβάτου, παιδάριον δὲ ἡγεῖσθαι θυμιατήριον ἔχον ἀτμίζον|| καὶ τὸν ἱερέα λέγειν τεθεράπευσαι, χρὴ δὲ ἀποδιδόναι τὰ ἴατρα.| καὶ ἐποίησα, ἃ εἶδον, καὶ χρείμενος μὲν τοῖς ἁλσὶ καὶ τῶι νάπυ|ϊ ὑγρῶι ἤλγησα, λούμενος δὲ οὐκ ἤλγησα. ταῦτα ἐν ἐννέα ἡμέ|ραις ἀφ' οὗ ἦλθον. ἥψατο δέ μου καὶ τῆς δεξιᾶς χιρὸς καὶ τοῦ| μαστοῦ, τῇ δὲ ἑξῆς ἡμέρᾳ ἐπιθύοντός μου φλὸξ ἀναδραμοῦ||σα ἐπέφλευσε τὴν χεῖρα, ὡς καὶ φλυκταίνας ἐξανθῆσαι· μετ' ὀ|λίγον δὲ ὑγιὴς ἡ χεὶρ ἐγένετο. ἐπιμείναντί μοι ἄνηθον με|τ' ἐλαίου χρήσασθαι πρὸς τὴν κεφαλαλγίαν εἶπεν. οὐ μὴν ἤλ|γουν τὴν κεφαλήν. συνέβη οὖν φιλολογήσαντί μοι συνπλη|ρωθῆναι· χρησάμενος τῷ ἐλαίῳ ἀπηλάγην τῆς κεφαλαλγί||ας.

ond Sophistic," in *Pilgrimage in Graeco-Roman and Early Christian Antiquity: Seeing the Gods*, ed. Jaś Elsner and Ian Rutherford (Oxford: Oxford University Press, 2005), 279–80; Clarisse Prêtre and Philippe Charlier, *Maladies humaines, thérapies divines: analyse épigraphique et paléopathologique de textes de guérison grecs* (Villeneuve d'Ascq: Presses Universitaries du Septentrion, 2009), 189–97; Gil Renberg, *Where Dreams May Come: Incubation Sanctuaries in the Greco-Roman World* (Leiden: Brill, 2016), 169–71.

12. The length of this inscription makes it the longest first-person account of Asclepius healing an individual in the form of an inscription ever discovered (Renberg, *Where Dreams May Come*, 169).

ἀναγαργαρίζεσθαι ψυχρῷ πρὸς τὴν σταφυλὴν—καὶ γὰρ περὶ| τούτου παρεκάλεσα τὸν θεὸν—τὸ αὐτὸ καὶ πρὸς παρίσθμια. ἐκέ|λευσεν δὲ καὶ ἀναγράψαι ταῦτα. χάριν εἰδὼς καὶ ὑγιὴς γε|νόμενος ἀπηλλάγην.

During the priesthood of Publius Aelius Antiochus, I, Marcus Julius Apellas of Idrias of Mylasa, was sent for by the god [because] I was often sick and suffered from indigestion.[13] While sailing, [the god] ordered me in Aigina not to be agitated all the time. When I went into the sanctuary, he ordered: that my head be covered for two days (on these days thunderstorms occurred); προλαβεῖν cheese, bread, and celery with lettuce; to bathe myself; to train myself by running; προλαμβάνειν the rind of a citrus tree in water; to rub against the wall near the Ears (?) in the bath; to walk in the upper room; [to swing] on the swings; to smear myself with mud; to walk barefoot; to pour wine on myself before I go into the hot water in the bath; to bathe alone; to give an Attic drachma to the bath attendant; to sacrifice jointly to Ascelpius, Epione, and Eleusinian goddesses; and προλαβεῖν milk with honey on one day when I drank milk only, [the god] said, "Put honey in the milk so that it can break through [your bowels]." When I beseeched the god to cure me faster, I saw (the following) in a vision. I had rubbed my entire [body] with mustard and salt and went out of the Ears (?) of the untrodden [place] (?). Now a little boy having a smoking censer led me out and the priest said, "You have been healed. Now you need to pay the doctor-bill." So, I did what I saw (in my vision) and when I was covered with salt and moist mustard, I was in pain. After I washed, I was not in pain. These things occurred within nine days after [I came to the sanctuary]. Now [the god] touched me and my right hand and breast. On the next day while I was sacrificing, the flame shot up and burned my hand so that blisters appeared. In a little while the hand was made well. I stayed and [the god] said to use dill with olive oil for my headache. Truly, I did not suffer in my head. However, it turned out that after I studied I was congested. I used olive oil and rid myself of the headache. [The god told me] to gargle with cold water for my uvula—for I had beseeched the god about this—and [to do] the same far my tonsils. Now he ordered me to write these things: I had wished to be made well and I became healthy. I know that I am grateful" (*SIG*^{3} 1170 = *IG* IV 955 = *IG* IV^2.1 126).

13. Marcus Julius Apellas is known from two, possibly three inscriptions from Labraunda in Caria (*ILabraunda* 58; 59; 94). See Renberg, *Where Dreams May Come*, 170n117.

Προλαμβάνω appears three times in this inscription: lines 7 (τυρὸν καὶ ἄρτον προλαβεῖν), 9 (κιτρίου προλαμβάνειν τὰ ἄκρα), and 15 (γάλα μετὰ μέλιτος προλαβεῖν). Each appearance of the verb is in an infinitive form, either present (προλαμβάνειν) or aorist (προλαβεῖν). Bruce Winter notes, "It certainly makes no sense to translate any of the uses of the verb in this inscription as 'to take before.' "[14] The first occurrence of προλαμβάνω indicates that Asclepius commanded (ἐκέλευσεν) Apellas "προλαβεῖν cheese, bread, and celery with lettuce." The third and last appearance of προλαμβάνω attests that the god directed Apellas "προλαβεῖν milk with honey."[15] Winter is correct that προλαμβάνω does not have a temporal meaning in these two uses of the verb. The first use means "eat" and the third most probably means "drink," granted that drinking is a form of consumption.[16]

Despite these two translations of προλαμβάνω, the inscription's second use of the verb probably has a temporal meaning. Winter translates the clause in question—κιτρίου προλαμβάνειν τὰ ἄκρα εἰς ὕδωρ ἀποβρέξαι—as, "to take lemon peels and to soak them in water."[17] He does not comment on what this means. It seems to me that Asclepius is not commanding Apellas to eat lemon peels, but rather directing him to take the lemons or rind from a citrus tree (as I have translated) and make some kind of brew with them: "to brew the rind of a citrus tree in water." Brewing a drink with a citrus rind and using a form of προλαμβάνω to describe the process suggest that the verb has a temporal meaning, which is indeed how most historians translate this use of προλαμβάνω. Mary Hamilton renders the clause as: "I was . . . to drink citron-lemonade."[18] Gil Renberg translates it as: "to take lemon peels in advance (and) to soak (them) in water."[19]

---

14. Winter, *After Paul Left Corinth*, 145; Winter, "Lord's Supper," 74–75.

15. Most translations of this inscription render two of the three occurrences of προλαμβάνω as "eat," "drink," or "consume": Wilamowitz-Moellendorff, *Isyllos von Epidauros*, 117–18; Hamilton, *Incubation*, 40–43; Galli, "Pilgrimage," 279; Luck, *Arcana Mundi*, 191–92, no. 45; Prêtre and Charlier, *Maladies humaines*, 191; Renberg, *Where Dreams May Come*, 170–71.

16. Winter ("Lord's Supper," 74–75; *After Paul Left Corinth*, 145–48) renders: "to eat cheese and bread" and "to eat milk with honey." Moulton and Milligan ("προλαμβάνω," *MM* 542) note that this third use of προλαμβάνω is best translated "to drink."

17. Winter, "Lord's Supper," 74–75; Winter, *After Paul Left Corinth*, 145–48. Wilamowitz-Moellendorff (*Isyllos von Epidauros*, 118) notes that one must take κιτρίου προλαμβάνειν τὰ ἄκρα εἰς ὕδωρ ἀποβρέξαι together because ἀποβρέξαι has no object.

18. Hamilton, *Incubation*, 40–43.

19. Renberg, *Where Dreams May Come*, 171. See also Luck, *Arcana Mundi*, 191–92, no. 45; Galli, "Pilgrimage," 279; Edelstein and Edelstein, *Asclepius*, 1:248, no. 432.

Clarisse Prêtre and Philippe Charlier render the clause in question as: "to take the zest of a lemon and after I have brewed them in water."[20] In short, the case for translating προλαμβάνω as "eat" when food is its object is not as clear as Winter and others propose.[21] The inscription that they use as evidence has two different uses of προλαμβάνω: two that should be translated as "eat" and one that should be translated as "to take before," or, more appropriately, "to brew."

There is another epigraph that uses προλαμβάνω with food (or money used to buy food) as its object. The inscription is from Samos, dates to the late third to early second century BCE, and is one of the most important pieces of information about the funding and distribution of grain in a Greek city during the Hellenistic period.[22] It is a public inscription in the form of a public law (see chapter 1.IV.1.1) regulating the purchase of grain with a fund that 120 to 121 contributors provided. The actual text is carved onto three faces of a square white marble pillar, totaling about 228 lines.[23] Much about the law remains obscure and historians debate many aspects of it, such as

20. Prêtre and Charlier, *Maladies humaines*, 191, 193.

21. Garland (*1 Corinthians*, 540) notes, "[προλαμβάνω] appears three times in an inscription (*SIG* 3.1170) on a stele in the Asclepius sanctuary at Epidaurus (second century) and clearly means 'to eat.'" Smith (*From Symposium to Eucharist*, 192) argues that προλαμβάνω with food as its object means "to eat," following Conzelmann (*1 Corinthians*, 195n22), who relies on the Epidaurus inscription noting that the verb does not mean "take before another . . . but of the 'consuming' of food; Ditt., *Syll.* 3.328f (no. 1170, line 7, 9, 15)."

22. Theodore Wiegand and Ulrich von Wilamowitz-Moellendorff, "Ein Gesetz von Samos über die Beschaffung von Brotkorn aus öffentlichen Mitteln," *Sitzungsberichte der königlich preussischen Akademie der Wissenschaften* 1 (1904): 917–31; Gerhard Thür and Christian Koch, "Prozessrechtlicher Kommentar zum 'Getreidegesetz' aus Samos," *Anzeiger* 118 (1981): 61–88; Graham Shipley, *A History of Samos: 800–188 BC* (Oxford: Clarendon, 1987), 211–13, 218–21; Daniel J. Gargola, "Grain Distribution and the Revenue of the Temple of Hera on Samos," *Phoenix* 46 (1992): 12–28. Christian Habicht ("Samische Volksbeschlüsse der hellenistischer Zeit," *MDAI(A)* 72 [1957]: 233–41) dates this epigraph between the last few years of the third and early second century BCE because of prosopography.

23. The most conservative estimate places the grain fund between 18,000 to 21,000 drachmas. The difficulty with totaling the amount is that some donations are illegible. The extant ones range from 100 to 1000 drachmas and so to arrive at a number one must supply those missing contributions by estimating an average of the known donations. Shipley (*History of Samos*, 213) estimates that the number is 18,000 drachmas, while Gargola ("Grain Distribution," 19–20) proposes that it is 21,000 drachmas. In addition, Gargola proposes that another epigraph was placed atop the one in question, is now missing, and that it contained a list of contributors. If he is correct, then the total for both stones may have been 50,000 drachmas.

whether the grain distribution was for every citizen of Samos or only the poorer ones.[24] The portion of the inscription that concerns me (and the only part that I quote) is the provision for lending out interest accrued from the grain fund. Once again, I have left προλαμβάνω untranslated so as not to prejudice the reader's opinion about its meaning.

> ἀ|ποδεικνύτω δὲ ὁ δῆμος καθ' ἕκαστον ἐνιαυτὸν ἐν τῆι πρώτη[ι]| τῶν ἀρχαιρεσιῶν μετὰ τὸ καταστῆσαι τὰς χειροτονητὰς|| ἀρχὰς ἄνδρας δύο, ἐξ ἑκατέρας φυλῆς ἕνα, τοὺς ἐσομέ|νους ἐπὶ τοῦ σίτου μὴ ἐλάσσονα οὐσίαν ἔχοντα ἑκάτερον| ταλάντων τριῶν· οὗτοι δὲ παραλαβόντες τὸν τόκον παρὰ| τῶν μελεδωνῶν διδότωσαν τὴν τιμὴν τοῦ σίτου καὶ ἐ|άν τι ἄλλο δαπάνημα γίνηται, παραμετρείσθωσαν δὲ|| ḳαὶ τὸν σῖτον. ἀποδεικνύτω δὲ καὶ σιτώνην ὁ δῆμος ἐν| [[ταυ]]τῆι αὐτῆι ἐκκλησίαι, μὴ ἐλάσσονα οὐσίαν ἔχοντα τα|λάντων δύο. γινέσθω δὲ, ἐὰν δόξηι, καὶ μίσθωσις τοῦ ἀρ|γυρ̣ίου τοῦ ἐκ τοῦ τόκου, ἐάν τινες βούλωνται ὑποθέμα|τα δόντες ἀξιόχρεα καὶ διεγγυήσαντες προλαβεῖν|| καὶ λυσιτελέστερον καταστῆσαι τὸν σῖτον. τὴν δὲ δ[ι]|εγγύησιν ποιείσθω̣σαν οἱ ἄνδρες οἱ χειροτονηθέντες ἐπ[ὶ]| τοῦ σίτου κινδύν[ω]ι τῷι ἑαυτῶν.
>
> At the first of the yearly elections of magistrates after the appointment of the elected rulers, every year let the body of citizens appoint two men, one from each tribe, who will be over the grain (each of these men not having property valued at less than three talents). Now after they receive the interest from the grain-attendants, let these men pay the price for the grain and any other expense, and let them measure out the grain. Now let the body of citizens in the same assembly appoint the grain-buyer (this man not having property valued at less than two talents). Now if it seems good, let the income of the money that is from the interest be lent out, if some, who after giving considerable securities and guarantors, desire προλαβεῖν and to render the grain more financially advantageous. Now let the men elected to be over the grain fund accept the security at their own risk (*SIG*³ 976 = *IG* XII.6 1 172.A.38–52).

According to the inscription, two elected wealthy men are to oversee the grain fund, while grain-attendants (μελεδωνοί) are to manage it. From another part of the grain law it is clear that the grain-attendants are to lend money from the grain fund out at interest (τόκος) and then

24. See Wiegand and Wilamowitz-Moellendorff, "Gesetz von Samos," 917–31; Shipley, *History of Samos*, 218–21; Gargola "Grain Distribution," 12–28.

turn over that interest to the two-man oversight committee (*IG* XII.6 1 172.A.21–24). This procedure is what the above portion of the law refers to when it says that, "after [the overseers] receive the interest from the grain-attendants."[25] The two-man oversight committee is to give this money to a grain-buyer (σιτώνης) appointed by the citizen body. In another portion of the inscription, two measures of grain are to be distributed monthly to every male citizen of Samos until the supply is exhausted (*IG* XII.6 1 172.A.53–57).

A provision of the grain law in the above quoted portion allows for taking the interest accrued from the grain fund and, instead of buying grain with it, lending it out. The purpose of this provision is "to render the grain more financially advantageous" (λυσιτελέστερον καταστῆσαι τὸν σῖτον). This provision can occur under two conditions. The first is that the citizen body of Samos decides to lend out the interest (γινέσθω δὲ, ἐὰν δόξηι). The second condition is that some (τινες) of the members of the citizen body provide collateral: "giving considerable securities and guarantors" (ὑποθέμα|τα δόντες ἀξιόχρεα καὶ διεγγυήσαντες). The two-man oversight committee, however, is ultimately responsible for what happens to the interest and so they must "accept the security at their own risk." Provided that these provisions are met, the interest from the grain fund can be lent out to make more money.

The question is: What does προλαβεῖν mean in this inscription? To answer this question, we must understand how it relates to the entire provision προλαβεῖν|| καὶ λυσιτελέστερον καταστῆσαι τὸν σῖτον and what the object of the infinitive προλαβεῖν is. There are two possibilities for the object of προλαβεῖν. The first is "the grain" (τὸν σῖτον) in the phrase προλαβεῖν|| καὶ λυσιτελέστερον καταστῆσαι τὸν σῖτον. The translation "to eat the grain supply" makes no sense because eating the grain supply does not "render the grain more financially advantageous." If "the grain" (τὸν σῖτον) is the object of προλαβεῖν, then προλαβεῖν has a temporal meaning of "to buy the grain earlier." There are a number of historians who adopt this translation. Roger S. Bagnall and Peter Derow translate the clause in question, "If any wish, after giving sufficiently valuable securities and providing guarantors, to buy earlier and arrange the grain supply more profitably . . ."[26] Ilias Arnaoutoglou renders the clause, "If there are citizens who, having provided

25. The committee purchases grain from the fields of Samos's patron goddess Hera (*IG* XII.6 1 172.A.24–26).

26. Roger S. Bagnall and Peter Derow, eds., *The Hellenistic Period: Historical Sources in Translation* (Malden, MA: Blackwell, 2004), 128.

sufficient mortgages and guarantors, wish to buy earlier and offer grain at a more advantageous price to the people . . ."[27]

The second option for the object of προλαβεῖν is μίσθωσις τοῦ ἀρ|γυρίου τοῦ ἐκ τοῦ τόκου "the income of the money that is from the interest" mentioned at the beginning of provision (*IG* XII.6 1 172.A.47–48).[28] The translation "to eat the income" does not "render the grain supply more financially advantageous." If the income is the object of the infinitive, then the most probable translation for προλαβεῖν is "to anticipate," which is found among historians as well. In the original publication of this inscription, Theodore Wiegand and Ulrich von Wilamowitz-Moellendorff translate προλαβεῖν with the German verb *vorwegnehmen*, which means "to take before," or "to anticipate," rendering the clause in question: "If it seems good, there should be a loan of the money raised from the interest, if the people, in light of sufficient mortgage and security, wish to anticipate the money and so make the grain more profitable."[29] In their detailed commentary on the epigraph, Gerhard Thür and Christian Koch render the provision, "By decision: an allocation of the money received at interest can be assigned if any wish to receive this [money] in advance and to procure the grain cheaper by giving appropriate *hypothemata* in value and arranging guarantors."[30] Whatever the object of προλαβεῖν is in the grain law from Samos, the verb must have a temporal meaning, whether "to buy earlier" or "to anticipate the money accrued from interest."[31] Given that this inscription is a public law and therefore was prepared with the city's best resources and meant to be understood, this epigraph proves that προλαμβάνω had a temporal meaning in the third to second century BCE, at least in Samos.

---

27. Ilias Arnaoutoglou, *Ancient Greek Laws: A Sourcebook* (London: Routledge, 1998), 49–52, no. 45.

28. Thür and Koch, "Prozessrechtlicher Kommentar," 75.

29. Wiegand and Wilamowitz-Moellendorff ("Gesetz von Samos," 925) translate: "*Es soll, wenn es gut scheint, auch eine Ausleihung des aus den Zinsen erwachsenen Geldes stattfinden, falls Leute gegen Stellung hinreichender Hypothek und Bürgschaft das Geld vorwegnehmen und so das Getreide nutzbringender machen wollen.*"

30. Thür and Koch ("Prozessrechtlicher Kommentar," 66, 75) translate: "*Auf Beschluß kann auch eine Vergabe des an Zinsen eingehenden Geldes stattfinden, wenn irgendwelche, indem sie im Wert entsprechende Hypothemata geben und Bürgen stellen, dieses vorher in Empfang nehmen und das Getreide günstiger beschaffen wollen . . . Es liegt deshalb näher, das Z. 47/48 erwähnte Geld auch als Objekt zu* προλαβεῖν *zu denken.*"

31. "Now if any of the borrowers does not repay the money, that is the entire loan or part of it . . ." (ἐὰν δέ τις τῶν| δανεισαμένων μὴ ἀποδιδοῖ τὸ ἀργύριον ἢ πᾶν ἢ μέρος τι . . .) (*IG* XII.6 1 172.A.64–65). Thür and Koch ("Prozessrechtlicher Kommentar," 75) note, "The constant interest on incoming money is an essential component of this transaction" (*Das an Zinsen ständig eingehende Geld ist wesentlicher Bestandteil dieses Geschäfts*).

The following final inscription demonstrates clearly that προλαμβάνω had a temporal meaning in Asia Minor in the late first century BCE (9 BCE). The epigraph in which the verb is found is the famous calendar inscription of Asia. It is a public sacred inscription (see chapter 1. IV.1.3) that contains the decree of the league of Asia, altering the calendar of the cities of the league so that their New Year corresponds to the emperor Augustus's birthday (September 23). The import of this epigraph for the meaning of προλαμβάνω is that the league of Asia, which consisted of representatives from the leading cities of Roman Asia, issued the decree and sent it out to the entire province. To date, portions of the decree have been found at six cites. The largest is from Priene, 84 lines on marble and limestone, but other fragments have been discovered at Apamea (with Latin portions), Dorylaion (with Latin portions), Maeonia, Eumeneia, and Metropolis.[32] The decree itself stipulates that an epigraph with this decision is to be set up at the temple complex of Roma and Augustus at Pergamum as well as being engraved on marble stelae in the cities of the province and placed in the temples of Caesar (*RDGE* 328–37, no. 65.63–67). Therefore, this decree with its temporal use of προλαμβάνω was circulated widely in an official communique from the league of Asia, and intended to be understood. I quote only the portion of the inscription that concerns me and I have left προλαμβάνω untranslated.

> ἔδοξεν τοῖς ἐπὶ τῆς Ἀσίας| Ἕλλησιν, γνώμῃ τοῦ ἀρχιερέως Ἀπολλωνίου τοῦ Μηνοφίλου Ἀζανίτου·| ἐπε[ιδὴ ἡ θείως] διατάξασα τὸν βίον ἡμῶν πρόνοια σπουδὴν εἰσεν[ενκα]|| [μ]ένη καὶ φιλοτιμίαν τὸ τεληότατον τῶι βίωι διεκόσμη[σεν ἀγαθὸν]|| ἐνενκαμένη τὸν Σεβαστόν, ὃν εἰς εὐεργεσίαν ἀνθρώ[πων] ἐπλή||ρωσεν ἀρετῆς <ὥ>σπερ ἡμεῖν καὶ τοῖς μεθ' ἡ[μᾶς σωτῆρα χαρισαμένη]|| τὸν παύσαντα μὲν πόλεμον, κοσμήσοντα [δὲ εἰρήνην, ἐπιφανεὶς δὲ]|| ὁ Καῖσαρ τὰς ἐλπίδας τῶν προλαβόντων [εὐανγέλια πάντων ὑπερ]||έθηκεν, οὐ μόνον τοὺς πρὸ αὐτοῦ γεγονότ[ας εὐεργέτας ὑπερβα]||λόμενος, ἀλλ' οὐδ' ἐν τοῖς ἐσομένοις ἐλπίδ[α ὑπολιπὼν ὑπερβολῆς,]| ἦρξεν δὲ τῶι κόσμωι τῶν δι' αὐτὸν εὐανγελί[ων ἡ γενέθλιος ἡμέ]ρα|| τοῦ θεοῦ.

> It seemed good to the Hellenes of Asia, in light of the motion of the high priest Apollonius Azanitus the son of Menophilus. Since Providence, which orders divinely our lives, having worked zealously and

32. *OGIS* 458 = *IPriene* 105 = *RDGE* 328–37, no. 65. For the Metropolis fragment see Boris Dreyer and Helmut Engelmann, "Augustus und Germanicus im ionischen Metropolis," *ZPE* 158 (2006): 173–82.

> honorably, has arranged the most complete good thing for life because she produced Augustus, whom for the beneficence of humans she filled with virtue, as if she bestowed a savior on us and those after us, a savior who caused war to cease, arranged peace now with his appearances, Caesar surpassed the hopes of all those who προλαβόντων good news, not only surpassing those who were benefactors before him, but also leaving no hope of surpassing for those who will come, and the birthday of the god was the beginning of good news for the world because of him. (*RDGE* 328–37, no. 65.30–41)

According to the epigraph, it is evident that divine providence has ordered the birth of Augustus because his appearances in Asia brought an end to civil war and made peace in the province.[33] There is no doubt that the decree has these benefactions in mind when, using a participial form of προλαμβάνω, it says, "Caesar surpassed the hopes of all those who προλαβόντων good news" (ὁ Καῖσαρ τὰς ἐλπίδας τῶν προλαβόντων [εὐανγέλια πάντων ὑπερ]|| ἔθηκεν). It is clear that προλαμβάνω has a temporal meaning here because the epigraph stresses that Augustus's past accomplishments have "surpass[ed] those who were benefactors before him" (τοὺς πρὸ αὐτοῦ γεγονότ[ας εὐεργέτας ὑπερβα]|λόμενος) and that the emperor has left "no hope of surpassing for those who will come" (ἐν τοῖς ἐσομένοις ἐλπίδ[α ὑπολιπὼν ὑπερβολῆς]). Therefore, we should render the clause in question: "Caesar surpassed the hopes of all those who received good news before [us]" (ὁ Καῖσαρ τὰς ἐλπίδας τῶν προλαβόντων [εὐανγέλια πάντων ὑπερ]|ἔθηκεν), which is how Robert Sherk translates προλαμβάνω in this case: "Caesar *exceeded* the hopes of [all] those who received [glad tidings] before us."[34] Therefore, προλαμβάνω clearly has a temporal meaning in the late first century BCE (9 BCE) among the Greeks living in Asia.

Three final observations about this epigraph, its use of προλαμβάνω, and the connection to 1 Cor 11:21 are in order. First, this inscription dates

33. Roman Asia in the late republic was in economic peril. The province had suffered from inept governors and cruel tax collectors, Asia had been one of the main theaters of the Roman civil war, and citizens had to quarter soldiers. Octavian's victory at Actium changed the province's situation. The new emperor remitted taxes, doled out grain, and returned looted divine images to their proper places. These benefactions led to fiscal stability and growth that lifted Asia out of its economic slump. See G. W. Bowersock (*Augustus and the Greek World* [Oxford: Clarendon, 1965], 1–13) for an extended discussion of Asia's plight after the civil war and Octavian's responses.

34. Robert Sherk, ed., *Rome and the Greek East to the Death of Augustus* (Cambridge: Cambridge University Press, 1984), 125.

closer to the composition of 1 Corinthians (56 CE) than the epigraph from Epidaurus (160 CE) that some scholars use to support their translation προλαμβάνω as "eat."[35] Second, the calendar inscription is a public sacred inscription, while the Epidaurus epigraph is a private inscription. The cities in the league of Asia had the best resources in the province available for drafting and engraving the decree (see chapter 1.III). The same cannot be said of the Epidarus inscription. Finally, the individual(s) responsible for the wording of the calendar decree knew that προλαμβάνω possessed a temporal meaning and, desiring to communicate effectively, believed that their Asian compatriots did likewise.[36]

In sum, the argument that προλαμβάνω means "eat" in certain cases, especially when it appears with food as its object, has substantial limitations. To date, there remains only one known inscription in which προλαμβάνω means "eat." Even in that one inscription, however, one of the three uses of προλαμβάνω has a temporal meaning. Therefore, the argument that προλαμβάνω means "eat" when it appears with food as its object is not as compelling as some claim. In addition, the verb clearly had a temporal meaning in the Greek cities of Asia in 9 BCE, which is closer in time to the composition of 1 Corinthians than the one inscription in which προλαμβάνω means "eat."

III. Προλαμβάνω and 1 Cor 11:21: My Reconstruction

Given the above evidence, the most probable translation of προλαμβάνω in 1 Cor 11:21 is "go ahead with."[37] There are three factors that support this

35. For the dating of 1 Corinthians see Fitzmyer, *First Corinthians*, 37–47.

36. Peter Lampe ("korinthische Herrenmahl," 191n28; "Eucharist," 48n13) has previously addressed this problem, concluding that προλαμβάνω has a temporal meaning in 1 Cor 11:21 because the translation "eat" appears in only one source, the epigraph from Epidaurus that I discussed above. He tries to discredit this inscription by positing that the engraver may have mistook προσλαμβάνειν, which means "to take in/receive," for προλαμβάνειν. Lampe, however, does not point out that one instance of προλαμβάνω in the inscription has a temporal meaning. Nor does he stress that there are public inscriptions closer to the time of the composition of 1 Corinthians in which προλαμβάνω clearly has a temporal meaning. The conclusion that an engraver made a mistake should always be a last resort, let alone that an engraver made the same mistake three times in the same inscription. Lampe ("korinthische Herrenmahl," 198–203), however, builds a strong case for the translation of προλαμβάνω as "go ahead with" from the Roman custom of first and second tables and the *eranos* meal.

37. Winter ("Lord's Supper," 75) acknowledges that context "must be the final arbiter" of the meaning of a word.

translation. First, as noted above, the calendar decree attests to widespread knowledge of the temporal meaning of προλαμβάνω among the Greeks of Asia closer to the composition of 1 Corinthians than the Epidaurus inscription. Second, the context of Paul's discussion in 1 Cor 11:17–34 makes better sense if προλαμβάνω has a temporal meaning. This is because Paul's solution to the problem is that the more affluent Corinthians "wait" (ἐκδέχεσθε) for their brothers and sisters before they begin the Lord's Banquet (1 Cor 11:33). Winter argues that ἐκδέχεσθε does not mean "wait" here, but "share." However, if ἐκδέχεσθε means share, then Paul's directive that those who are hungry should eat in their own homes makes little sense. The verb appears a second time in 1 Corinthians, where it clearly means something like to wait or to expect (1 Cor 16:11).[38]

The final factor supporting the translation of προλαμβάνω as "go ahead with" is the Roman character of Corinth. As is widely known, Corinth was a Roman colony. Ancient Roman sources describe the function of a Roman colony as a "mini-Rome," meaning that a colony was a center of Roman culture, which includes dining customs.[39] While the banqueting customs of Greeks and Roman were similar in some ways, there were markedly different in others.[40] Most often Greeks did not allow respectable upper class women to attend banquets.[41] The tradition in the Synoptic Gospels about the banquet that Herod Antipas hosted at which he decided to behead John the Baptist is a prime example (Mark 6:21–29). The individuals present are the king, the nobles, the chief officers, and the most eminent persons in Galilee (Mark 6:21). The only exception to this party of elite males is the entertainment:

38. Here Paul says, "I am waiting for/expecting [Timothy] with the brothers" (ἐκδέχομαι γὰρ αὐτὸν μετὰ τῶν ἀδελφῶν). This translation of ἐκδέχομαι as wait for/expect is one that the KJV, ASV, NIV, NRSV, and ESV adopt. Conzelmann (*1 Corinthians*, 294, 297) adopts the translation "to wait for" in 1 Cor 16:11. Outside the Pauline corpus, ἐκδέχομαι appears four more times in the NT and each carries a similar meaning: Acts 17:16; Heb 10:13; 11:10; Jas 5:7.

39. For a discussion of the Roman character of Corinth see D. Clint Burnett, "Divine Titles for Julio-Claudian Imperials in Corinth: Neglected Factors in Reconstructions of Corinthian Imperial Worship and Its Connections to the Corinthian Church," *CBQ* 82 (2020), forthcoming.

40. See Katherine M. D. Dunbabin, "Ut Graeco More Biberetur: Greeks and Romans on the Dining Couch," in *Meals in Social Context: Aspects of the Communal Meal in the Hellenistic and Roman World*, ed. Inge Nielsen and Hanne Sigismund Nielsen (Oxford: Aarhus University Press, 1998), 81–101.

41. Katherine M. D. Dunbabin, *The Roman Banquet: Images of Conviviality* (Cambridge: Cambridge University Press, 2003), 22–23.

Herodias's daughter, who dances for the banqueters (Mark 6:22, 24).[42] On the other hand, Roman women and men dined together.[43]

Not only did participants in Greek and Roman banquets differ, but also there were distinctive Roman and Greek layouts of dining rooms, at least during the early Roman Empire when Paul wrote 1 Corinthians. Katherine Dunbabin, the foremost expert in Roman dining customs, points out that the archaeology of Greek and Roman dining rooms highlights stark differences. Greek dining rooms tend to be larger than Roman ones, having five to eleven couches that held one or two banqueteers. Therefore, the number of participants at typical Greek banquet was eleven to twenty-two. The couches in a Greek dining room were laid out in a square and each couch (and thus pair of participants) had its own table. This layout allowed banqueteers to converse with each other, even across the room, while maintaining decor and giving deference to the guest of honor.[44]

The layout of Roman dining rooms was different, to which many that have been discovered inside and outside Pompeiian homes attest.[45] They were shaped like a U and tend to have three couches (hence the Latin word for dining room *triclinium*: *tri* = three; *clinium* = couch). Each couch was about 2.5 m long and 1.5 m deep. The first couch is called the highest (*summus*), the second the middle (*medius*), and the third couch the lowest (*imus*). These couches typically held three people who reclined on their left elbows and ate food with their right hands. The position of individuals on the couches and the relation of the three couches among each other displayed one's social status relative to other banqueteers. The clear place of honor is the middle couch and the third position (see Figure 3.1).[46]

42. It is clear from Mark's text that Herodias's mother is not at the banquet, for she has to leave (ἐξελθοῦσα) the dinner to talk with her mother and then return (εἰσελθοῦσα) to the banquet to announce her request. For a discussion see Adela Yarbro Collins, *Mark: A Commentary*, Hermeneia (Minneapolis: Fortress, 2007), 308–14.

43. Jérôme Carcopino, *Daily Life in Ancient Rome*, trans. E. O. Lorimer, 2nd ed. (New Haven: Yale University Press, 2003), 265–76; Dunbabin, *Roman Banquet*, 22–23.

44. Dunbabin, "Ut Graeco," 82–83; Katherine M. D. Dunbabin and William J. Slater, "Roman Dining," in *The Oxford Handbook of Social Relations in the Roman World*, ed. Michael Peachin (Oxford: Oxford University Press, 2011), 438–49.

45. For the dining rooms of some houses from Pompeii see Andrew Wallace-Hadrill, *Houses and Society in Pompeii and Herculaneum* (Princeton: Princeton University Press, 1994), esp. 197–216.

46. Dunababin, "Ut Graeco," 89; Dunababin, *Roman Banquet*, 36–67.

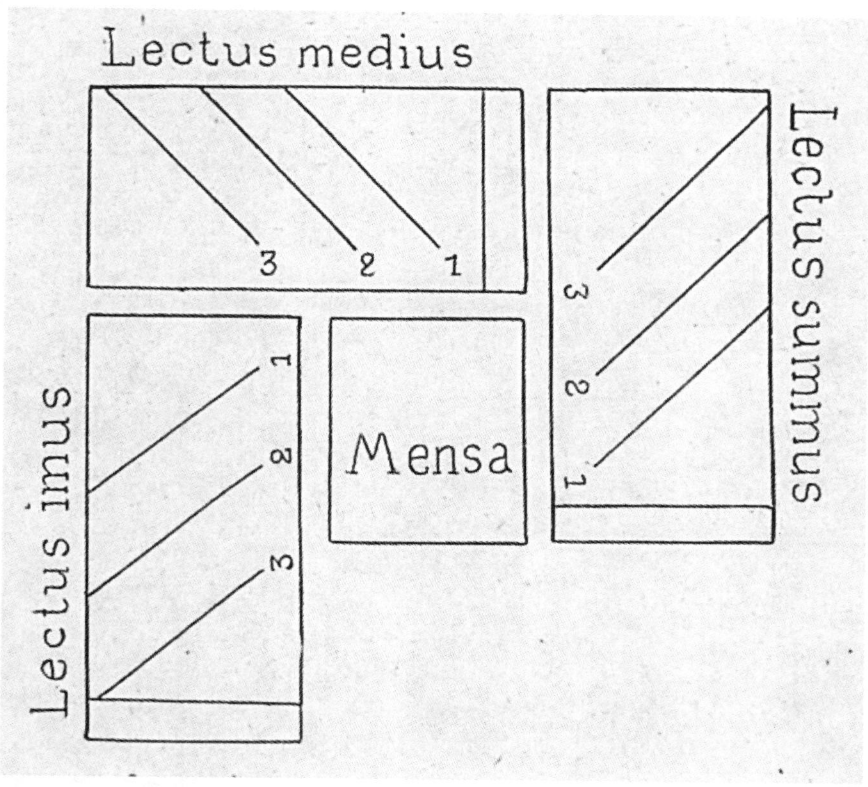

Figure 3.1. Drawing of a Pompeiian dining room from Henry Thédenat, *Pompéi* (Paris: Renouard, 1906, 77: Public Domain).

There are artistic depictions of Roman banquets on frescos in Pompeii (that date before the eruption of Mount Vesuvius in 79 CE) that conform to and confirm this description of a Roman banquet (see Figure 3.2).[47] The following fresco was found on the north wall of the dining room of a house in a region of Pompeii known as Regio V. It depicts two of the three couches of the Roman dining room, the highest (*summus*) and the middle (*medius*). There is one table in the middle of the couches, from which all participants dine. The banqueteers are reclining to eat and drink, while a slave, pictured in the bottom right hand corner, waits on them hand and foot. There are two Latin inscriptions above the heads of the participants. One says, "Enjoy yourselves and I will sing," and the other, "That's how life is: be well!"

47. Dunababin, *Roman Banquet*, 36–67.

Figure 3.2. Fresco dating 50 CE from the north wall of the dining room of House 2, Room 4 in Regio V in Pompeii, Italy (© D. Clint Burnett).

I must note that Roman dining customs were in the process of evolving during the early Roman Empire. By the second century CE, Roman dining rooms became larger and had longer couches that could hold more than nine people.[48] Given that no identifiable dining rooms have been excavated at Corinth, it is unclear when this evolution in Roman dining practices arrived in Corinth. Due to the Roman character of Corinth and until proven otherwise, we must assume that the dining customs of the Corinthians were Roman and resembled those described above.

Finally, Jerome Murphy-O'Connor has presented the most plausible reconstruction of the problem with the Lord's Banquet at Corinth. He

48. Dunababin, "Ut Graeco," 93–98; Dunababin and Slater, "Roman Dining," 438–49.

considers the architectural layout of Roman dining rooms, noting that the average size of known excavated dining rooms is thirty-six square m. This size suggests that only nine people could dine in them. He counts the number of Corinthians known from Paul's letters, fourteen, and posits that if they were married then the Corinthian church would have consisted of at least twenty-eight people. Providing for children, slaves, and other relations who lived in the homes of the known Corinthians, there may have been as many as fifty people in the Corinthian church. When the entire church gathered for the Lord's Banquet at their host's house, all of them could not fit into one dining room, provided that the host's dining room was average sized. Murphy-O'Connor proposes that the host of the church gathered with his friends who are probably wealthy Corinthians (Paul's "haves") in the dining room and began to feast before the majority of Corinthians, the poorer ones (Paul's "have nots"), arrive. Therefore, these latter Corinthians dined outside the dining room most probably in the atrium.[49] In short, Roman dining practices and the architectural layout of dining rooms contributed to the social division in the church. Paul's solution is that the "haves" must "wait for" (ἐκδέχομαι) (1 Cor 11:33) the "have nots" and if the "haves" are hungry, then they are to eat at their own homes (1 Cor 11:34).[50] Presumably, this waiting for all to gather for the Lord's Banquet would have negated the splintering of one group of affluent Christians in the dining room with poorer Christians scattered around the rest of the house.

49. Murphy-O'Connor, "House Churches and the Eucharist," 32–38; Murphy-O'Connor, *St. Paul's Corinth: Texts and Archaeology* (Wilmington, DE: Glazier, 1983), 153–61; Murphy-O'Connor, "House Churches and the Eucharist," in *Keys to First Corinthians: Revisiting the Major Issues* (Oxford: Oxford University Press, 2009), 183–93. In 2004, David G. Horrell ("Domestic Space and Christian Meetings at Corinth: Imagining New Contexts and the Buildings East of the Theatre," *NTS* 50 [2004]: 349–69) challenged Murphy-O'Connor's reconstruction, pointing out correctly that what had been identified as a villa at Anaploga near Corinth is not one. Horrell proposes that rooms in Greco-Roman houses were functional and that the Corinthian Christians were not wealthy enough to own homes with dining rooms such as those to which Murphy-O'Connor points. Murphy-O'Connor ("House Churches and the Eucharist," in *Keys to First Corinthians*, 183–93) responds to Horrell's criticism noting that the dining room in villa from Anaploga should no longer be considered one. However, he disagrees with Horrell that no Corinthian Christian could afford a house similar to ones excavated at Pompeii, Ephesus, and Olynthus, pointing to 1 Cor 1:26.

50. Theissen, *Social Setting*, 145–74.

IV. Conclusion

To summarize, this chapter has demonstrated the ability of inscriptions to adjudicate philological discussions. In the process, I have examined the proposal based on epigraphy that προλαμβάνω in 1 Cor 11:21 means "to eat." This proposal is problematic because one of the three uses of προλαμβάνω in the epigraph scholars point to as evidence has a temporal meaning. In addition, a use of προλαμβάνω in a public sacred inscription dating closer to the time of the composition of 1 Corinthians assumes that the Greeks living in the cities in the league of Asia knew that προλαμβάνω had a temporal meaning. Given that Paul's solution to the problem of the Lord's Banquet is that the Corinthians "wait for" (ἐκδέχομαι) each other (1 Cor 11:33) and that Roman dining customs were most probably practiced in Paul's Corinth, the most appropriate translation of προλαμβάνω in 1 Cor 11:21 is "go ahead with." This means that the problem with the Corinthian Lord's Banquet is that some wealthier Christians (probably no more than nine people) were arriving before the majority of the congregation and beginning to consume the Lord's Banquet in the dining room of the church's host. When the rest of the church arrived, most of the food had been consumed, and they are forced to eat elsewhere in the house. Paul harangued the wealthier Corinthians, commanding them to wait for their poorer brothers and sisters and indicating that such treatment of the latter is the reason why some among the wealthier Corinthian Christians have become ill and even died (1 Cor 11:30).

CHAPTER 4

Imperial Loyalty Oaths, Caesar's Decrees, and Early Christianity in Thessalonica: Contextualizing Inscriptions

One of the greatest epigraphers of the last century, Louis Robert, gives two words of warning to historians about inscriptions that apply to the student of the NT. The first danger of epigraphs is not using them, and the second is using them improperly.[1] By improper use, Robert means failing to contextualize inscriptions and neglecting to treat them as documents providing evidence for local laws, religions, practices, and customs.[2] However, some NT scholars have not heeded Robert's caution, and they approach inscriptions as if they were immediately applicable to every city and region of the early Roman Empire.[3] In the process, some scholars take a practice or custom attested in an inscription from one city, say, Ephesus, and conclude that this practice or custom applies to another city or even all cities of the Roman Empire. To provide a concrete example, a growing number of NT exegetes propose that one of the charges that Luke says was brought against Christians in Thessalonica, that they disregarded "Caesar's decrees" (Acts 17:7), refers to a group of inscriptions that contain oaths of loyalty that provincials swore to the reigning emperor. These epigraphs, however, are not imperial decrees, but decisions of local communities. Therefore, these oaths cannot be "Caesar's decrees." This negative conclusion notwithstanding does not mean that inscriptions cannot illumine what "Caesar's decrees" means. By contextualizing Thessalonica's loyalty to Rome in inscriptions, I contend that "Caesar's decrees" relates the city's status as "free" in the Roman Empire and that "Caesar's decrees" refers to imperial decrees or letters that Roman emperors, beginning with Augustus, sent to Thessalonica, confirming and reaffirming this privilege.

---

1. Louis Robert, "Les épigraphies et L'épigraphie grecque et romaine," in *Opera minora selecta. Epigraphie et antiquités grecque* (Amsterdam: AM Hakkert, 1990), 5:84.

2. Ibid., 5:72–79.

3. For scholarly generalizations of inscriptions and other archaeological materials see Laura S. Nasrallah, *Archaeology and the Letters of Paul* (Oxford: Oxford University Press, 2019), 18–39.

I. Affliction of Christians in Thessalonica

According to Luke, around 49 CE Paul and Silas (and Timothy too, although Luke does not mention him) made their way to the thriving port city of Thessalonica (Acts 17:1; 1 Thess 1:1; 2 Thess 1:1).[4] Paul's preaching was successful and he gained a number of converts (Acts 17:2–4). Because of this success, a group of non-Christ-confessing Jews who lived in Thessalonica formed a mob and started a riot in the city with the purpose of arresting Paul (Acts 17:5a). They stormed the home of one of the new converts to the Christian movement, Jason, looking to bring formal charges against Paul and Silas before the local Thessalonian body of citizens. Not finding Paul or Silas, the mob vented their wrath on Jason, accusing him and his Christian colleagues of three charges: (1) subverting the empire, (2) disregarding Caesar's decrees, and (3) proclaiming Jesus as king (Acts 17:6–7).[5] My focus is on the meaning of the second charge, disregarding Caesar's decrees.

---

4. For discussions of the date of Paul's tenure in Thessalonica see Abraham J. Malherbe, *The Letters to the Thessalonians: A New Translation with Introduction and Commentary*, AB 32B (New York: Doubleday, 2000), 67–74. For a discussion of Thessalonica see Winfried Elliger, *Paulus in Griechenland: Philippi, Thessaloniki, Athen, Korinth* (Stuttgart: Katholisches Bibelwerk, 1987), 78–105; Holland Lee Hendrix, "Thessalonica," in *ABD*, 6:523–27; Christoph vom Brocke, *Thessaloniki—Stadt des Kassander und Gemeinde des Paulus*, WUNT 2/125 (Tübingen: Mohr Siebeck, 2001); D. V. Grammenos, ed., *Roman Thessaloniki*, trans. David Hardy, Thessaloniki Archaeological Museum Publications 1 (Thessaloniki: Archaeological Museum, 2003). Luke (Acts 17:1–10) does not record that Timothy accompanied Paul and Silas to Thessalonica. First Thessalonians, however, confirms that Timothy did.

5. There is scholarly disagreement about the number of charges that Luke records. Ernst Haenchen (*Acts of the Apostles: A Commentary* [Philadelphia: Westminster, 1971], 510); C. K. Barrett (*A Critical and Exegetical Commentary on the Acts of the Apostles*, ICC [Edinburgh: T&T Clark, 1998], 2:815); and C. Kavin Rowe (*World Upside Down: Reading Acts in the Graeco-Roman Age* [Oxford: Oxford University Press, 2009], 96) conclude that there is one charge, claiming that there is another king. Jeffrey A. D. Weima ("The Political Charges against Paul and Silas in Acts 17:6–7: Roman Benefaction in Thessalonica," in *Stones, Bones, and the Sacred: Essays on Material Culture and Ancient Religion in Honor of Dennis E. Smith*, ed. Alan H. Cadwallader, ECL 21 [Atlanta: SBL Press, 2016], 241–68) counts two offenses: causing trouble all over the world and defying Caesar's decrees by proclaiming that there's another king, Jesus. A. N. Sherwin-White (*Roman Society and Roman Law in the New Testament* [Oxford: Clarendon, 1963], 103) and Joseph A. Fitzmyer (*The Acts of the Apostles: A New Translation with Introduction and Commentary*, AB 31 [New York: Doubleday, 1998], 592) tally three charges: causing trouble all over the world, acting in defiance of Caesar's decrees, and claiming there is another king, Jesus.

Most scholars agree that Paul and the early Thessalonian congregation faced external afflictions of some kind.[6] Paul's own testimony in 1 Thessalonians confirms that the apostle and his converts faced difficulty (1 Thess 2:2, 16–18).[7] Paul says that the Thessalonian Christians "received the message in much affliction" (1:6) and that this reception of the gospel resembled that of the Jewish Christians in Roman Judea, for the Thessalonian Christians "suffered" from their "own countrymen" as the Jewish Christians did from theirs (2:14–16). The apostle desires that his new converts remain steadfast "in the midst of these afflictions" because they are "destined for this" treatment (3:3; cf. 3:4–5; 5:15). If one accepts Pauline authorship of 2 Thessalonians and if the letter was written soon after 1 Thessalonians, then Paul's converts continued to face conflict in the form of harassments and afflictions (2 Thess 1:4–5).[8] Given that 1–2 Thessalonians and Acts lack any mention of deaths as a result of this harsh treatment of Christians, most scholars propose that the nature of these afflictions are social harassment,

---

6. Haenchen, *Acts*, 505–14; F. F. Bruce, *The Acts of the Apostles: The Greek Text with Introduction and Commentary*, 3rd ed. (Grand Rapids: Eerdmans, 1990), 369–72; Dieter Lührmann, "The Beginnings of the Church at Thessalonica," in *Greeks, Romans, and Christians: Essays in Honor of Abraham J. Malherbe*, ed. David L. Balch, Everett Ferguson, and Wayne A. Meeks (Minneapolis: Fortress, 1990), 237–49; John J. Kilgallen, "Persecution in the Acts of the Apostles," in *Luke and Acts*, ed. Gerald O'Collins and Gilberto Marconi, trans. Matthew J. O'Connell (New York: Paulist, 1993), 143–60; Fitzmyer, *Acts*, 591–96; Barrett, *Acts*, 2:806–17; Rainer Riesner, *Paul's Early Period: Chronology, Mission Strategy, Theology*, trans. Doug Stott (Grand Rapids: Eerdmans, 1998), 352–59; Craig S. Keener, *Acts: An Exegetical Commentary*, vol. 3, *15:1–23:35* (Grand Rapids: Baker Academic, 2014), 2532–58.

7. George Milligan, *St Paul's Epistles to the Thessalonians: The Greek Text with Introduction and Notes* (London: Macmillan, 1908), xxviii-xxxii; Ernst von Dobschütz, *Die Thessalonischer-Briefe*, KEK 7 (Göttingen: Vandenhoeck & Ruprecht, 1909), 11–31; F. F. Bruce, *1 and 2 Thessalonians*, WBC 45 (Waco, TX: Word, 1982), xxxv-xxxvi, 15–16, 20–22, 45–51, 62–64; Karl P. Donfried, "The Cults of Thessalonica and the Thessalonian Correspondence," *NTS* 31 (1985): 336–56; Robert Jewett, *The Thessalonian Correspondence: Pauline Rhetoric and Millenarian Piety* (Philadelphia: Fortress, 1986), 117–18; Lührmann, "Beginnings of the Church," 242–49; John M. G. Barclay, "Conflict in Thessalonica," *CBQ* 55 (1993): 512–30; Barclay, "Thessalonica and Corinth: Social Contrasts in Pauline Christianity," *JSNT* 47 (1992): 50–56; Craig Steven de Vos, *Church and Community Conflicts: The Relationships of the Thessalonian, Corinthian, and Philippian Churches with Their Wider Civic Communities*, SBLDS 168 (Atlanta: Scholars Press, 1997), 123–77; Todd D. Still, *Conflict at Thessalonica: A Pauline Church and Its Neighbours*, JSNTSup 183 (Sheffield: Sheffield Academic, 1999), 67–73.

8. Milligan, *Thessalonians*, xxxviii–xxxix; von Dobschütz, *Thessalonischer-Briefe*, 11–31; Jewett, *Thessalonian Correspondence*, 117–18; Bruce, *Thessalonians*, xxxiii-xxxiv, xxxix-xli, 149–54; Barclay, "Conflict in Thessalonica," 525–28.

external threats, and possibly violence.[9] A minority of exegetes, however, most notably Karl P. Donfried, posit that some Thessalonian Christians were killed.[10]

That Christians in Thessalonica were opposing "Caesar's decrees" is unique among all the charges that Luke says pagans and Jews bring against Christians in Acts. Therefore, scholars have attempted to reconstruct what Luke means by "Caesar's decrees."[11] One proposal gaining wide assent among interpreters is that "Caesar's decrees" refers to imperial loyalty oaths, which are oaths found in inscriptions that provincials took to remain loyal to the reigning emperor.[12] Donfried argues that the inhabitants of Thessalonica took such oaths and that the city's magistrates, *politarchs* (Acts 17:6), administered them. Donfried points to parts of the early Christian kerygma that could be interpreted as anti-imperial.[13]

If we reconstruct Paul's preaching from 1 (and, depending on one's view of authorship, 2) Thessalonians, it was filled with terms that the Thessalo-

---

9. Barclay, "Conflict in Thessalonica," 513–15; de Vos, *Church and Community Conflicts*, 1–26, 155–60; Still, *Conflict at Thessalonica*, 208–27. Riesner, *Paul's Early Period*, 373.

10. Karl P. Donfried, "The Theology of 1 Thessalonians," in *The Theology of the Shorter Pauline Letters* (Cambridge: Cambridge University Press, 1993), 22–23. See also Bruce, *Acts*, 372. The main exception to the notion that the Thessalonian Christians suffered external affliction is Malherbe (*Thessalonians*, 62, 77, 127–28), who notes that Paul and the Thessalonian Christians faced opposition even though he concludes that the references to affliction in 1 Thessalonians refer to internal struggles related to conversion to Christianity.

11. For a recent discussion of the various proposals of what "Caesar's decrees" means see Weima, "Political Charges," 241–68.

12. E. A. Judge ("The Decrees of Caesar at Thessalonica," *RTR* 30 [1971]: 1–7) is the first historian to connect Acts 17:1–7 to these oaths, providing three possible historical reconstructions of Luke's testimony, one of which involves oaths to emperors. Pointing to an imperial loyalty oath that the provincials on Cyprus took and in which they promised to support, to reverence, and to give their allegiance to Tiberius, Judge suggests that the Thessalonian *politarchs* may have administered such an oath with its stipulations.

13. Donfried ("Theology of 1 Thessalonians," 16) notes, "In all likelihood the politarchs in Thessalonica were responsible for administering an oath of loyalty and for dealing with its violations. In view of this situation we need to ask whether there were elements in the proclamation of Paul and his co-workers in Thessalonica that might have been perceived as so politically inflammatory as to provoke the crisis described in Acts and whether the unusually strong civic cult in the city would have created an environment particularly hostile to early Christian proclamation and language." It is generally recognized that Luke accurately notes that the civic magistrates of Thessalonica were *politarchs*.

nian pagans and even Christians may have interpreted as seditious.[14] Paul preached of God's kingdom (1 Thess 2:12; cf. 2 Thess 1:5), which would soon appear when God's Son returned from heaven on the day of wrath (1 Thess 1:10) in a manner that resembled a monarch's triumphant entry into a city (1 Thess 4:13–18).[15] Given that one imperial loyalty oath calls for hunting down and attacking those who were guilty of sedition, such evidence best explains the ill treatment of Christians in Thessalonica.[16]

The problem with this hypothesis is that it overlooks the content, occasion, and contextual nature of the actual imperial loyalty oaths. These vows are not imperial decrees, but decisions local Greco-Roman communities made in response to the ascension of a new emperor, the appointment of one while the current emperor was still alive, or a concrete benefaction that an emperor provided, all of which served to curry favor with the reigning emperor.

II. Imperial Loyalty Oaths and Caesar's Decrees

Imperial loyalty oaths are vows in Latin and Greek that individuals living in the Roman Empire swore by their gods to remain loyal to the reigning emperor and his household.[17] Vows of fealty to sovereigns are not unique

---

14. Given that Paul frequently reminds the Thessalonian Christians of his initial visit to them and what he preached (more often than any other letter) (οἶδα: 1 Thess 1:4, 5; 2:1, 2, 5, 11; 3:3, 4; 4:2; 5:2; cf. 2 Thess 2:6; 3:7), his preaching probably resembled what he wrote to his converts in Thessalonica. Most scholars conclude that we can reconstruct Paul's kerygma from the Thessalonian correspondence.

15. For a discussion see Milligan, *Thessalonians*, 145–48; Oepke, "παρουσία," *TDNT* 5:859–60.

16. Donfried, "Theology of 1 Thessalonians," 22–23. For similar positions see Bruce, *Acts*, 372; Jewett, *Thessalonian Correspondence*, 125; James K. Harrison, *Paul and Imperial Authorities at Thessalonica and Rome: A Study in the Conflict of Ideology*, WUNT 273 (Tübingen: Mohr Siebeck, 2011), 53–54; Keener, *Acts*, 2555–56; Bruce W. Winter, *Divine Honours for Caesars: The First Christians' Responses* (Grand Rapids: Eerdmans, 2015), 252–59. It appears that Fitzmyer (*Acts*, 596–97) agrees with this position when he quotes a section of one loyalty oath without qualification.

17. For more on Greek and Roman oaths see Fritz Graf, "Oath/Serment/Eid/Giuramento," in *Thesaurus Cultus et Rituum Antiquorum (ThesCRA)* (Los Angeles: J. Paul Getty Museum, 2005), 3:237–46. For imperial loyalty oaths see Franz Cumont, "Un serment de fidélité à l'empereur Auguste," *REG* 14 (1901): 26–45; T. B. Mitford, "A Cypriot Oath of Allegiance to Tiberius," *JRS* 50 (1960): 75–79; Peter Herrmann, *Die römische Kaisereid: Untersuchungen zu seiner Herkunft und Entwickung*, Hypomnemeta 20 (Göttingen: Vanderhoeck & Ruprecht, 1968); B. F. Harris, "Oaths of Allegiance to Caesar," *Prudentia* 14 (1982): 109–22; Julián Gonzalez, "The First Oath *pro salute Augusti* Found

to the Roman Empire. Most historians agree that imperial loyalty oaths in the Roman Empire are indebted to two different traditions that predate it: one Greek and the other Latin. Greek cities had a long history of swearing fealty to Hellenistic kings, especially promising to be well-disposed (εὔονια) toward them.[18] On the other hand, Latin oaths can be traced back to the Republican period and the Roman military oath (*sacramentum*) that Roman soldiers, and later civilians, swore to generals.[19]

These scholars are not incorrect that imperial loyalty oaths stem from two older traditions. However, Moshe Weinfeld has demonstrated that these Latin and Greek traditions are indebted to an even older tradition. Subjects living in the ancient Near Eastern empires of the Egyptians, Hittites, Babylonians, and Assyrians swore fealty to their sovereigns, and some of these oaths date as early as the fifteenth century BCE. Weinfeld distinguishes a threefold pattern of loyalty oaths to monarchs from the ancient Near East to the Roman world consisting of (1) swearing loyalty to the ruler and his dynasty, (2) obliging oneself to act against the monarch's enemies, and (3) cursing those who foreswear the oath.[20] Thus, these vows of loyalty

---

in Baetica," *ZPE* 72 (1988): 113–27; Greg Rowe, *Princes and Political Cultures: The New Tiberian Senatorial Decrees* (Ann Arbor: University of Michigan Press, 2002), 124–53; Hubert Cancik, "Der Kaiser-Eid: Zur Praxis der römischen Herrscherverehrung," in *Die Praxis der Herrscherverehrung in Rom und seinen Provinzen*, ed. Hubert Cancik and Konrad Hitzl (Tübingen: Mohr Siebeck, 2003), 29–45; Ralf Scharf, "Conobaria 5 v. Chr. – Der erste römische 'Kaisereid,'" in *Hommages à Carl Deroux, III. Histoire et épigraphie, Droit*, ed. Pol Defosse, Latomus 270 (Leuven: Peeters, 2003), 415–24; Serena Connolly, "Ὀμνύω αὐτὸν τὸν Σεβαστὸν: The Greek Oath in the Roman World," in *Horkos: The Oath in Greek Society*, ed. Alan H. Sommerstein and Judith Fletcher (Exeter: Bristol Phoenix Press, 2007), 203–16; Barbara Levick, "Some Augustan Oaths," in *Scritti di storia per Mario Pani*, ed. Silvana Cagnazzi et al. (Bari, Italy: Edipuglia, 2011), 245–56; Takashi Fujii, *Imperial Cult and Imperial Representation in Roman Cyprus*, Heidelberger Althistorische Beiträge und Epigraphische Studien 53 (Stuttgart: Steiner, 2013), 77–91; Søren Lund Sørensen, "A Re-examination of the Imperial Oath from Vezirköprü," *Philia* 1 (2015): 14–32.

18. Herrmann, *römische Kaisereid*, 21–49; Gonzalez, "First Oath," 117–19; Levick, "Some Augustan Oaths," 246–48. Connolly ("Ὀμνύω αὐτὸν τὸν Σεβαστὸν," 215–16) has collected thirty-six such Greek oaths that date from 411 to 91 BCE.

19. Herrmann, *römische Kaisereid*, 50–89; Harris, "Oaths," 109–11; Gonzalez, "First Oath," 113–27; Levick, "Some Augustan Oaths," 246–48.

20. Moshe Weinfeld ("The Loyalty Oath in the Ancient Near East," in *Normative and Sectarian Judaism in the Second Temple Period*, LSTS 54 [London: T&T Clark, 2005], 2–44, quote from 30) concludes, "The formal similarity between oaths and treaties in East and West is so great that it seems to be impossible not to assume an eastern influence on the west (Greece and Rome) in this area." Connolly ("Ὀμνύω αὐτὸν τὸν Σεβαστὸν," 210–12) agrees with Weinfled, noting that ancient Near Eastern

were not unknown among God's people throughout their existence. Indeed, scholars have noted that Deuteronomy, one of the most influential books in the Second Temple period, resembles an ancient Near Eastern fealty oath.[21] There is, however, one major difference between imperial loyalty oaths and those from the ancient Near East: ancient Near Eastern sovereigns demanded that their subjects swear fealty to them, while Roman emperors appear to have made no such requirements.

To date, there are six known imperial loyalty oaths and these are the sum total for the entire existence of the Roman Empire.[22] There are two additional epigraphs that, although not containing oaths themselves, refer to them.[23] Two imperial fealty oaths and the two references to them in inscriptions date to Augustus's reign (31 BCE–14 CE);[24] one oath is from Tiberius's reign (14–37 CE);[25] two oaths are from the first year of Gaius's (Caligula's) reign (37 CE);[26] and the emperor of the sixth oath is unknown,

---

fealty oaths and imperial loyalty oaths have a strikingly similar mode of expression and are "almost formulaic."

21. For Deuteronomy's resemblance to a fealty oath see Moshe Weinfeld, *Deuteronomy 1–11: A New Translation with Introduction and Commentary*, AB 5 (New York: Doubleday, 1991), 6–9, 328–52. For the place of Deuteronomy in the Second Temple period see Timothy H. Lim, "Deuteronomy in the Judaism of the Second Temple Period," in *Deuteronomy and the New Testament: The New Testament and the Scriptures of Israel*, ed. Steve Moyise and Maarten J. J. Menken, LSTS 358 (New York: T&T Clark, 2007), 6–26; Weinfeld, *Deuteronomy 1–11*, 80–81.

22. Conobaria, Spain: González, "First Oath," 113–27; Paphlagonia: Cumont, "serment de fidélité," 26–45 = *ILS* 8781 = *IGRR* III 137 = *OGIS* 532 = Herrmann, *römische Kaisereid*, 123–24, no. 4 = Sørensen, "Re-examination of the Imperial Oath," 14–32; Paphos: Mitford, "Cypriot Oath," 75–79 = Herrmann, *römische Kaisereid*, 124–25, no. 5 = *SEG* 18.578; Assos: J. R. S. Sterrett, "Inscriptions of Assos," *Papers of the American School of Classical Studies at Athens* 1 (1882–1883): 50–53, no. 26 = *IGRR* IV 251 = *SIG*[3] 797 = Herrmann, *römische Kaisereid*, 123, no. 3 = *IAssos* 26; Aritium, Lusitania: *CIL* 2.172 = *ILS* 190 = Herrmann, *römische Kaisereid*, 122, no. 1; Sestinum: *CIL* 11.5998a = Herrmann, *römische Kaisereid*, 122, no. 2.

23. Samos: Peter Herrmann, "Die Inschriften römischer Zeit aus dem Heraion von Samos," *MDAI(A)* 77 (1960): 70–84, nos. 1–3 = Herrmann, *römische Kaisereid*, 125–26, no. 6; Mytilene: *OGIS* 456 = *IGRR* IV 39.

24. Gonazález, "First Oath," 113–27; Cumont, "serment de fidélité," 26–45 = *ILS* 8781 = *IGRR* III 137 = *OGIS* 532 = Herrmann, *römische Kaisereid*, 123–24, no. 4 = Sørensen, "Re-examination of the Imperial Oath," 14–32.

25. Mitford, "Cypriot Oath," 75–79 = Herrmann, *römische Kaisereid*, 124–25, no. 5 = *SEG* 18.578.

26. Sterrett, "Inscriptions of Assos," 50–53, no. 26 = *IGRR* IV 251 = *SIG*[3] 797 = Herrmann, *römische Kaisereid*, 123, no. 3 = *IAssos* 26; *CIL* 2.172 = *ILS* 190 = Herrmann, *römische Kaisereid*, 122, no. 1.

but is probably Gaius.[27] Therefore, all the extant imperial loyalty oaths date to a specific time, from 31 BCE to 37 CE.

These imperial loyalty oaths are spread out across the Mediterranean basin. Five are from the Greek East in various provinces. One oath (Assos) and two references to oaths (Samos and Mytilene) are from Roman Asia, one oath is from Galatia (Paphlagonia), and one is from Cyprus (Paphos). The three remaining vows are from the West. One oath is from Sestinum, Umbria in Italy; one oath is from Aritium, Lusitania; and the final oath is from Conobaria, Spain. All of these inscriptions evidence that these cities (and, in one case, a province) took the oath to a reigning emperor and wished to monumentalize the oaths semi-permanently by engraving them on bronze, limestone, sandstone, and marble so that they could be constant reminders to these communities and their gods.[28]

As noted above, historians conclude that extant imperial loyalty oaths stem from two traditions: a Greek one a Roman one. Three Greek imperial loyalty oaths attest to this Greek tradition and these are written in Greek.[29] They date from to March 6, 3 BCE to 37 CE. The oaths begin with the takers swearing by the Greek gods, which can be local (e.g., Paphos and Assos) or personifications of heaven and earth (e.g., Paphlagonia).[30] Those who took

27. *CIL* 11.5998a = Herrmann, *römische Kaisereid*, 122, no. 2.

28. Levick, "Some Augustan Oaths," 246. Connolly ("Ὀμνύω αὐτὸν τὸν Σεβαστὸν," 212) notes, "Surely the text of an oath required no inscribing to ensure its efficacy: the swearing ceremony, as a religious act, should have sufficed. But earlier Greek oaths were inscribed, as were Hittite and Neo-Assyrian oaths. Inscription onto a *stele* made the terms of an oath permanently known to those who swore it and future generations, and to third parties as well." Ancient Near Eastern fealty oaths indicate that these texts were inscribed as reminders for future generations (*COS* 2:82) and the gods (*ANESTP*, 539–41).

29. Cumont, "serment de fidélité," 26–45 = *ILS* 8781 = *IGRR* III 137 = *OGIS* 532 = Herrmann, *römische Kaisereid*, 123–24, no. 4 = Sørensen, "Re-examination of the Imperial Oath," 14–32; Sterrett, "Inscriptions of Assos," 50–53, no. 26 = *IGRR* IV 251 = *SIG*³ 797 = Herrmann, *römische Kaisereid*, 123, no. 3 = *IAssos* 26; Mitford, "Cypriot Oath," 75–79 = Herrmann, *römische Kaisereid*, 124–25, no. 5 = *SEG* 18.578.

30. The oath from Paphlagonia was sworn by "Zeus, Earth, the Sun, al[l] gods [and al]l [goddesses], and Augu[s]tus himself" (Δία Γῆν Ἥλιον θεοὺς πάντα[ς καὶ πά]|σας καὶ αὐτὸν τὸν Σεβασ[τ]ὸν) (Cumont, "serment de fidélité," 26–45 = *ILS* 8781 = *IGRR* III 137 = *OGIS* 532 = Herrmann, *römische Kaisereid*, 123–24, no. 4 = Sørensen, "Re-examination of the Imperial Oath," 14–32). The one from Cyprus was sworn by "our Acraea Aphrodite, ou[r] Core, our Hylate[s Apoll]o, our Ce[r]ynetes Apollo, our savior Dioscuroi, the common Bouleia Hestia of the island, all the gods and goddesses who are common and ancestral to the island, the offspring of Aphrodite, Augustus god Caesar, the everlasting Roma, and all the other gods and all [the other goddesses]" ([τ]ὴν ἡμετέραν Ἀκραίαν Ἀφροδίτην κα[ὶ]| τὴ[ν ἡμ]ετέραν Κόρην *v.* καὶ τὸν ἡμέτερον Ὑλά|τη[ν Ἀπόλλ]ω καὶ τὸν ἡμέτερον Κε[ρ]υνήτην| Ἀπόλλω *v.* καὶ τοὺς ἡμετέρους

the oaths swore to remain well-disposed (εὔονειν) to the reigning emperor and to his dynasty (except in one case), sharing his friends and enemies. The oaths end with the takers invoking curses upon themselves if they foreswear their vows. To provide an example, the people of Assos swore the following oath to Gaius (Caligula):

> ὄμνυμεν Δία Σωτῆρα καὶ θεὸν Καίσαρα Σεβαστὸν καὶ τὴν|| πάτριον ἁγνὴν Παρθένον εὐνοήσειν Γαΐωι Καίσαρι Σεβασ|τῶι καὶ τῶι σύμπαντι οἴκωι αὐτοῦ, καὶ φίλους τε κρίνειν,| οὓς ἂν αὐτὸς προαιρῆται, καὶ ἐχθρούς, οὓς ἂν αὐτὸς προβά|ληται· εὐορκοῦσιν μὲν ἡμῖν εὖ εἴη, ἐφιορκοῦσιν δὲ τὰ ἐναν|τία·
>
> We swear by Zeus the Savior, the god Caesar Augustus, and by our pure ancestral Virgin: to be well-disposed to Gaius Caesar Augustus and to all his house and to consider friends whom he chooses and enemies whom he chooses. May it go well for us who swear truly and may it be the opposite for us who swear falsely.[31]

The content of Greek imperial oaths suggests that citizens gathered in assemblies and took them communally, for two of our three Greek imperial loyalty vows use first-person plural verbs and pronouns.[32] In addition, two local decrees of Greek cities that proscribe the taking of oaths locate the swearing of them during festivals (e.g., Samos and Mytilene).[33] Greek imperial loyalty oaths tend to be connected to imperial divine honors for the living emperor to whom the oaths are sworn (e.g., Paphlagonia, Paphos, Samos, and Mytilene). For example, the Paphlagonians swore their oath in the temple complexes of Augustus beside the altars of Augustus, while it

---

σωτῆρας|| Διοσκούρους *v.* καὶ τὴν κοινὴν τῆς νῃ̣σου| Βουλαίαν Ἑστίαν *v.* καὶ θεοὺς θεάς τε τοὺ[ς]|| κοινοὺς τῆς νήσου πατρῴους *vv.* καὶ τὸν| ἔκγονον τῆς Ἀφροδίτης σεβαστὸν θεὸν| Καίσαρα *vv.* καὶ τὴν ἀέναον Ῥώμην *v.* καὶ τοὺ[ς]|| ἄλλους θεοὺς πάντας τε καὶ πάσας) (Mitford, "Cypriot Oath," 75–79 = Herrmann, *römische Kaisereid*, 124–25, no. 5 = *SEG* 18.578). And the oath from Assos was sworn by Zeus the Savior, the god Augustus, and Athena Polias (for the Greek of this inscription see below) (Sterrett, "Inscriptions of Assos," 50–53, no. 26 = *IGRR* IV 251 = *SIG*³ 797 = Herrmann, *römische Kaisereid*, 123, no. 3 = *IAssos* 26).

31. Sterrett, "Inscriptions of Assos," 50–53, no. 26 = *IGRR* IV 251 = *SIG*³ 797 = Herrmann, *römische Kaisereid*, 123, no. 3 = *IAssos* 26.

32. ἡμῖν, ἡμετέρας, ὄμνυμεν, ἡμῖν (Sterrett, "Inscriptions of Assos," 50–53, no. 26 = *IGRR* IV 251 = *SIG*³ 797 = Herrmann, *römische Kaisereid*, 123, no. 3 = *IAssos* 26); ἡμετέραν, [ἡμ]ετέραν, ἡμέτερον, ἡμέτερον, ἡμετέρους, ἡμῶν (Mitford, "Cypriot Oath," 75–79 = Herrmann, *römische Kaisereid*, 124–25, no. 5 = *SEG* 18.578).

33. Herrmann, "Inschriften römischer Zeit," 70–84, nos. 1–3 = Herrmann, *römische Kaisereid*, 125–26, no. 6; *OGIS* 456 = *IGRR* IV 39.

appears that the Cypriots decided not to vote divine honors for anyone else except Roma and the emperor to whom they swore fealty, Tiberius.[34] This is not the case for every Greek imperial loyalty oath, however. The one that was taken in Assos appears not to be connected to any imperial divine honor. Nonetheless, it is clear that Greek imperial loyalty oaths are not imperial decrees. Rather, they are government decisions of local Greek communities that have been commemorated in public inscriptions (see chapter 1.IV.1.1). For instance, the oath from Assos is clearly labeled "decree of the Assians" (ψήφισμα Ἀσσίων).[35]

These decisions were made for three reasons.[36] First, these oaths were taken during political transition in Rome: either the appointment of a successor to the imperial purple (e.g., Paphlagonia) and/or the ascension of a new emperor (e.g., Assos and Paphos).[37] Second, imperial loyalty oaths show appreciation for imperial benefaction (e.g., Samos and Mytilene).[38] Third, the oaths were intended to curry favor with the reigning emperor. The best example of this purpose is, once again, the imperial fealty vow from Assos. The Assian oath's preamble indicates that the city sent an embassy to Gaius to inform him of the oath and to congratulate the emperor on his ascension. The embassy consisted of the "eminent and best Romans and Greeks" who lived in the city. One of the stated goals of these ambassadors

34. Κατὰ τὰ αὐτὰ ὤμοσαν καὶ οἱ ἐ[ν τῆι χώραι]| πάντες ἐν τοῖς κατὰ τὰ CYI [- - - Σε]|βαστήοις παρὰ τοῖς βωμοῖ[ς τοῦ Σεβαστοῦ].| ὁμοίως τε Φαζιμωνεῖται οἱ [τὴν καὶ Νεάπο]||λιν λεγομένην κατοικοῦν[τες ὤμοσαν σύμ]|παντες ἐν Σεβαστήωι παρὰ τ[ῶι βωμῶι τοῦ]|Σεβαστοῦ (Cumont, "serment de fidélité," 26–45 = *ILS* 8781 = *IGRR* III 137 = *OGIS* 532 = Herrmann, *römische Kaisereid*, 123–24, no. 4 = Sørensen, "Re-examination of the Imperial Oath," 14–32). Τιβέριον Καίσαρα Σεβαστοῦ ὑὸν Σεβας|τὸν σὺν τῶι ἄπαντι αὐτοῦ οἴκωι *vv.* καὶ *vv.*| τὸν αὐτὸν ἐκείνοις φίλον τε καὶ ἐχθρὸν *v.*| ἕξειν *v.* μετά τε τῶν ἄλλων θεῶν μ̣όνοις|Ῥώμῃ καὶ Τιβερίωι Καίσαρι *v.* Σεβ̣α̣στοῦ υἱῷ̣ι| Σεβαστῶι – *v.* *12* - ὑο̣ῖ̣ς τε τοῦ|| αἵματος αὐτοῦ *v.* καὶ οὐδενὶ ἄ̣λ̣λ̣ῳ̣ τῶν|| πάντων *v.* εἰσηγήσεσθαι *v.* ψηφ̣ίσ̣[α]σ̣[θαι]?| [ἱερὰ . . .] (Mitford, "Cypriot Oath," 75–79 = Herrmann, *römische Kaisereid*, 124–25, no. 5 = *SEG* 18.578).

35. Sterrett, "Inscriptions of Assos," 50–53, no. 26 = *IGRR* IV 251 = SIG^3 797 = Herrmann, *römische Kaisereid*, 123, no. 3 = *IAssos* 26.

36. Ancient Near Eastern parallels support the notion that the body politic took the oath communally: Deut 29:9–28; 2 Chr 15:14. Amenhotep II (1447–1421 BCE) boasts that after his successful military expedition in which he conquered Kadesh, the city's inhabitants, including children, swore fealty to him (*ANESTP*, 245–48).

37. Sterrett, "Inscriptions of Assos," 50–53, no. 26 = *IGRR* IV 251 = SIG^3 797 = Herrmann, *römische Kaisereid*, 123, no. 3 = *IAssos* 26; Mitford, "Cypriot Oath," 75–79 = Herrmann, *römische Kaisereid*, 124–25, no. 5 = *SEG* 18.578.

38. Herrmann, "Inschriften römischer Zeit," 70–84, nos. 1–3 = Herrmann, *römische Kaisereid*, 125–26, no. 6; *OGIS* 456 = *IGRR* IV 39.

was "to gain an audience with [Gaius], to become friendly with him, and to entreat him to have our city in the midst of his mind and his charge just like he himself professed when he first visited the district of our city with his father Germanicus."[39] The visit in question occurred in 18 CE, at which time Gaius was only six years old! The delegates were also supposed to sacrifice to Jupiter in Assos's name for the health of Gaius.[40] Therefore, the Assian oath indicates that the stated purpose of the city's loyalty oath was to acquire Gaius's goodwill.

The Latin tradition that forms the basis of Latin imperial loyalty oaths differs from its Greek counterpart. These were written in Latin and result from local decisions by Latin communities that chose to inscribe their decrees publicly (see chapter 1.IV.1.1).[41] Therefore, Latin imperial loyalty oaths are not imperial decrees. The earliest surviving oath dates to 5 BCE, while the latest dates to May 11, 37 CE. The content of Latin imperial loyalty oaths and the tradition from which they stem suggest that they were sworn individually. The actual vows use the first-person singular verbs, pronouns, and phrases.[42] Latin imperial loyalty oaths are traced to the military oath (or *sacramentum*) that a Roman soldier swore that, according to the most detailed description of it from Polybius (6.21), was taken individually, albeit in a communal setting. The oath-taker vows to have the same friends and

---

39. ἔδοξεν τῆι βουλῆι καὶ τοῖς πραγματευομένοις παρ' ἡμῖν| Ῥωμαίοις καὶ τῶι δήμωι τῶι Ἀσσίων κατασταθῆναι πρεσ|βείαν ἐκ τῶν πρώτων καὶ ἀρίστων Ῥωμαίων τε καὶ Ἑλλή|νων τὴν ἐντευξομένην καὶ συνησθησομένην αὐτῶι,| δεηθησομένην τε ἔχειν διὰ μνήμης καὶ κηδεμονίας|| τὴν πόλιν, καθὼς καὶ αὐτὸς μετὰ τοῦ πατρὸς Γερμανικοῦ| ἐπιβὰς πρώτως τῆι ἐπαρχείαι τῆς ἡμετέρας πόλεως| ὑπέσχετο (Sterrett, "Inscriptions of Assos," 50–53, no. 26 = *IGRR* IV 251 = *SIG*^{3} 797 = Herrmann, *römische Kaisereid*, 123, no. 3 = *IAssos* 26).

40. "These ambassadors offered themselves at their own expense: Gaius Varius Castus the son of Gaius from the Voltinia tribe, Herophanes the son of Zolius, Kretus the son of Pisistratus, Aischrion the son of Kalliphanes, and Artemidorus the son of Philomousus. These prayed to Zeus Capitolinus on behalf of health of Gaius Caesar Augustus Germanicus and they sacrificed in the name of the city" (πρεσβευταὶ ἐπηνγείλαντο ἐκ τῶν ἰδίων| Γάϊος Οὐάριος Γαΐου υἱὸς Οὐολτινία Κάστος| Ἑρμοφάνης Ζωΐλου| Κτῆτος Πισιστράτου| Αἰσχρίων Καλ<λ>ιφάνους|| Ἀρτεμίδωρος| Φιλομούσου| οἵτινες καὶ ὑπὲρ τῆς Γαΐου Καίσαρος Σεβαστοῦ Γερμανικοῦ| σωτηρίας εὐξάμενοι Διὶ Καπιτωλίωι ἔθυσαν τῶι τῆς πόλε|ως ὀνόματι) (Sterrett, "Inscriptions of Assos," 50–53, no. 26 = *IGRR* IV 251 = *SIG*^{3} 797 = Herrmann, *römische Kaisereid*, 123, no. 3 = *IAssos* 26).

41. Gonazález, "First Oath," 113–27; *CIL* 2.172 = *ILS* 190 = Herrmann, *römische Kaisereid*, 122, no. 1; *CIL* 11.5998a = Herrmann, *römische Kaisereid*, 122, no. 2.

42. *[e]x mei, eg[o], faciam, habebo, m[eos], [animad]|vertero* (Gonazález, "First Oath," 113–27); *ex mei, ego, ero, cognovero, internecivo, meos, habebo, mihi, meos* (*CIL* 2.172 = *ILS* 190 = Herrmann, *römische Kaisereid*, 122, no. 1); *internecivo, desistam, iudica||bo* (*CIL* 11.5998a = Herrmann, *römische Kaisereid*, 122, no. 2).

enemies as the reigning emperor. Latin imperial loyalty oaths tend to have a clause that calls for the person swearing the oath to stamp out seditious behavior, especially "on land and sea." To provide an example, on May 11, 37 CE the people of Aritium swore the following oath to Gaius (Caligula):

> *Ex mei animi sententia, ut ego iis inimicus| ero, quos C. Caesari Germanico inimicos esse| cognovero, et si quis periculum ei salutiq(ue) eius| in[f]ert in[f]er[e]tque, armis bello internecivo| terra mariq(ue) persequi non desinam, quoad|| poenas ei persolverit, neq(ue) me <neque> liberos meos| eius salute cariores habebo, eosq(ue), qui in| eum hostili animo fuerint, mihi hostes esse| ducam; si s[cie]ns fa[ll]o fefellerove, tum me| liberosq(ue) meos Iuppiter Optimus Maximus ac|| Divus Augustus ceteriq(ue) omnes di immortales| expertem patria incolumitate fortunisque| omnibus faxint.*
>
> By reason of my own intention, I will be an enemy to those whom I ascertain to be enemies of C(aius) Caesar Germanicus. If anyone causes or will cause danger to him or his safety, I will not desist to pursue in deadly battle with implements of war on land and sea until he has paid the penalty on account of him [Gaius Caesar Germanicus]. Neither will I cherish myself nor my freed-born children dearer than his safety. Those who have a hostile intention towards him, I will consider to be my enemies. If I intentionally swear falsely or will have done so in the future, then may Jupiter Optimus Maximus, Deified Augustus, and all the rest of immoral gods cause me and my free-born children to be destitute of our fatherland, health, and all our possessions.[43]

These vows, like their Greek counterparts, were taken at times of political transition: either a successor to the reigning emperor was appointed (while the current emperor still reigned) or a new emperor had ascended to the imperial purple. Finally, Latin imperial loyalty oaths were not connected to cultic honors for the emperor to whom the oath is sworn, although some were connected to divine honors for deceased and officially deified emperors.

In sum, imperial loyalty oaths are not imperial decrees, but decisions that local Latin and Greek communities took during times of political transition or to thank the reigning emperor for an imperial benefaction, both of which served to curry favor with the new regime in Rome. Therefore, Luke's "Caesar's decrees" cannot refer to imperial loyalty oaths.[44]

---

43. *CIL* 2.172 = *ILS* 190 = Herrmann, *römische Kaisereid*, 122, no. 1.

44. This observation has been stated by Weima ("Political Charges," 258–59), but not demonstrated.

III. Caesar's Decrees

If "Caesar's decrees" are not imperial loyalty oaths, then to what is Luke referring? Reconstructing Luke's meaning is difficult. The Roman historian A. N. Sherwin-White, who tended to trust the reliability of Acts, concludes of Luke's reference to "Caesar's decrees," "The accusation brought against the apostles at Thessalonica is somewhat obscure, and possibly garbled . . . [and] the most confused of the various descriptions of charges in Acts."[45] He concludes that Thessalonica's status as a "free city" (*civitas libera*) is what determined the *politarchs*' course of action. They only took bail from Jason to secure good behavior of Christians in the city because the charge of opposing Caesar's decrees was not "strictly relevant in the court of a free city" because it lay outside direct Roman control.[46] I agree with Sherwin-White's conclusion that the charge of violating "Caesar's decrees" is obscure, confused, and possibly garbled, but not his assessment that Thessalonica's status as a "free city" made them disinterested in charging Christians in the city with treason. Rather, the history of Thessalonica's relationship with Rome suggests that the city in which Paul established the church was acculturated to Roman values and wanted to preserve its status as a "free city," which was an honor that the emperor bestowed and could take away. Therefore, I contend that "opposing Caesar's decrees" has everything to do with Thessalonica's status as a "free city" and that it relates to the imperial decrees and letters granting this status.

To begin, I must note that because the modern city of Salonika stands atop the early Roman city a systematic excavation of Thessalonica is impossible. This situation means that we do not know as much about Roman Thessalonica as we would like. A number of inscriptions have been discovered in the city and its environs either by chance during modern-day construction projects or by destruction of some kind (such as a fire) that opened up the ancient city. In addition, some of our most important inscriptions (e.g., *IG* X.2.1 31) have been lost since their initial publication. Given that many inscriptions have not been found in scientific excavations and others cannot be re-examined by epigraphers, a reconstruction of Thessalonica's social history is impossible. Therefore, one must depend on the testimony of ancient Greek and Roman literary sources, especially historians. These sources, supplemented by inscriptions, paint a picture of Thessalonica as a

45. Sherwin-White, *Roman Society*, 96, 103.
46. Ibid., 96.

city that owes its prominence to Rome and is eager to maintain good relations with the capital of the empire.

Rome first began to exert influence in the region in which Thessalonica is located, Macedonia, in the late third century BCE. Rome was a republic at this time and in 229 BCE and 219 BCE, Roman soldiers fought successful campaigns in Illyria on the coast of the Adriatic Sea, northwest of Macedonia. The result of this incursion was that Rome made Illyria one of its protectorates. The kingdom of Macedon still existed at that time and its king, Philip V, considered Illyria his sphere of influence. He resented this show of Roman force and looked for a way to curb it. Therefore, Philip allied himself with Rome's mortal foe, Carthage, in 215 BCE in an attempt to force Roman troops out of Illyria.[47] This alliance resulted in the First Macedonian War (215–205 BCE) between Macedon and Rome. There was no real winner in this conflict and the peace treaty that the two sides signed in 205 BCE was tenuous. Within five years, Macedon and Rome were at war again in the Second Macedonian War (200–197 BCE). The cause of this second conflict was the city of Athens, which had declared war on Macedon and requested that Rome join the war as an ally. Rome obliged and the Republic defeated Macedon at the battle of Cynoscephalae on the eastern coast of Macedonia (in modern-day Greece). Rome forced a peace treaty on Macedon that required Philip V to surrender control of some cities in Greece and Asia Minor and prevented him from making war outside his territory without Rome's permission.[48]

In 179 BCE, Philip V died and his son, Perseus, succeeded him to the throne. Discontented with Macedon's relationship with Rome, Perseus wished to free himself from Roman influence. He declared war on Rome in 172 BCE and so began the Third Macedonian War (172–168 BCE). Rome defeated Perseus in 168 BCE in a battle near the city of Pydna on the eastern coast of Macedonia (in northern modern-day Greece). Given the number of wars that Rome fought against Macedon, the Republic decided to make the territory of the kingdom of Macedon into a province ruled directly by Rome. Macedon was broken up into four administrative sections (or *merides*), each with its own capital.[49] Thessalonica became the capital of the second district of the Roman province of Macedonia.

---

47. My discussion about Roman martial intervention in Macedonia draws on the excellent survey by Adrian Goldsworthy, *In the Name of Rome: The Men Who Won the Roman Empire* (New Haven: Yale University Press, 2003), 71–80.

48. Ibid., 75–80.

49. Ibid., 80–94.

Sometime in the mid-second century BCE, a man named Andriscus claimed to be the rightful heir to the kingdom of Macedon. He amassed a following and declared war on Rome, for the purpose of restoring political autonomy of the former kingdom. Rome, however, quelled this revolt in 148 BCE in a battle south of Pydna, the city where Rome had defeated Perseus about twenty years earlier. After this victory, Rome reorganized Macedonia, eliminating the administration sections and making it one province governed by a proconsul from Thessalonica.[50] The geography of the city probably led to Rome's choice of it as capital. Thessalonica's deep-water port on the Thermic Gulf accommodated the traffic coming and going from Rome that was needed for governing a province. The result was that the city prospered materially, financially, and in status.[51]

Thessalonica knew that Rome had defeated Andriscus and honored the general, Quintus Caecilius Metellus, who did so. In 148 BCE, the city erected a statue of Metellus and placed a public honorary inscription (see chapter 1.IV.1.2) on its base calling him "savior and benefactor" of Thessalonica (Κόιντον Καικέ[λιον Κοίντου Μέτελλον]| στρατηγὸν ἀ̣[νθύπατον Ῥωμαίων]| τὸν αὐτῆς σω̣[τῆρα καὶ εὐεργέτην]| ἡ π̣[όλις]) (*IG* X.2.1 134). It is unclear if the city bestowed cultic honors on the general, but it is possible and even probable. In his magisterial survey of divine honors for Hellenic kings of the Hellenistic period, Christian Habicht demonstrates that cultic honors such as sacrifice, games, etc. often accompanied the bestowal of the titles "savior" (σῶτηρ) and "benefactor" (εὐεργέτης).[52]

During the 130s BCE, the proconsul of Macedonia Gnaeus Egnatius oversaw the construction of a great Roman road linking the Adriatic coast (at the port city of Dyrrhachium on the western coast of Macedonia) to Byzantium. The road was named after the proconsul and called the Via Egnatia (or Egnatian Way). It is unclear why Egnatius had the road constructed, but its main purpose was probably military. The road ensured that the Romans could transport men and materiel quickly across the province, but civilians (like Paul and his missionary colleagues in the mid-first

50. Arthur M. Eckstein, "Macedonia and Rome, 221–146 BC," in *A Companion to Ancient Macedonia*, ed. Joseph Roismas and Ian Worthington (Malden, MA: Blackwell, 2010), 246–48; John Vanderspoel, "*Provincia Macedonia*," in Roismas and Worthington, *Ancient Macedonia*, 251–75.

51. P. Adam-Veleni, "Thessalonike," in *Brill's Companion to Ancient Macedon: Studies in the Archaeology and History of Macedon, 650 BC–300 AD*, ed. Robin J. Lane Fox (Leiden: Brill, 2015), 545–62.

52. Christian Habicht, *Divine Honors for Mortal Men in Greek Cities: The Early Cases*, trans. John Noël Dillon (Ann Arbor: Michigan Classical Press, 2017), 116–17.

century CE) were able to use it. The Via Egnatia passed through Thessalonica, with the result that the city became a major trading hub on land as well as on the sea.[53] Therefore, a number of Roman traders and merchants moved to Thessalonica.

Several Romans in the city provided benefactions to Thessalonica. To show appreciation for this munificence, the city set up a public cult dedicated to its "Roman benefactors." This cult is unparalleled in the Greco-Roman world and as Andrew Erskine notes, "This cult is at present not known to have existed anywhere but in Thessalonica."[54] The cult of Roman benefactors is first attested in 95 BCE in a public honorary inscription (see chapter 1.IV.1.2) that lauds a local gymnasiarch (or official in charge of Thessalonica's gymnasium) named Paramonus. The epigraph indicates that Paramonus funded and then increased the customary sacrifices to the gods and the Roman benefactors (*IG* X.2.1 4). This decree indicates that the cult of Roman benefactors was based in Thessalonica's gymnasium, at least in 95 BCE. The gymnasium was a training ground for young Greek boys. By placing the cult of Roman benefactors in it, the authorities of Thessalonica were attempting to ensure that their youth, who would grow up to run the city, knew from a young age that they should be grateful to Rome. Even though this inscription is the first known attestation of cultic honors for Romans in Thessalonica, the cult must predate the inscription by some time because the epigraph stresses that Paramonus paid for the *accustomed* sacrifices. How far back the cult of Roman benefactors can be traced is unclear, although we know that it lasted into the third century CE and became associated with imperial cultic honors (*IG* X.2.1 31, 128, 133, 226).

Later in the first century BCE, Pompey the Great made Thessalonica his base of operations during his war with Julius Caesar (49–45 BCE) (Dio Cassius 41.18.5–6; 41.44.1). Pompey and his partisans, some two hundred Roman senators and consuls, lived in Thessalonica and even made a portion of the city a "mini-Rome." Dio records that this group consecrated a tract of land for the express purpose of determining the will of the gods by the flight of birds (the Roman custom of augury). Dio stresses that this consecration of land was in complete accordance with Roman law, which states that augury can only be performed inside the sacred limits of the *pomerium*

53. Vanderspoel, "*Provincia Macedonia*," 264–67.

54. Andrew Erskine ("The Romans as Common Benefactors," *Historia* 43 [1994]: 70–87, quote from 80) goes on to note that the presence of this cult of benefactors suggests that the city in question viewed Rome as responsible for any benefit that it received.

(41.43.1–5). Thessalonica appears not to have suffered from its association with Pompey. The decisive battles between Julius Caesar and Pompey were fought in Macedonia, but not in or near Thessalonica. Presumably, Caesar, with his great clemency, held no ill-will toward the city.[55]

After the assassination of Julius Caesar (March 15, 44 BCE), civil war between Romans came to Thessalonica's doorstep. The Liberators, Brutus and Cassius (who killed Julius Caesar), and their armies fled Rome to Macedonia. The decisive battle between the Liberators and the Caesarians, Marc Antony and Octavian (later called the emperor Augustus), was fought outside the city of Philippi. Plutarch records that on the way to Philippi the Liberators attempted to stop at Thessalonica. The city, however, refused to admit them and Brutus, enraged by this refusal, offered to allow his troops to pillage Thessalonica after they defeated Antony's and Octavian's forces (Plutarch, *Brut.* 46; cf. Appian, *Bell. civ.* 4.118). This confidence was ill-fated and the Caesarians defeated the Liberators at the battle of Philippi (42 BCE).[56] Because of Thessalonica's refusal to harbor the Liberators and the city's loyalty to the cause of the Caesarians, Antony rewarded the city by bestowing on it the status of a "free city" (*civitas libera*). Being a "free city" meant that Roman troops could not be billeted in Thessalonica and that the city did not have to pay tribute to Rome.[57] Thessalonica took pride in this gift of status and boasted of being "free" (ἐλεύθεροι) in a fragmentary public inscription (*IG* X.2.1 6) and minting a coin in 37 BCE depicting the goddess of freedom, Eleutheria (*RPC* 1.1551). In addition, the city honored Antony, thanking him by altering its calendar. The years of the Thessalonian calendar from 42 to 32 BCE were given in those "of Antony" (*IG* X.2.1 83, 109, 124). It is clear that the appreciation for Antony extended into the private sphere, for two inscriptions are dedications that private individuals (see chapter 1.IV.2.3) set up to Isis, Osiris, and the gods associated with their cult (*IG* X.2.1 83, 109).

After Octavian defeated Antony at the battle of Actium (31 BCE), Thessalonica dropped its association with Antony. Two of the three surviving inscriptions that were dated by "years of Antony" were defaced, thereby erasing his name and his memory (*IG* X.2.1 83, 109). Octavian must have

55. For a description of Julius Caesar's operations against Pompey in Macedonia see Adrian Goldsworthy, *Caesar: Life of a Colossus* (New Haven: Yale University Press, 2006), 405–47.

56. For a description of the battle of Philippi see Adrian Goldsworthy, *Augustus: First Emperor of Rome* (New Haven: Yale University Press, 2014), 134–47.

57. Adam-Veleni, "Thessalonike," 554.

allowed Thessalonica to retain the status of "free city," and in return the city altered its calendar once again to honor the new sole ruler of the Roman Empire. This alteration of the calendar is epigraphically attested after 27 BCE, when the senate in Rome bestowed the title Augustus (Sebastos in Greek) on him. Several Thessalonian inscriptions, many of which are epitaphs (see chapter 1.IV.2.1), provide evidence that the inhabitants of the city knew that they were living in the age of Augustus and that events were dated according to his reign (*IG* X.2.1 285, 448, 450, 457, 483, 495, 573, 608, 826, 923; *IG* X.2.1s 1075, 1321, 1339).

In addition to the calendar, Thessalonica built a triumphal arch on the west side of the city in honor of Augustus most probably after the battle of Actium (but some propose that it was after the battle of Philippi and in honor of Antony and Augustus) known as the Golden Gate or the Gate of the Vardar. The arch no longer exists because it was demolished around 1877. However, eighteenth and nineteenth century French and English travelers to Salonica documented its existence (see Figure 4.1).

Figure 4.1. Golden Gate from Thessalonica that was set up most probably after Octavian's victory at Actium (© Wikimedia Commons: Public Domain).

Some of the gate was buried under the street level of eighteenth and nineteenth century Salonica, but what was visible was decorated with garlands at the top of the arch and two men on horses, whose identities remain unknown, at the bottom of each of its sides.[58] Despite some uncertainty about the arch, we can be sure that it was a public monument that the civic authorities set up, because there was an inscription on the arch that listed Thessalonica's *politarchs* (*CIG* 1967).

Besides the arch and calendar, Thessalonica advertised its fidelity to Augustus by minting coins (27 BCE–14 CE) with inscriptions on them acknowledging the divine status of Augustus's adoptive father, Julius Caesar. Epigraphs on two coin series call the deceased dictator a god, which is the Greek translation of the Latin *divus* meaning deified (*RPC* 1.1554, 1555). This suggests that there was a cult honoring Deified Julius at this time. The translation of the Latin *divus* on Thessalonica's coins indicates that the city followed the political decisions of Rome closely. The senate in Rome deified Julius Caesar in 42 BCE and it bestowed on him the title *divus* (Suetonius, *Jul.* 88; Dio 47.18.2–47.19.3). Most Greek cities voted divine honors for living emperors who benefited them in some way, which served as a quid pro quo. On the other hand, Romans in the official state religion in the capital city voted divine honors to deceased and officially deified emperors, not living ones.[59] Therefore, these Thessalonian coins witness Roman influence that was unique to Macedonia because there are no other examples of Greek cities in the province in the early Roman Empire minting coins depicting Deified Julius.

The city of Thessalonica and some of its inhabitants undertook several major construction projects honoring the imperial family. Between 27 BCE and 14 CE, Thessalonica built a temple for Augustus that has yet to be identified.[60] The evidence for the temple, a public honorary inscription (see chapter 1.IV.1.2), honors those people involved in its construction:

58. Edward Daniel Clarke, *Travels in Various Countries of Europe, Asia, and Africa* (London, 1816), 2:359.

59. See Ittai Gradel, "Roman Apotheosis," in *Thesaurus Cultus et Rituum Antiquorum (ThesCRA)* (Los Angeles: J. Paul Getty, 2004), 2:186–99.

60. Most scholars propose that this temple was dedicated to Julius Caesar because of the coinage, e.g., Holland Lee Hendrix, "Thessalonicans Honour Romans" (PhD Thesis, Harvard University, 1984), 292–311; Donfried, "Cults of Thessalonica," 345–46. If those coins did not exist, then the most logical reading of the inscription is that the temple belonged to the Caesar who had the priesthood and president of games: Augustus. That Thessalonica's epigraphic record attests to no priests of Julius Caesar supports this conclusion. For more information see D. Clint Burnett, "Imperial Divine Honours in Julio-Claudian Thessalonica: A Reassessment of Thessalonian Imperial Cultic Activity," *JBL*, forthcoming.

> – – – –| [.c.3–4.]ΒΟΣΑ – – – – – – – – – –| ἀ[ν]θύπατος – – – – – – – – [.c.7–8]| λατομίας ἐπόησ[εν τὸν]| Καίσαρος να[όν].|| ἐπὶ ἱερέως καὶ ἀγων[οθέτου · Αὐ]|τοκράτορος · Καίσα[ρος · Θεοῦ]| υἱοῦ Σεβασ{βασ} το[ῦ – – – – – – – – – .c.7–8]|ως τοῦ Νεικοπόλ[εως · ἱερέως]| δὲ τῶν θεῶν · Δω[– – – – – – .c.5–6 . τοῦ – – – – –.c.4–5]||που, Ῥώμης δὲ κ[αὶ Ῥωμαίων]| εὐεργετῶν · Νεικ[– – – – – – – – –.c.6–8 . τοῦ]| Παραμόνου· *v.*| πολειτα[ρχούντων]| Διογένους το[ῦ – – – – – – – – – – – – c.9–10],|| Κλέωνος τοῦ Π– – – – – – – – – – – c.8–9],| Ζωπᾶ τοῦ Καλ – – – – – – – – – – c.9–10,| Εὐλάνδρου τοῦ – – – – – – – – – c.7–8,| Πρωτογένους τοῦ – – – – – – c.5–6,| τοῦ καὶ προστα[τήσαντος]|| τοῦ ἔργου· ταμ[ίου τῆς πόλεως]| Σώσωνος τ[οῦ – – – – – – – – – – – – – – c.11–12],| ἀρχιτεκ[τονοῦντος]| Διονυσίο[υ τοῦ – – – – – – – c.6]| – – – –

> BOSA . . . The proconsul . . . he made the temple of Caesar of quarried stone in the time of the priest and president of victorious general Caesar Augustus son of god . . . –os son of Neikopolis priest of the gods. De- . . . son of . . . –pos Roma and the Roman benefactors. Neik- . . . son of Paramonus. When Diogenes son of . . . Kleon son of . . . Zopas son of Kal- . . . Eulandrus son of . . . Protogenes son of . . . served as *politarchs* . . . and supervised the work, Sosonus son of . . . was treasurer of the city . . . Dionysus son of . . . was the architect. (*IG* X.2.1 31)

Thessalonica even honored some of the priests of Caesar Augustus who served at the temple during Augustus's reign (31 BCE–14 CE) (*IG* X.2.1s 1059).

Between 12 BCE and 14 CE, a rich Thessalonian woman who was a Roman citizen, Avia Posilla, paid for the construction of temple, bath, cistern, and stoas and dedicated them to Augustus, Hercules, and the city of Thessalonica. The dedicatory, private (see chapter 1.IV.2.2), and bilingual Greek and Latin inscription was found outside of the city limits:

> Αὐτοκράτορι Καίσαρι θεοῦ υἱῶι| Σεβαστῶι καὶ Ἡρακλεῖ καὶ τῆι πόλει| Αὐία Αὔλου θυγάτηρ Πώσιλλα τὸν| ναὸν καὶ τὰ θερμὰ καὶ τὴν δεξαμενὴν|| καὶ τ[ά]ς περει[κειμέν]ας στọᾶς τῶι ὕδατι ἐκ τοῦ ἰδίου.| *v.*| *Imp(eratori) · Caesari · divi · f(ilio) · Aug(usto) · pontif(ici) · max(imo)| et · Herculi et civitati Thessalonicensium| Avia A(uli) · f(ilia) · Posilla · aedem · aquas · piscinam · et| porticus · circa · piscinam de suo.*

> Avia Posilla daughter of Aulus (set up) this temple, the baths, the cistern, and the stoas surrounding the basin to victorious general Caesar

Augustus son of god, Hercules, and the city from her own funds. Avia Posilla daughter of Aulus (set up) this temple, the baths, the basin, and the portico around the pool to victorious general Caesar Augustus *pontifex maximus* son of the deified one, Hercules, and the city of the Thessalonians from her own funds. (*IG* X.2.1s 1650)

Sometime between 14 and 29 CE, Thessalonica dedicated some structure to Augustus's wife, Livia. A public honorary inscription (see chapter 1.IV.1.2) found reused in a Byzantine church in Thessalonica attests to this dedication: "The city (dedicated this) to the goddess Julia Augusta wife of the god Caesar Augustus and the mother of Tiberius Caesar Augustus" ([θεᾷ Ἰουλίᾳ Σεβαστῇ]| [γυναι]κὶ θεοῦ Σεβαστοῦ Καίσα[ρος]| [καὶ μ]ητρὶ Τιβερίου Καίσαρος| [Σε]βαστοῦ : ἡ πόλις) (*IG* X.2.1s 1060). Finally, during Claudius's reign (41–54 CE), Thessalonica minted three coin series with inscriptions calling the long deceased Augustus a god (*RPC* 1.1578–1580), reflecting his status as a *divus* in the public religion of the city of Rome (Suetonius, *Aug.* 99.1–101.4; Dio 56.46.1–5).

From the beginning of the Roman province of Macedonia (146 BCE) to the time that Paul established the church in Thessalonica (49 CE), Thessalonica owed its prosperity and prominence to Rome. Rome made the city the provincial capital, a Roman proconsul constructed the main thoroughfare that ran through Thessalonica (Via Egnatia) and Rome bestowed the city's "free" status, which meant that it was self-governing and did not pay tribute to Rome. The status of being a "free city" in the Roman Empire was particularly coveted because it was awarded sparingly. I have already noted in chapter 1 that the Greek city of Samos petitioned Augustus for this status. Samos enlisted the emperor's wife, Livia, to influence Augustus, and appealed to the fact that Aphrodisias had the status. Augustus declined this request via a letter that was later inscribed on a wall of Aphrodisias's theater, stating that being a "free city" was not given lightly. The emperor said that he bestowed the honor on Aphrodisias because the city "thought about my affairs during the war [with Marc Antony] and was taken captive because of their goodwill toward us" (ὅς ἐν τῷ πολέμῳ τὰ ἐμὰ φρονήσας δοριάλωτος διὰ τὴν πρὸς ἡμᾶς εὔνοιαν ἐγένετο). Augustus goes on to say that he grants the status only for the most deserving cities, "For it is not right to bestow the greatest benefaction of all in vain and without reason. . . . I do not wish to give the worthiest benefaction without good reason" (οὐ γάρ ἐστιν δίκαιον τὸ πάντων μέγιστον φιλάνθρωπον εἰκῇ καὶ χωρὶς αἰτίας χαρίζεσθαι . . . ἀλλὰ τὰ τειμιώτατα φιλάνθρωπα χωρὶς αἰτίας εὐλόγου δεδωκέναιν οὐδενὶ βούλομαι) (*IAph2007* 8.32). Provided that this was Augustus's policy, the emperor must have considered Thessalonica to be exceptionally loyal and thus deserving of the "greatest" and "worthiest" "benefaction of all," freedom.

Neither Augustus nor any Julio-Claudian emperor visited Thessalonica.[61] This fact raises the question of how the city received the official documentation related to its "free" status. There is only one answer this question. Thessalonica must have sent an embassy to Augustus either in Rome or when the emperor was traveling in the provinces. Long ago, the Roman historian Fergus Millar demonstrated that the Roman emperor was passive in doling out verdicts and privileges. Most often the emperor adjudicated requests that provincials sent to him via embassies that made known the requests of cities and provinces. The emperor's task was to either oblige or refuse these petitions.[62] One fantastic example of an embassy sent to Augustus is found in the late first-century-BCE work of the geographer Strabo. He recounts that while he was journeying from Asia Minor to Rome by boat around 31 BCE his ship docked at a small fishing village called Gyaros on an island in the Aegean Sea. While anchored, a local fisherman came aboard. As they set sail, this fisherman informed his fellow travelers that his village had chosen him to go on an embassy to Augustus, who was in Corinth at that time. The purpose of his embassy was to ask the emperor for a reduction in tribute to Rome from one hundred fifty drachmas to one hundred (*Geogr.* 10.5.3).

It remains unknown if this fisherman gained an audience with Augustus in Corinth or that if he did, the emperor obliged his request. However, a similar process must have occurred in order for Augustus to grant Thessalonica its status as a "free city." The city had to have sent a deputation to the emperor asking for the right to retain the status that Antony had bestowed on it. In addition, Thessalonica would have needed to send other embassies with the same request upon the ascension of Tiberius, Gaius, Claudius, Nero, etc. It is probable that when these deputations returned with the favorable imperial decisions the local Thessalonian authorities set up public inscriptions commemorating and advertising the city's "free" status as they had done after Antony first declared it in 42 BCE (*IG* X.2.1 6).

---

61. Victoria Allamani-Souri, "The Province of Macedonia in the Roman Imperium," in *Roman Thessaloniki*, Thessaloniki Archaeological Museum Publications 1, ed. D. V. Grammenos, trans. David Hardy (Thessaloniki: Archaeological Museum, 2003), 67–79.

62. Fergus Millar concludes that the emperor answering petitions from provincials is "an essential aspect of the life of the empire." *The Emperor and the Roman World (31 BC–AD 337)* (London: Duckworth, 1977), 385.

Bringing this evidence to bear on the charge of "opposing Caesar's decrees," the accusation, while still obscure, probably refers to imperial letters containing edicts confirming and reaffirming Thessalonica's "free" status. If the Thessalonian correspondence informs our understanding of Paul's preaching (as is generally assumed), then it is easy to see how local Thessalonians could have interpreted Paul's preaching and the early Christian message of another king, the Lord Jesus, who would take the city and thus the empire by storm and establish a new kingdom (1 Thess 1:10; 2:12; 4:13–18; 5:2; 2 Thess 1:5), as seditious and as a possible threat to the city's status in the empire. The Thessalonians knew that what the emperor gave, he could take away.

In 73 BCE Mithradates VI, the king of Pontus, invaded Roman Asia. Strabo says that Mithradates came upon the city of Cyzicus (in modern-day northwest Turkey) and besieged it. The Roman general Leucullus sent a detachment of his army to aid Cyzicus. Mithradates was forced to withdraw and Leucullus granted Cyzicus the status of being "free" (ἐλευθέρα), which Strabo says it retained until his day in the late first century BCE (*Geogr.* 12.8.11). Suetonius (*Tib.* 37.3) and Dio Cassius (54.7.6) confirm Strabo's testimony. However, Dio says in 20 BCE Augustus "enslaved" (ἐδουλώσατο) the people of the city because some Roman citizens were flogged and killed during a riot (54.7.6). By enslaved (δουλόω), Dio means that Augustus revoked the city's privileged status as "free" (ἐλεύθερος). Dio later testifies that Agrippa, Augustus's son-in-law, restored Cyzicus's freedom (ἐλευθερία) in 15 BCE (54.23.7–8). The city's "free" status was revoked once again in 25 CE by Tiberius. Suetonius (*Tib.* 37.3) and Tacitus (*Ann.* 4.36) agree that this was because of offenses that the city committed against Roman citizens and Tacitus adds that Tiberius charged Cyzicus with neglecting the cult of Deified Augustus (*Ann.* 4.36).[63]

Not wanting to have their city's status stripped like Cyzicus, the Thessalonian mob accused the Christians of, among other things, "opposing Caesar's decrees" or acting in such a way as to endanger the city's free status that Augustus confirmed and successive emperors had reaffirmed in the form of imperial decisions communicated via letters. The result was that the *politarchs* acted against the early Christians so that they would not be guilty of harboring a possible seditious cult. They took bail from Jason to ensure good behavior and appear to have barred Paul from returning to the city (1 Thess 2:17–18).

---

63. For a discussion see F. W. Hasluck, *Cyzicus* (Cambridge: Cambridge University Press, 1910), 178–91.

IV. Conclusion

To summarize, inscriptions have been misused in the discussion of Luke's reference to Christians in Thessalonica "opposing Caesar's decrees." A number of scholars claim that these imperial decrees are imperial loyalty oaths, but analyses of the extant imperial loyalty oaths show that this cannot be the case. Imperial loyalty oaths are decisions of local communities, not imperial decrees. Instead, I suggest that "Caesar's decrees" refers to imperial letters and decrees granting and reconfirming Thessalonica's status as a "free city" in the Roman Empire.

CHAPTER 5

Benefactresses, Deaconesses, and Overseers in the Philippian Church: Inscriptions and Their Insights into the Religious Lives of Women in the Roman World

Inscriptions illuminate the lives of people in the Greco-Roman world who were not elite males, especially women, in ways that literary sources cannot. Elite males produced most surviving Greco-Roman literature and androcentrism colors their presentation of women. It is for this reason that inscriptions play a critical and sometimes corrective role in the reconstruction of the lives of women in the Roman Empire, because they shed light on the activity of women in society.[1] One specific area epigraphs illuminate is the prominent role that some upper-class women had in Greco-Roman cults. Such information helps to fill out our limited evidence from the NT and illumine the leadership roles of women in the earliest years of the church.

In this chapter, I use inscriptions from Philippi to demonstrate the prominent position of women in the Philippian church. I have chosen Philippi as my test case for two reasons. First, large portions of the city have been systematically excavated, which has yielded a substantial number of inscriptions. Most of these epigraphs have been published, providing an abundance of material with which to work. Second, two of our NT documents give a goodly amount of attention to women in the Philippian church. In Paul's letter to the Philippians, the apostle calls out Euodia and Syntyche, two of his female coworkers, and asks them to reconcile with

---

1. For discussions of women in the Roman world and the problem of sources see Ross Shepherd Kraemer, *Her Share of the Blessings: Women's Religions among Pagans, Jews, and Christians in the Greco-Roman World* (New York: Oxford University Press, 1992); Lynn H. Cohick, *Women in the World of the Earliest Christians: Illuminating Ancient Ways of Life* (Grand Rapids: Baker Academic, 2009). For a recent discussion of women in Roman epigraphy see Maria Letizia Caldelli, "Women in the Roman World," in *The Oxford Handbook of Roman Epigraphy*, ed. Christer Bruun and Jonathan Edmondson (Oxford: Oxford University Press, 2015), 582–604.

each other (Phil 4:2–3).[2] Luke, the author of Acts, records the founding of the Philippian congregation (around 49 CE), noting that the first convert is Lydia, a woman from Thyatira living in Philippi who became the church's patron (Acts 16:11–16, 40).[3] More women are known in the Philippian church than any other church connected to Paul. This suggests that women must have played prominent roles in the church's life and leadership, but to what extent? I argue that in light of the epigraphic evidence of women having leadership roles in Philippian cults, Lydia is probably the church's benefactress, while Euodia and Syntyche are probably deaconesses and possibly overseers.[4]

I. Women in the Philippian Church

Since the 1970s, scholars have noted the prominence of women associated with the Philippian church.[5] While some question the historicity of

---

2. For the most recent discussion of date and provenance of Philippians see Paul A. Holloway, *Philippians*, Hermeneia (Minneapolis: Fortress, 2017), 10–31. I disagree with Holloway that Paul wrote Philippians in Rome and opt for an Ephesian imprisonment. However, I agree with Holloway (10–19) that Philippians is one, not two, letters.

3. In addition to the NT, Polycarp writes to the Philippian church about 117 CE and singles out its widows, calling them "God's altar" (θυσιαστήριον θεοῦ) (Pol. *Phil.* 4:3) and he commends Crescens's sister who, for reasons unknown, is visiting the Philippian church (Pol. *Phil.* 14).

4. I use the translation "overseer" for ἐπίσκοπος because it does not conjure up the hierarchical structure that began to appear in the church in various places in the second century CE, most notably in the churches to whom Ignatius of Antioch sent letters: Ign. *Eph.* 4:1; 5:1, 2; 6:1; Ign. *Magn.* 2:1; 3:1, 2; 6:1; 13:1, 2; Ign. *Trall.* 2:1, 2; 3:1, 2; 7:1; 12:2; 13:2; Ign. *Phld.* 1:1; 4:1; 7:1; 8:1; Ign. *Smyrn.* 8:1, 2; 9:1; 12:2; Ign. *Pol.* 5:2; 6:1. For the threefold structure of bishop, council of presbyters, and deacons in Ignatius's letters see Ign. *Magn.* 2:1; 6:1; 13:1; Ign. *Trall.* 2:1–3; 3:1; 7:1–2; Ign. *Phld.* 4; 7:1; Ign. *Smyrn.* 8:1; 12:2; Ign. *Pol.* 6:1. For the notion that the sacraments are only valid in the presence of the bishop in Ignatius's letters see Ign. *Eph.* 5:1–3; 20:2; Ign. *Phld.* 4:1; Ign. *Smyrn.* 8:1–2; Ign. *Pol.* 5:2. For a further discussion of bishops in the early church see Everett Ferguson, "Bishop," in *Encyclopedia of Early Christianity*, ed. Everett Ferguson, 2nd ed. (New York: Routledge, 1999), 182–85.

5. W. Derek Thomas, "The Place of Women in the Church at Philippi," *ExpTim* 83 (1971–1972): 117–20; Francis X. Malinowski, "The Brave Women of Philippi," *BTB* 15 (1985): 60–64; Lilian Portefaix, *Sisters Rejoice: Paul's Letter to the Philippians and Luke-Acts as Seen by First-Century Philippian Women* (Stockholm: Almqvist & Wiksell, 1988); Florence M. Gillman, *Women Who Knew Paul* (Collegeville, MN: Liturgical Press, 1992), 30–38, 45–49; Ben Witherington III, *Women in the Earliest Churches*, SNTSMS 59 (Cambridge: Cambridge University Press, 1988), 111–13, 147–49; Ivoni Richter Reimer, *Women in the Acts of the Apostles: A Feminist Liberation Perspective*,

Luke's account about the establishment of the Philippian congregation (Acts 16:11–40), most scholars agree that Luke works with reliable tradition and that the nascent church met in Lydia's house where she served as its patron.[6] Most exegetes agree that when Paul wrote Philippians, Euodia and Syntyche played prominent roles in the church and were even leaders. Some scholars do not explicate further about Euodia's and Syntyche's leadership roles,[7] but others suggest that they were patrons of house churches,[8] deacons,[9]

---

trans. Linda M. Maloney (Minneapolis: Fortress, 1995), 71–149; Nils A. Dahl, "Euodia and Syntyche and Paul's Letter to the Philippians," in *The Social World of the First Christians: Essays in Honor of Wayne A. Meeks*, ed. L. Michael White and O. Larry Yarbrough (Minneapolis: Fortress, 1995), 3–15; Davorin Peterlin, *Paul's Letter to the Philippians in Light of Disunity in the Church* (Leiden: Brill, 1995), 102–32; Cynthia Briggs Kittredge, *Community and Authority: The Rhetoric of Obedience in the Pauline Tradition*, HTS 45 (Harrisburg, PA: Trinity, 1998), 91–108; Carolyn Osiek, *Philippians, Philemon*, ANTC (Nashville: Abingdon, 2000), 109–12; Mary Ann Getty-Sullivan, *Women in the New Testament* (Collegeville, MN: Liturgical Press, 2001), 243–51; Richard S. Ascough, *Lydia: Paul's Cosmopolitan Hostess* (Collegeville, MN: Liturgical Press, 2009); Jean-Pierre Sterck-Degueldre, *Eine Frau namens Lydia*, WUNT 2/176 (Tübingen: Mohr Siebeck, 2004); Cohick, *Women*, 188–90; Craig S. Keener, *Acts: An Exegetical Commentary*, vol. 3, *15:1–23:35* (Grand Rapids: Baker Academic, 2014), 2375–2532; Teresa J. Calpino, *Women, Work and Leadership in Acts*, WUNT 2/361 (Tübingen: Mohr Siebeck, 2014), 180–224.

6. Valerie A. Abrahamsen (*Women and Worship at Philippi: Diana/Artemis and Other Cults in the Early Christian Era* [Portland, ME: Astarte Shell Press, 1995], 19) questions the historicity of this account. However, Ernst Haenchen (*Acts of the Apostles: A Commentary* [Philadelphia: Westminster, 1971], 502) notes, "The way in which the status of the colony of Philippi and the smallness of the Jewish community are spoken about reveals exact knowledge of the conditions. Nor does the story of Lydia give any cause to suspect that here pious imagination has simply conjured up a romance." Hans Conzelmann (*Acts of the Apostles: A Commentary on Acts of the Apostles*, trans. James Limburg, A. Thomas Kraabel, and Donald H. Juel, Hermeneia [Philadelphia: Fortress, 1987], 126–33) determines that while much of Acts 16:11–40 passed through many hands before Luke received it, the exception is the report of Lydia's conversion. Bradley B. Blue ("Acts and the House Church," in *The Book of Acts in Its Graeco-Roman Setting*, vol. 2 of *The Book of Acts in Its First Century Setting*, ed. David W. Gill and Conrad Gempf [Grand Rapids: Eerdmans, 1994], 186) concludes that there is no reason to doubt that the church met in Lydia's house.

7. Witherington, *Women*, 112–13; Getty-Sullivan, *Women*, 250; Gordon D. Fee, *Paul's Letter to the Philippians*, NICNT (Grand Rapids: Eerdmans, 1995), 389; Markus Bockmuehl, *The Epistle to the Philippians*, BNTC (Peabody, MA: Hendrickson, 1998), 238; Richard S. Ascough, *Paul's Macedonian Associations*, WUNT 2/161 (Tübingen: Mohr Siebeck, 2003), 131–33, 136.

8. Gillman, *Women*, 46; Getty-Sullivan, *Women*, 250; Osiek, *Philippians*, 111–12.

9. Gillman (*Women*, 46) and Getty-Sullivan (*Women*, 250) note that they are "perhaps" deacons. Portefaix (*Sisters Rejoice*, 138n13) concludes that they could have been deacons. Gerald F. Hawthorne and Ralph P. Martin (*Philippians*, rev. ed., WBC 43

and even overseers.[10] To support these proposals, exegetes rightly appeal to the leadership roles of women in the Pauline corpus, especially Phoebe, whom Paul calls a deaconess and a patron of the church in Cenchrae (Rom 16:1–2).[11] There is a difficulty with this approach, however. What we know of male leadership, let alone female leadership, in Paul's churches and in the Pauline corpus is vague. There appears to be variety in how churches associated with Paul organized themselves.

Paul addresses "managers" (προϊστάμενοι) only in Romans (12:8) and 1 Thessalonians (5:12), but their exact functions are unclear. Paul tells the Corinthians to submit to Stephanus and people like him (1 Cor 16:15–16), but Stephanus and people like him do not appear to have a formal office.[12] Even among the Pastoral Epistles, there is diversity of church order and the roles of elders, overseers, and deacons seem to be functional.[13] Titus is told to appoint elders, which appear to be the same as overseers (Titus 1:5–9). Titus mentions no deacons, however. On the other hand, 1 Timothy provides qualifications of an overseer (always in the singular) (1 Tim

---

[Grand Rapids: Zondervan, 2004], 241) propose that they may be deaconesses. Peterlin (*Philippians*, 106–28) asserts that they are deacons, that the relationship between deacons and overseers is unclear because the former may not be subordinated to the latter, and suggests that some leaders of house churches are deacons and overseers.

10. Osiek (*Philippians*, 111–12) posits that they were overseers. Kittredge (*Community and Authority*, 108) proposes that they may be overseers and deacons. Ascough (*Paul's Macedonian Associations*, 138) points to the role of women in voluntary associations and concludes that men and women were overseers and deacons among the Philippians. John Reumann (*Philippians: A New Translation with Introduction and Commentary*, AYB 33B [New Haven: Yale University Press, 2008], 626) argues that Euodia and Syntyche may be deacons or overseers.

11. Peterlin, *Philippians*, 106–28.

12. Hans Conzelmann, *1 Corinthians: A Commentary on the First Epistle to the Corinthians*, trans. James W. Leitch, Hermeneia (Minneapolis: Fortress, 1975), 298.

13. Contrary to older German scholarship (see Martin Dibelius and Hans Conzelmann, *The Pastoral Epistles: A Commentary on the Pastoral Epistles*, trans Philip Buttolph and Adela Yarbro, Hermeneia [Philadelphia: Fortress, 1972], 50–57), more recent Anglo-American scholarship on the Pastoral Epistles emphasizes the diversity of church leadership in them, the functional nature of that leadership, and that legitimating church order is not the sole purpose for their composition. See I. Howard Marshall, *A Critical and Exegetical Commentary on the Pastoral Epistles*, ICC (Edinburgh: T&T Clark, 1999), 52–57, 77, 170–81, 486–88, 512–21; Luke Timothy Johnson, *The First and Second Letters to Timothy: A New Translation with Introduction and Commentary*, AB 35A (New York: Doubleday, 2001), 74–76, 212–25; Philip Towner, *The Letters to Timothy and Titus*, NICNT (Grand Rapids: Eerdmans, 2006), 50–53, 239–70. Raymond E. Brown ("*Episkopē* and *Episkopos*: The New Testament Evidence," *TS* 41 [1980]: 331) notes, "The very fact that Titus has to be told to do this [to appoint presbyters in each city] means that there were not yet presbyters-bishops in all the churches of the Pauline mission."

3:2–7) and deacons (1 Tim 3:8–13). The only clear address to a group of congregation leaders in the Pauline corpus is the Philippian "overseers and deacons" (1:1).[14]

John Reumann has focused on church offices in Paul's letters and especially Philippians at length. Pointing to the diversity of leadership in churches that Paul established, he concludes that Paul did not bring a uniform concept of leadership to his churches. Rather, the apostle allowed his congregations to develop their own leadership structures. The result of this process is that some of these churches may have looked to their environment, particularly the church in Philippi. Reumann examines the possible backgrounds for the "overseers and deacons" of the Philippian church and notes that there is little evidence for these leadership positions in Second Temple Judaism. He proposes that the most probable background for these leadership roles is that Paul's converts patterned their organization after the leadership positions in local, Philippian cults.[15]

Other scholars build their case for Euodia and Syntyche as leaders, deacons, and/or overseers from the supposedly more liberated place of women in Macedonian culture.[16] There is, however, a major difficulty with this approach. The Philippi that Paul missionized was not considered Macedonian soil. Rather, it was a Roman colony and thus a city that functioned as a mini-Rome (Gellius, *Attic Nights* 16.13.9). This means that Philippi would have been a beacon of Roman, not Greek or Macedonian, culture.[17] The Roman character of Philippi is something that Luke (or his source) knows

14. I take overseers and deacons to be two distinct offices and that Paul is not referring to the "overseers who serve." Contra Hawthorne and Martin, *Philippians*, 8–10.

15. John Reumann, "Church Offices in Paul, Especially in Philippians," in *Origins and Method: Toward a New Understanding of Judaism and Christianity; Essays in Honour of John C. Hurd*, ed. John Coolidge Hurd and B. H. McLean (Sheffield: JSOT Press, 1993), 82–91. See also Reumann, *Philippians*, 62–64.

16. Witherington, *Women*, 112–13; Getty-Sullivan, *Women*, 251; Peterlin, *Philippians*, 127; Fee, *Philippians*, 390–91; Reumann, *Philippians*, 627; Keener, *Acts*, 2390.

17. For the religions of Roman colonies see Mary Beard, John North, and Simon Price, *Religions of Rome* (Cambridge: Cambridge University Press, 1998), 1:315, 328–34. For more on Philippi see Paul Collart, *Philippes ville de Macédoine depuis ses origines jusqu'à la fin de l'époque romaine*, 2 vols. (Paris: de Boccard, 1937); Michel Sève, *1914–2014 Philippes Φιλιπποι Philippi. 100 ans de recherches françaises 100 χρονια γαλλικων επευνων 100 Years of French Research* (Athens: École française d'Athènes, 2014); Julien Fournier, ed., *Philippes, de la Préhistoire à Byzance: études d'archéologie et d'histoire*, BCHSup 55 (Athens: École française d'Athènes, 2016); Cédric Brélaz, "'Outside the City Gate': Center and Periphery in Paul's Preaching in Philippi," in *The Urban World and the First Christians*, ed. Steve Walton, Paul R. Trebilco, and David W. J. Gill (Grand Rapids: Eerdmans, 2017), 123–40; Brélaz, *Philippes, colonie romaine*

well, because he records the mob's charge against Paul and Silas as the advocation of customs unlawful for Romans to accept or practice (Acts 16:21).

The most productive approach to the question of female leadership in the Philippian church is to examine the social context of Roman Philippi. To date, two scholars, Lilian Portefaix and Valerie Abrahamsen, have focused on women in the Philippian church and tried to glean concrete information about them from the inscriptional (and archaeological) remains of the city. Both historians conclude that women played prominent roles in Philippian cults. Portefaix proposes that Paul's description of Euodia and Syntyche struggling side-by-side with him (Phil 4:3) fits with what we know women in Philippi were doing and that Euodia and Syntyche were possibly deacons who cared financially for the congregation.[18] Abrahamsen argues that women were active in a number of Philippian cults, even dominating the cult of Diana, and that women were leaders of Philippian cults, including the early Christian church.[19] There are problems with Portefaix's and Abrahamsen's treatments.[20] Both are dated because more inscriptions have been discovered at Philippi that illuminate the place of women in the colony since their works were published.[21] Abrahamsen omits pertinent evidence that was available to her—an inscription that supports the notion that Euodia and Syntyche were leaders in the Philippian church—and she overstates the female dominance of Diana's cult.[22] Therefore, the place of women in the Philippian church needs a reappraisal that takes into account the latest evidence from Philippi. To this task, I now turn.

---

d'Orient. Recherches d'histoire institutionnelle et sociale, BCHSup 59 (Athens: École française d'Athènes, 2018).

18. Portefaix, *Sisters Rejoice*, 135–53, 202, esp. 138n13.

19. Abrahamsen, *Women*, 25–44, 53–127, 193–95; Abrahamsen, "Priestesses and Other Female Cult Leaders at Philippi in the Early Christian Era," in *The People Beside Paul: The Philippian Assembly and History from Below*, ed., Joseph A. Marchal (Atlanta: SBL Press, 2015), 25–62. Abrahamsen agrees with Mary Rose D'Angelo ("Women Partners in the New Testament," *JFSR* 6 [1990]: 72, 75–77, 81–85) that Euodia and Syntyche were a lesbian missionary couple whom Paul attempts to reconcile to himself, not to each other. Most scholars reject this conclusion.

20. Osiek (*Philippians*, 110) goes too far when she notes about the material that Portefaix and Abrahamsen have collected: "This material makes interesting background information against which to reconstruct the lives of Philippian women, but probably has little bearing on the customs in force about women's social freedom and leadership."

21. Portefaix's magisterial work is thirty years old, while Abrahamsen's book is almost twenty-five. Even Abrahamsen's latest discussion (2015; "Priestesses," 25–62) draws from her earlier work and she considers no newer archaeological and epigraphic discoveries.

22. Abrahamsen would not include Lydia in her findings because she doubts the reliability of Luke's testimony in Acts.

II. Inscriptions and Female Leadership of Philippian Cults

Inscriptions from Philippi provide insights into the religion of women and their leadership positions within certain cults. Overall, epigraphs attest that Roman cultural values dominated women's public religion in the colony from its founding in 42 BCE to the third century CE. Almost all public inscriptions from 42 BCE to the end of the first century CE are in Latin, not Greek. Before the Roman colony was founded, the residents of Philippi consisted of three different types of people: Thracians, Macedonians, and Greeks. Inscriptions show that Thracian, Macedonian, and Greek women continued to live in and around Philippi after the colony's creation. Some of these women acquired Roman citizenship (although they still lacked the right to vote) and they even adopted the Latin language and Roman religious customs (*CIPh* II.1.75; *Philippi II* 048, 519, 638, 649). The evidence suggests that the women who did not adopt Latin as their language were nevertheless familiar with Roman customs and Latin. A private epitaph (see chapter 1.IV.2.1) from the imperial period indicates that a husband named Aliupaides set up a marble stele containing a funeral banquet scene for his deceased wife, Tertia.[23] The same epigraph says that another woman, Secus, set up an account to pay for a sacrifice in honor of the dead, which follows the distinctive Roman festival of Rosalia.[24] What is interesting about this inscription is that it is written in Latin, but with Greek letters, suggesting that Aliupaides and Secus thought in Latin concepts.

Greek Inscription

Αλιουπαιβες Ζει|παλα ουξωρι Τερ|τιε σουε · φηκυτ · αν| Χ · ο΄. Σεκους Φυρμι|| φειλια ρελικυτ βικανι|βους Σατρικηνις ρμ΄.| ουτ μ(ενσις) Ι(ουνιου) δεκιμου Κα|λανδας παρεν[τ]ητορ.

Equivalent Latin Transcription

Aliupaibes Zei|pala <filius> uxori Ter|tiae suae fecit an(no)| ch(oloniae) LXX. Secus Firmi|| filia reliquit vicani|bus Satricenis CXL,| ut m(anibus) i(nferis) decimo ka|landas paren[t]etur.

---

23. Pilhofer (*Philippi II* 048) suggests that this inscription dates to 41 CE, but Brélaz (*Philippes*, 26n43) notes that this date is conjectural.

24. Although the epigraph does not say so specifically, four other Philippian inscriptions refer to the Rosalia (*Philippi II* 512, 524, 529, 644).

Translation

> Aliupaides the son of Zeipalas set up (this monument) for his own wife Tertia in the seventieth year of the colony(?) Secus the daughter of Firmius bequeathed to the Satrician villagers one hundred and forty denarii so that they might sacrifice to the underground gods for the dead on the tenth day before the Kalends (*Philippi II* 048).

Most surviving inscriptions relate to women of some financial means. A few of these women were able to gain prominence in Philippi in two ways: by patronizing the colony and serving in official and nonofficial religious cults. While being a benefactress is not explicitly a religious leadership role, we must remember that what we call religion did not exist in the Roman Empire. As there was no separation of church and state, religion permeated all aspects of life. If women in Philippi were benefactresses to the colony, then there is a good chance that their benefactions were religious in some sense. To date, there is one inscription that attests to a benefactress. It is a public honorary epigraph (see chapter 1.IV.1.2) on the base of an honorific statue that says "For the mother Licinia" (· *Liciniae* · *matri* ·) (*CIPh* II.1.26 = *Philippi II* 207). Little is known about Licinia and her statue has not survived. The title "mother," however, is honorary (cf. Rom 16:13) and suggests that Licinia was a benefactor of the colony in some way. It is unclear when Licinia lived. Given that some members of the third-century-CE imperial family in Rome share the distinctive name Licinii, she may have lived at that time.[25]

Archaeologists found the Licinia inscription in 1934 on the main Roman road, the Via Egnatia, that passes through the middle of Philippi. It divides the religious and political heart of the colony, the forum, into a rectangular upper terrace and a lower square terrace. The forum was initially built during the reign of the first Roman emperor Augustus (31 BCE–14 CE), but later went through two major building phases. The first was during Claudius's reign (41–54 CE) and the second was during the reign of Marcus Aurelius (161–180 CE). During this second building phase, the forum was completely dismantled and rebuilt.[26] The Via Egnatia is not the original

25. See Brélaz's discussion in *CIPh* II.1.26.

26. Michel Sève and Patrick Weber, *Guide du forum de Philippes,* Sites et Monuments 18 (Athens: École française d'Athenes, 2012), 11–27. Little is known of the upper, rectangular terrace during Claudius's reign, but the lower square was paved with marble and buildings on its south, east, and west sides framed it.

location of Licinia's statue. Archaeologists propose that it was probably set up in the forum, along with other statues honoring benefactors.[27]

Besides being benefactresses of Philippi, some upper-class women gained leadership roles in official and nonofficial cults. The difference between official and nonofficial cults boils down to who funded them. Official cults are those that the colony of Philippi supported financially. Nonofficial ones, including Judaism and Christianity, were not supported by the colony.[28] Portefaix points out that official Roman cults dominated Philippi's forum, with a few exceptions. Those cults of non-Roman deities, including the Jewish God (Acts 16:11–40), were located outside the forum, thereby creating a spatial division between the two types of cults.[29] Roman women in Philippi were probably encouraged to worship Roman gods and not to adopt foreign ones, for three husbands in Philippi who were Roman citizens praised their deceased spouses in Latin epitaphs (see chapter 1.IV.2.1) as "most pious" (*uxori pissimae*) (*Philippi II* 286, 314, 513). The idea of Roman women being "pious" had a threefold meaning: they were committed to their familial duties; they were devoted to traditional Roman religion that Roman authorities deemed proper, what the Romans called *religio*; and they shunned non-traditional Roman cults, which were considered to be *superstitiones* or nonofficial.[30]

The most prominent official cults in which women participated were those devoted to members of the Roman imperial family. The cult about which we are most informed is that of Augustus's wife Livia.[31] This cult was founded in 42 CE. Tiberius, Livia's son, had refused to allow the senate in Rome to deify Livia after her death in 29 CE (Tacitus, *Ann.* 5.1–2; Dio 58.2.1–6). When Claudius ascended to the imperial purple (41 CE), the senate in Rome deified Livia and gave her the official name Deified Augusta

27. See Brélaz's discussion in *CIPh* II.1.26.

28. See Beard, North, and Price, *Religions of Rome*, 1:250–59, 278–79; John Scheid, *An Introduction to Roman Religion*, trans. Janet Lloyd (Bloomington: Indiana University Press, 2003), 61–63.

29. Most Romanized Greek gods were worshiped on the acropolis and outside of sacred the boundary of the colony or the *pomerium*: Portefaix, *Sisters Rejoice*, 71–72.

30. See Beard, North, and Price, *Religions of Rome*, 1:215–19, 297; Scheid, *Introduction*, 23, 173–76. Philippian inscriptions showcase that women participated in Roman or Romanized cults irrespective of the status of the cults as official or nonofficial: Diana Caszoria (*Philippi II* 451), Diana (*Philippi II* 172, 184), Diana Lucifera (*Philippi II* 227), Venus (*Philippi II* 057), and Diana Minveria (*Philippi II* 519).

31. *CIPh* II.1.118, 126. Juno Sabina (128/129 or 136/137 CE) (*CIPh* II.1.12 = *Philippi II* 208) and Faustina Augusta or Faustina the Younger (161–176 CE) (*CIPh* II.1.20 = *Philippi II* 231) were worshiped in Philippi as well, but the evidence is minimal.

(42 CE) (Suetonius, *Claud.* 11.2; Dio 60.5.1–5). Soon after Livia's deification, Philippi established a cult for her and, in keeping with Roman religious tradition, a priesthood for the new divinity that consisted only of women. To date, we know of at least five priestesses of Deified Augusta (*CIPh* II.1.118 = *Philippi II* 002; *Philippi II* 222; *CIPh* II.1.126 = *Philippi II* 226).

The cult of Deified Augusta alongside her priestesses was highly visible in the colony. To date, archaeologists have found two monuments honoring these priestesses. The first is a limestone sarcophagus of a priestess named Cornelia Asprilla that was found in modern Kavala, ancient Philippi's port, and dates between 80 and 90 CE. The epitaph (see chapter 1.IV.2.1) says that she died at thirty-five years old.[32] We can trace some of Cornelia Asprilla's family history in Philippi. She was a member of an elite Philippian family. Her father, Publius Cornelius Asper Atiarius Montanus, was a Roman knight, magistrate in the colony, and held two priestly offices, one to the deceased and deified emperor Claudius (*CIPh* II.1.53 = *Philippi II* 001).

The second monument is one that a Philippian woman, Maecia Auruncina Calaviana, paid to erect in the forum (for which she would have needed permission from local authorities). This monument remains the largest known statue group found in Philippi, and it once held the statues of at least five women. None of these have survived, but fragments of the public honorary inscriptions (see chapter 1.IV.1.2) that accompanied the monument provide the names of priestesses of Deified Augusta: Julia Auruncina, Julia Modia, Maecia Auruncina Calaviana, an unknown priestess, and Octavia Polla, who is not explicitly said to be a priestess.[33] Each of these women are Roman citizens and probably from prominent local families.[34]

32. "Here rests Cornelia Asprilla daughter of Publius [and] priest of Diva Augusta. She lived thirty-five years" (*Cornelia · P(ublii) · fil(ia) · Asprilla ·| sac(erdos) · diuae ·| v. Aug(ustae) · ann(orum) · XXXV · h(ic) ·| s(ita) · e(st). v.*) (*CIPh* II.1.118 = *Philippi II* 002).

33. "(A) For Julia Auruncina the daughter of Caius and priestess of Deified Augusta. (B) For Julia Modia the daughter of . . . and priestess of Deified Augusta. (C) . . . priestess of Deified Augusta. (D) For Maecia Auruncina Calaviana the daughter of Caius and priestess of Deified Augusta. (E) For Octavia Polla daughter of Publius. (F) Maecia Auruncina Calaviana the daughter of Caius set up (this monument)" ((A) *[Iu]ḷiaẹ C(aii) · f(iliae) ·| Auruṇcinae| sạc̣ẹrdoti · diuae ·| v. Ạụg(ustae). v.* | (B) *Iuliạẹ [.] f.(iliae)||Modiạẹ| sacerd(oti) [diuae Aug(ustae)].*| (C)*[---]CV+++[---]| [sacerd(oti) diuae]| Ạụg(ustae)* | (D) *Maeciae · C(aii) · f(iliae)| Auruncinae| Calauianae · sacerd(oti) ·| v. · diuae · Aug(ustae) · v.*| (E) *Octauiae · P(ublii) · f(iliae) ·| v. Pollae · v.*| (F) *[v.] Maecia · C(aii) f(ilia)| Auruncịn[a Cal]auiana · fecit · v.*) (*CIPh* II.1.126 = *Philippi II* 226).

34. Two of these women, Julia Auruncia and Julia Modia, owe their Roman citizenship to Augustus. Based on the size of the remaining portions of the monument, it

This monument was set up in the northeast corner of the forum in the last third of the first century CE (66–99 CE) next to what was probably an imperial temple dating to Claudius's reign (41–54 CE).[35] What is noteworthy about this monument is that it remained in place after the renovation of the forum during Marcus Aurelius's reign (161–180 CE), which included a restoration of the imperial temple beside which the statue group was set up.[36] This means that the colony did not take the easy option of removing this monument when they restored the imperial temple. Rather, Philippi took the harder and more time-consuming option of working around it. This suggests that at least one of the families whom the women represented were important enough in the colony that the monument remained in place almost one hundred years after it was erected. The woman who paid for the monument, Calaviana, must have been a woman of great influence in the first century CE because she also paid for the erection of an honorary statue of her brother that was set up on the edge of the forum (for which she needed colonial permission) and this statue remained in place after the forum was renovated.[37]

The fact that these women served as priestesses of Deified Augusta's cult does not mean that they served in the same capacity as male priests. Roman historians have stressed that there was one limit to women's participation in official Roman public cults. They were excluded from the central ritual: they did not carry out sacrifices.[38] John Scheid in particular notes, "Public sacerdotal responsibilities were always exercised by men. . . .

---

probably held two more statues for a total of seven. See Michel Sève and Patrick Weber, "Un monument honorifique au forum de Philippes," *BCH* 112 (1988): 467–79.

35. Sève and Weber, *Guide du forum*, 76–77.

36. Abrahamsen (*Women*, 80) dates this monument to the second century CE and concludes that there were two imperial temples in the forum: one to Marcus Aurelius and the other to Faustina the Younger. Newer archaeological discoveries have overturned these proposals. Abrahamsen's ("Priestesses," 27–34) latest work comes to the same conclusion except she acknowledges that the monument dates to the late first century.

37. "Maecia Auruncina Calaviana daughter of Caius set up (this statue) for her brother [. . .]lturius Crispus son of Caius of the Voltinia tribe" (*[. . .]ḷturio| [C(ai) f(ilio)] Vol(tinia) Crispo| [M]aecia C(ai) f(ilia) Au|runcina Cala|viana fratri*) (*Philippi II* 222).

38. Beard, North, and Price, *Religions of Rome*, 1:297–98; Eve D'Ambra, *Roman Women* (Cambridge: Cambridge University Press, 2007), 142, 166, 179–80. I am indebted to Riet van Bremen's *The Limits of Participation: Women and Civic Life in the Greek East in the Hellenistic and Roman Periods* (Amsterdam: J. C. Gieben, 1996) for the phrase "limits of participation." Given that her work focuses on Greek cities and not Roman colonies, I am not suggesting that her work applies directly to Philippi.

Women (along with foreigners and prisoners) were forbidden to participate in sacrificial rituals."[39] Therefore, male imperial priests and in some cases male slaves known as *victimari* would have handled sacrifices, especially blood sacrifices (if any were offered), to Deified Augusta instead of these imperial priestesses.

This limit to female participation did not apply to nonofficial cults, however.[40] Inscriptions from Philippi indicate that women were cultic officials of nonofficial cults and exercised some authority over men. One Philippian woman was the patron and overseer of a god's temple. A marble block dating to the Roman Empire found near the village of Drama in 1898 contains a public sacred inscription (see chapter 1.IV.1.3). The epigraph states that by the decree of the colonial authorities Valeria Severa, the overseer (*antistes*) of the temple of the goddess Diana Caszoria, set up a statue (*imagio*) of the goddess with her own money.[41] This goddess, Diana Caszoria, is a Romanized manifestation of a local Macedonian goddess named Artemis Gazoria. Inscriptions from Macedonia indicate that female slaves were often manumitted sacredly to the goddess (see chapter 1.IV.2.5).[42] For whatever reason, Artemis Gazoria/Diana Caszoria must have been a goddess attractive to women and this may explain why Valeria Severa was the overseer of her temple. The term overseer, the Latin *antistes*, means that Valeria Severa

39. John Scheid, "The Religious Roles of Roman Women," in *A History of Women in the West*, vol. 1, *From Ancient Goddesses to Christian Saints*, ed. Pauline Schmitt Pantel (Cambridge: Belknap Press of Harvard University Press, 1992), 378–79.

40. Beard, North, and Price, *Religions of Rome*, 1:298–301.

41. "By the request from the most sacred order and decree of the decurions, Valeria Severa overseer of Diana Caszoria's temple set up this image for herself and her own grandson Atiarius Acmeus." (*Valeria| Seuera an|tistes Deane| Caszoriae pe||titu a sancti|simo ordine| et decreto d[ec(urionum)]| IO imaginem| ++ sibi · et Atiar[i]o|| Acmeo · nepot[i]| suo · f(aciendam) · c(urauit) ·)* (*CIPh* II.1.135 (with corrections) = *Philippi II* 451).

42. See Brélaz's informed discussion of this epigraph in *CIPh* II.1.135. An inscription from the village of Arseni, Macedonia, indicates that a couple named Ulpia Euporia and Aurelius Dionysus dedicated their slave Onesima to the goddess in 232 CE, whereby she became "the goddess's slave" (δούλην τῆς θεᾶς) and was free with regard to matters outside Artemis Gazoria's cult (πρὸς τ[ὰ] ἐκτ{ρ}ὸς (*sic*) ἐλευθέραν). See Alfred Delacoulonche, "Mémoire sur le berceau de la puissance macédonienne des bords de l'Haliacmon et ceux de l'Axius," *Archives des missions scientifiques et littéraires* 8 (1859): 93, 244, no. 29. A marble block from the village of Episkopi, Macedonia, says that a woman named Aurelia Philippa discharged (ἀφίημι) her slave girl (παιδίσκην) Ariagne to the goddess as a sanctuary slave (ἱερόδουλον) (*SEG* 2.396; cf. *SEG* 52.618). For a discussion of these texts see Stefano G. Caneva and Aurian Delli Pizzi, "Given to a Deity? Religious and Social Reappraisal of Human Consecrations in the Hellenistic and Roman East," *ClQ* 65 (2015): 182–83.

had a leading, active, and presiding role in the cult, administering and attending to its sacred rites, including sacrifices.[43] In fact, in later Christian inscriptions, *antistes* became synonymous with the Greek term ἐπίσκοπος (cf. Phil 1:1).[44]

A private sacred inscription (see chapter 1.IV.2.3) indicates that a Thracian woman named Manta served as a priestess of the cult of Diana Minervia at Philippi. The epigraph provides a list of eleven Thracian men from three villages (*vici*) surrounding Philippi who paid for the restoration of the roof of Diana Minervia's temple.[45] Whatever roles, if any, men in this cult had, Manta served as the goddess's priestess and probably exercised some authority over them.[46]

---

43. The Roman historian Livy recounts a speech of a certain Publius Decius Mus to support the passage of a bill in 300 BCE allowing one of the consuls every year in Rome to be a plebeian. One of Mus's arguments is that the plebeians are already members of the *decemviri*, interpreters of the Sibylline Oracles, and "the same people are *antistites* of Apollo's sacred rites and other divine rituals" (*antistites eosdem Apollinaris sacri caerimoniarumque aliarum*) (10.8.2–3). Livy says that when Romulus founded Rome he appointed the Vestal Virgins to be "perpetual *antistites* for her temple" (*adsiduae templi antistites*) (1.20.1.3). The Vestal Virgins were in charge of tending the sacred hearth of the city of Rome and with making *mola salsa* that Roman priests sprinkled on her blood sacrifice offered in state cult. See Beard, North, and Price, *Religions of Rome*, 1:51–54. In Cicero's speech against Verres, he rails against the treatment of the city of Henna, claiming that it is sacred to the goddess Ceres. Cicero says, "But they do not seem to me citizens of that [city], but they are all priests; they are all temple-dwellers and *antistites* of Ceres" (*ut mihi non cives illius civitatis, sed omnes sacerdotes, omnes accolae atque antistites Cereris esse videantur*) (*Verr.* 2.3.111–12).

44. For numerous epigraphic examples of *antistes*, which is a synonym for *episkopos*, see George N. Olcott, *Thesaurus Linguae Latinae Epigraphicae: A Dictionary of the Latin Inscriptions* (Rome: Loescher, 1904), 1:349–51.

45. "The villagers of Sc . . ., Nicaenses, Coreni, and Zcambu . . . at this place restored the roof of the temple for Diana Minervia who . . . during the time of the curators: Zaerazistes the son of Be . . ., BAAEIBI, Centozaeras the son of Zipaibes, Cetrilas the son of . . . CV[- -]VBRES the son of Dules, Dizalas the son of Brassis, and Zipyro the son of Dules. Bascilas the son of Bithus, Cerzus the son of Dininithus, Caius Cornelius the son of CVB . . . the son of Zerces, Cetrilas the son of Zeredules, and Manta the daughter of Zercedis the priestess" (*Deanae Ṃịnerviae, quae a[. . ., re]|situerunt ho[c] loco vicani Sc[. . . et]| Nicaenses et Coreni et Zcambu[. . . tectum ae]|dis sub curatoribus: Zaerạziste Be[. . .]|| BAAẸỊBI, Cẹntozaera Zipaibis, Cetrila [. . .]| CV[- -]VBRES Dulis, Dizala Brassis, Zipyro Dul[is . . .],| Bascilas Bithi, Cerzus Dininithi, C(aius) Corn[elius . . .]| CVB [. . .] Zer[ce]dis, Cetrilas Z[er]edu[lis, . . .],| Manta Zercedis, sacerdos v.*) (*Philippi II* 519). Pilhofer (*Philippi II* 519) points out that the names Zaerazistes, Centozaeras, Cetrilas, Dizalas, and Zipyro are in the ablative case, while Bascilas, Cerzus, Caius Cornelius, Cetrilas, and Manta are in the nominative case. Contra Abrahamsen (*Women*, 31), who suggests that some of these Thracian men could be women.

46. Portefaix, *Sisters Rejoice*, 84; Abrahamsen, *Women*, 31.

There was a coed association of maenads in Philippi who worshiped Liber, Libera, and Hercules, which may be the Romanization of a cult of Dionysus that was in Philippi before its conversion to a Roman colony. Macedonians, Greeks, and Thracians had worshiped Dionysus in Philippi and there was a local myth about the god's connection to a mountain near Philippi, Mount Pangaion.[47] The triad Liber, Libera, and Hercules probably had their own sanctuary inside the sacred boundary of the colony, the *pomerium*, because five private sacred inscriptions (see chapter 1.IV.2.3) have been found there, near what became a Christian basilica known as Basilica B.[48] Some of these epigraphs indicate that women set up ex-votos to Liber, Libera, and Hercules (*Philippi II* 341, 342).[49] One inscription in particular says that the divine triad commanded a woman named Pomponia Hilara to set up a monument to them, which evidently had an image of the gods.[50] While the social status of Pomponia Hilara and the other women in this association are unclear, it is clear that they are all Roman citizens who possessed enough money to make significant contributions to the cult of Liber, Libera, and Hercules.[51]

The final piece of Philippian evidence for female cultic activity comes from the acropolis. There are a number of reliefs carved into the rock of the acropolis depicting female figures and the goddess Diana, all of which date to the second and third century CE. The rock reliefs of female figures number about forty. Their exact function is unknown.[52] There may be a

47. Collart, *Philippes*, 1:413–22; Portefaix, *Sisters Rejoice*, 98–114.

48. Archaeologists found evidence of the substructure of another building under Basilica B that Collart (*Philippes*, 1:413–15) identifies as the sanctuary of Liber, Libera, and Hercules.

49. Men worshiped Liber Pater as well (*Philippi II* 338, 408, 524, 525).

50. "By the command of Liber, Libera, and Hercules, no one should touch the image (*facies*) unless it has been commanded. Pomponia Hilara set up (this monument) by command [of Liber, Libera, and Hercules]" (*ex imperio| Liberi et Liberae| et Herculis.| nequis nequ||eve velit faciem| tangere, nesi| siqui imperat|um fueret.| ex imperio|| Pomponia| Hilara posuit*) (*Philippi II* 339).

51. Pomponia Hilara may have been connected to the illustrious Pompeiian family either by birth or as a manumitted slave. See Portefaix, *Sisters Rejoice*, 100–101. Two other women, Salvia Pisidia and Pisidia Helpsis, are Romans as well. All known Salvii in Macedonia come from Philippi and one Salvius was the Macedonian proconsul named Caius Salvius Liberalis Nonius Bassus (82–83 or 83–84 CE) (*Philippi II* 091). If Salvia is related to him, then she may be from the upper echelons of Philippian society. Finally, Portefaix (*Sisters Rejoice*, 101) points out that these women had control of their own money and goes on to suggest that they had fulfilled the requirements of the Augustan marriage laws.

52. For the reliefs see Paul Collart and Pierre Ducrey, "Catalogue," BCHSup 2 (1975): 121–59, nos. 98–137. For their interpretation see Paul Collart and Pierre Ducrey, "Étude des types et de leur representation," BCHSup 2 (1975): 228–35. It is

connection between the reliefs of these female figures and those of the goddess Diana, because many of the female figures were carved next to or even abut reliefs of Diana.[53] Portefaix points to other funerary monuments in the Roman world and suggests that the female figures are women attempting to spend their afterlives with Diana.[54] Abrahamsen notes that the reliefs of female figures are placed in a frame resembling the front of a temple. Therefore, she proposes that the women are priestesses of Diana.[55] There is only one inscription associated with these reliefs. It mentions nothing of death or Diana explicitly, but it is an ex-voto to an unnamed god by a woman named Aelia Atena: "Aelia Atena dedicated this because of a vow" (*Aelia · Atena · ex ·| votum · fecit*) (*Philippi II* 184). The god in question may be Diana, but it is unclear. Nevertheless, the rock reliefs of female figures have some religious connotations.[56]

The reliefs of Diana on the acropolis, which number about ninety, picture the goddess in various poses with various items, for instance, a bow, a spear, a branch, etc.[57] This cult of Diana appears to be a Romanized form of one that existed in Philippi before the colony's creation. No evidence of a temple of Diana has been found at Philippi, even on the acropolis, and so it appears that Diana's devotees worshiped her in an open-air sanctuary on the acropolis.[58] As noted above, Abrahamsen sees a connection between the reliefs of Diana and those of the female figures. Because there are no males depicted in rock reliefs, she concludes that male participation in the cult of Diana was "tolerated," and that these female devotees had no temple because they could not afford one.[59] Abrahamsen's proposal overlooks one important factor: the epigraphs associated with Diana's reliefs. There are seven votive inscriptions (see chapter 1.IV.2.3) found on the reliefs of Diana, and a woman set up only one of them: "Galgestia Primilla paid her vow willingly and deservedly to Diana on behalf of her daughter" (*Galgest|ia*

---

the normality of the women's clothing that excludes the interpretation of these women as deities (ibid., 233).

53. Collart and Ducrey, "Étude des types et de leur representation," 233–35; Portefaix, *Sisters Rejoice*, 83–88.

54. Portefaix, *Sisters Rejoice*, 85–96.

55. Abrahamsen, *Women*, 30–32; Abrahamsen, "Women at Philippi: The Pagan and Christian Evidence," *JFSR* 3 (1987): 17–30, esp. 20–22.

56. Collart and Ducrey, "Étude des types," 234.

57. Collart and Ducrey, "Catalogue," 37–120, nos. 8–97.

58. Portefaix, *Sisters Rejoice*, 78.

59. Abrahamsen, "Women at Philippi," 21; Abrahamsen, *Women*, 26–33, 37–38, 64–65, 78.

Primil|la pro|filia Ḍẹ[a]n<a>e|| v(otum) s(olvit) l(ibens) m(erito)) (*Philippi II* 172/173). Men are responsible for the other six votive epigraphs and thus the accompanying rock reliefs (*Philippi II* 168, 170, 171, 174, 181, 183). Almost all inscriptional evidence, roughly 88 percent, indicates that men created the reliefs of Diana as votives to the goddess. Therefore, women cannot have dominated the cult.

In sum, public and private inscriptions from Philippi evidence that Roman or Romanized cults dominated the lives of women (and men) from the founding of the colony to the third century CE. Certain wealthy women were able to gain prominence in official and nonofficial cults by patronizing them and attaining leadership roles in them. In official Roman cults in Philippi, however, women could not offer any sacrifices. This restriction did not apply to nonofficial cults and some women became priestesses and benefactors of these cults, in which they had leadership roles and some authority over men.

IV. Women in the Philippian Church in Light of Philippian Epigraphy

In light of this survey of the evidence for leadership roles of women in cults in Philippi, what can we say about Lydia, Euodia, Syntyche, and their roles in the church? Provided that the church in Philippi patterned its leadership after official and nonofficial cults in the city, there is no reason to doubt that certain wealthy women in the church had leadership positions. The picture of women from Philippian epigraphy fits well with Luke's description of Lydia in Acts. Most scholars agree that after Paul preached to a group of women gathered at the *proseuche*, Lydia (and later her household) joined the early Christian movement. Because Lydia was in charge of a household, she appears to have been a widowed woman of some means. Luke records that the early church met in Lydia's house and intimates that she became its patron (Acts 16:14–15, 40).[60] The colony of Philippi honored Licinia as a

60. The Philippian *proseuche* is probably a synagogue, even though Luke uses *proseuche* twice (Acts 16:13, 16) instead of his usual συναγωγή (Acts 6:9; 9:2, 20; 13:5, 14, 43; 14:1; 15:21; 17:1, 10, 17; 18:4, 7, 19, 26; 19:8; 22:19; 24:12, 26:11). See Richard E. Oster, "Women, Diaspora Synagogues (Proseuche) and Acts 16:13 (Philippi)," in *Faith in Practice: Studies in the Book of Acts; A Festschrift in Honor of Earl and Ottie Mearl Stuckenbruck*, ed. David A. Fiensy and William D. Howden (Atlanta: European Evangelistic Society, 1995), 260–99; Reimer, *Women*, 78–92; Lee I. Levine, *The Ancient Synagogue: The First Thousand Years*, 2nd ed. (New Haven: Yale University Press, 2000), 135–39, 171.

benefactress and set up a statue of her in the forum, which means that she provided financial support to Philippi in some capacity. In addition, some women patronized private cults, setting up divine images (e.g., Valeria Severa and Pomponia Hilara). As the patron of the early house church in Philippi, Lydia probably hosted the Lord's Banquet and gave financial aid to those who needed it. In these ways, she probably resembles Phoebe in Cenchrae (Rom 16:1; cf. 1 Tim 3:7–14) and Nympha in Colossae (Col 4:15).

The inscriptional portrait of the activities of women in Philippi suggests that Euodia and Syntyche had leadership roles in the church. Paul says that these women were his coworkers (συνεργῶν μου) who "struggled side-by-side in the gospel" (ἐν τῷ εὐαγγελίῳ συνήθλησάν). Ben Witherington III and Davorin Peterlin both stress that coworker is a term that Paul reserves for his associates who teach and preach the gospel.[61] Gerald Hawthorne and Ralph Martin note that there is no justification in Philippians, Paul's letters, or Acts to suggest that Euodia and Syntyche preached only to women.[62] Paul's description of Euodia and Syntyche as coworkers preaching the gospel resembles the description of Timothy in 1 Thessalonians. It was as a "coworker of God in the gospel of Christ" that Paul and Silas dispatched Timothy to the Thessalonians (συνεργὸν τοῦ θεοῦ ἐν τῷ εὐαγγελίῳ τοῦ Χριστοῦ) (1 Thess 3:2a). As a coworker, Timothy "supported" (στηρίξαι) and "encouraged" (παρακαλέσαι) the Thessalonians not to be shaken by any affliction (1 Thess 3:2b–3). Epigraphic evidence from Philippi provides support for the theory that Euodia and Syntyche likewise supported and encouraged the Philippians.

Valeria Severa was an *antistes* or overseer of the temple of Diana Caszoria. According to Latin sources, an *antistes* was someone who oversaw the cult of a god, carried out sacrificial duties, and even spoke on behalf of the deity.[63] In addition, women in Philippi served as priestesses in official (e.g., Deified Augusta) and unofficial cults (e.g., Diana Minervia). In this latter type of cult, Manta served as a priestess in the cult of Diana Minervia, which appears to have had mostly male devotees. Given that women spoke on behalf of gods, were *antistes*, and had cultic leadership roles in coed cults, it is probable that Euodia and Syntyche were deacons and possible that they were overseers in the Philippian church. Female deacons are known in churches associated with Paul (Rom 16:1; cf. 1 Tim 3:11–13).

61. Witherington, *Women*, 111–12; Peterlin, *Philippians*, 118–23.
62. Hawthorne and Martin, *Philippians*, 243.
63. Livy 1.20.1.3;10.8.2–3; Cicero, *Verr.* 2.3.111–12.

What is more, the attention that Paul pays to Euodia and Syntyche in Philippians suggests that they were prominent in the congregation. Paul does not have a habit of calling out people in his churches and asking them to "get along."[64] The fact that he does so means that Euodia's and Syntyche's reconciliation is vital for the interests of the church. Moreover, there are good reasons for supposing that the argument between Euodia and Syntyche was one of the main reasons that Paul composed Philippians and that his argument in the letter builds up to Paul's calling them out (Phil 1:27–2:11; 3:20–4:3).[65] One last note about Euodia and Syntyche is appropriate. The only difficulty with the conclusion that they were overseers is that there is no confirmation of female overseers in the Pauline corpus (as there is for deacons; Rom 16:1–2). This does not necessarily mean that Euodia and Syntyche were not overseers, but that if they were, then the Philippian church's leadership appears to have been unique in comparison to other churches associated with Paul.

Finally, I must qualify my conclusion about female leadership in the Philippian church in two ways. First, I am not claiming that the leadership roles that Lydia, Euodia, and Syntyche probably exercised resemble the well-defined hierarchical ecclesiastical structures of the church that began to form in the second century CE. Rather, leadership roles in the Philippian church, like that of leadership roles in all churches associated with Paul, including in the Pastoral Epistles, are functional and diverse. There is nothing in Philippians that approaches the mono-episcopacy of Ignatius's letters, the threefold structure (bishop, council of presbyters, and deacons) of some of the churches of Roman Asia in the early second century CE, or the notion that the sacraments are only valid in the presence of the bishop. Indeed, when Polycarp wrote to the Philippian church around 117 CE, its leadership seems to have remained close to what it was when Paul wrote (Phil 1:1), for Polycarp addresses overseers/presbyters and deacons (Pol. *Phil.* 5:2–6:3). Second, given what little we know of leadership in churches associated with Paul and in the first-century church in general, it is unclear if there was a hierarchal relationship between the overseers and deacons at the time that Paul wrote Philippians.[66] In short, much is unknown about leadership in Pauline churches, but there is good reason to believe that some

64. Kittredge (*Community and Authority*, 93) notes, "The singularity of these verses [in the Pauline corpus] suggests that they are significant to the letter."

65. See Dahl, "Euodia and Syntyche," 3–15. Contra Reumann, *Philippians*, 632. For a history of scholarship on Euodia's and Syntyche's disagreement see ibid., 628.

66. Osiek, *Philippians*, 111–12; Peterlin, *Philippians*, 123–24.

wealthy women in the Philippian church attained leadership positions in the mid-first century CE.

V. Conclusion

To conclude, inscriptions illuminate the lives of non-elite men in the Roman world, especially those of women. This information has important historical and theological consequences because it highlights the more egalitarian nature of early Christianity. Using the Roman colony of Philippi as a test case, I have shown that epigraphs reveal that some wealthy women gained prominent roles in Philippi by patronizing the colony and its cults and by serving as priestesses in official and nonofficial cults. Given the roles that Philippian women possessed and the evidence from Acts and Philippians, it is probable that Lydia served as patroness of the nascent church and that Euodia and Syntyche were deacons and possibly overseers.

CHAPTER 6

Calculating Numbers with Wisdom: Inscriptions and Exegetical Impasses

One of the benefits of inscriptions that B. H. McLean notes is that they provide evidence for all aspects of life in the Roman world, some of which are not found in literature of the period.[1] This means that inscriptions have enormous interpretative potential for the NT, allowing us to sidestep exegetical impasses and discover new solutions to or nuanced interpretations of problematic texts. One such example is Rev 13:18's calculation of the beast's name. Some exegetes point to one or two graffiti from Pompeii to argue that John the prophet's use of calculating the number of the beast resembles a common Greco-Roman practice. Other scholars propose that calculating a person's Greek name is impossible unless one knows how many letters are in it. They argue that the name of the beast does not refer to a person, but is symbolic, highlighting that the beast is thrice evil. In this chapter, I collect a total of twenty-three cases of the calculation of a person's Greek name with numbers in the Roman Empire that are largely unknown to most NT scholars. These inscriptions indicate that John the prophet follows a standardized form of Greco-Roman name calculation and that the calculation of the beast's name refers to a particular person. The contexts in which some of these inscriptions were found by archaeologists indicate that the calculation of a person's Greek name is not impossible to decipher and that the practice was geared toward a group of insiders: the one who made the calculation, sometimes the one about whom the calculation is made, and their associates. John the prophet's use of name calculation for the beast functions similarly. He provides all the information that his audience needs to calculate the beast's name as Nero Caesar. Before I begin, I must address one methodological matter. I discuss only the most pertinent of the twenty-three Greco-Roman number calculations of Greek names

1. B. H. McLean, *An Introduction to Greek Epigraphy of the Hellenistic and Roman Periods from Alexander the Great down to the Reign of Constantine (323 B.C.–A.D. 337)* (Ann Arbor: University of Michigan Press, 2002), 1.

known to me. The rest, along with the full Greek and Latin inscriptions and my translations, are in an appendix at this chapter's end.

I. The Beast's Number and Its Interpretation

After the prophet John describes the first (Rev 13:1–10) and second beast (Rev 13:11–18) of Rev 13, he says of the first beast, "Here is wisdom: Let the one who has understanding calculate the number of the beast, for the number is that of a man and his number is 666."[2] The first recorded attempt to discover the beast's name is that of Irenaeus of Lyon. He determines that the number representing the name must be understood "according to the calculation of the Greeks by the letters that are in it" (κατὰ τὴν τῶν Ἑλλήκων ψῆφον διὰ τῶν ἐν αὐτῷ γραμμάτων / *secundum Graecorum computationem per literas quae in eo sunt*) (*Haer*. 5.30.1). Irenaeus notes that many names possess the numerical value of 666, but Christian scholars of his day prefer three: Euanthas (ΕΥΑΝΘΑΣ), Lateinos (ΛΑΤΕΙΝΟΣ), and a particular spelling of Titan, Teitan (ΤΕΙΤΑΝ). Irenaeus favors the last of these proposals and supports his argument by pointing to the name's antiquity, symmetry—six Greek letters and two syllables, each with three letters—and meaning. Titans are divine and associated with vengeance and royal tyranny. These aspects, Irenaeus claims, fit the beast's identity (*Haer*. 5.30.3).

Many modern interpreters of Revelation agree with Irenaeus that John uses Greco-Roman name calculation with numbers, which they call gematria, to cipher the beast's name.[3] Most of these interpreters point to one or

2. There is disagreement in Revelation's manuscript tradition as to the exact number of the beast. The fifth-century-CE Codex Ephraemi Rescriptus, an Oxyrhynchus papyrus (P115) (*P.Oxy* 66.4499), and Irenaeus evince that some Christians thought that the beast's number was 616 and not 666: David C. Parker, "A New Oxyrhynchus Papyrus of Revelation: P115 (P. Oxy. 4499)," *NTS* 46 (2000): 159–74. Revelation's manuscript tradition has stronger support for the latter number, which is the conclusion that Irenaeus (*Haer.* 5.30.1–3) and most modern exegetes of Revelation reach: Bruce Metzger, *A Textual Commentary on the Greek New Testament*, 2nd ed. (Stuttgart: Deutsche Bibelgesellschaft, 1994), 676; Michael George Michael, "666 or 616 (Rev. 13:18)," *BBS* 19 (2000): 77–83. One notable exception is J. Neville Birdsall ("Irenaeus and the Number of the Beast Revelation 13,18," in *New Testament Textual Criticism and Exegesis*, ed. A. Denaux [Leuven: Leuven University Press, 2002], 349–59), who argues that 616 is the better reading.

3. Ferdinand Benary, "Interpretation of the Number 666 (χξϛ) in the Apocalypse (13:18) and the Various Reading 616 (χιϛ)," trans. Henry Boynton Smith, *Bibliotheca Sacra and Theological Review* 1 (1844): 84–86; Wilhelm Bousset, *The Antichrist Legend:*

two Pompeian graffiti that they find in Adolf Deissmann's *Light from the Ancient East* that calculate the name of female lovers with numbers.[4] They propose that John the prophet's name calculation functions similarly and that the beast's name is the Greek spelling of Nero Caesar transliterated into Aramaic/Hebrew, which, like Greek, did not employ Arabic numerials but used the letters of the alphabet as numbers: Νέρων Καῖσαρ = *nrwn qsr*: *n* = 50 + *r* = 200 + *w* = 6 + *n* = 50 + *q* = 100 + *s* = 60 + *r* = 200 = 666.[5] Some of

---

A Chapter in Christian and Jewish Folklore, trans. A. H. Keane (London, 1896), 11–12; Bousset, *Die Offenbarung Johannis* (Göttingen: Vandenhoeck & Ruprecht, 1906), 105–6, 369–74; Henry Barclay Swete, *The Apocalypse of St John: The Greek Text with Introduction, Notes and Indices*, 3rd ed. (London: MacMillan, 1911), 174–76; R. H. Charles, *A Critical and Exegetical Commentary on the Revelation of St. John*, ICC, (Edinburgh: T&T Clark, 1920), 1:364–68; Eduard Lohse, *Die Offenbarung des Johannes*, NTD 11 (Göttingen: Vandenhoeck & Ruprecht, 1983), 81–82; Richard Bauckham, *The Climax of Prophecy: Studies on the Book of Revelation* (Edinburgh: T&T Clark, 1993), 384–407; Heinz Giesen, *Die Offenbarung des Johannes*, RNT (Regensburg: Pustet, 1997), 315–18; David E. Aune, *Revelation 6–16*, WBC 52B (Nashville: Thomas Nelson, 1998), 769–73; Hans-Josef Klauck, "Do They Never Come Back? 'Nero Redivivus' and the Apocalypse of John," *CBQ* 63 (2001): 692–93; Ian Boxall, *The Revelation of Saint John*, BNTC (Peabody, MA: Hendrickson, 2006), 198–99; Craig Koester, *Revelation: A New Translation with Introduction and Commentary*, AYB 38A (New Haven: Yale University Press, 2014), 538–40, 596–99; Koester, "The Number of the Beast in Revelation 13 in Light of Papyri, Graffiti, and Inscriptions," *Journal of Early Christian History* 6 (2016): 1–21; Hans Taeuber, "Ephesische Graffiti als Zeugnisse des Lebensgefühls in der hohen Kaiserzeit," in *Epigraphik und Neues Testament*, ed. Thomas Corsten, Markus Öhler, and Joseph Verheyden, WUNT 365 (Tübingen: Mohr Siebeck, 2016), 62–63.

4. Adolf Deissmann (*Light from the Ancient East: The New Testament Illustrated by Recently Discovered Texts of the Graeco-Roman World*, trans. Lionel R. M. Strachan, 4th ed. [New York: Hodder & Stoughton, 1910; repr. Grand Rapids: Baker Books, 1978], 276–78) relies on the work of A. Sogliano, "Isopsepha Pompeina," *Rendiconti della Reale Accademia dei Lincei, Classe di scienze morali, storiche e filologiche* 10 (1901): 256–59. For those who rely on Deissmann see Aune, *Revelation 6–16*, 772; Bauckham, *Climax of Prophecy*, 384–85. G. B. Caird (*A Commentary on the Revelation of St. John the Divine*, HNTC [New York: Harper & Row, 1966], 174) uses Deissmann's work, but does not come to a decisive conclusion about the beast and his number. Lohse (*Offenbarung*, 81) and Edmondo F. Lupieri (*A Commentary on the Apocalypse of John*, trans. Maria Poggi Johnson and Adam Kamesar [Grand Rapids: Eerdmans, 1999], 212) reference one Pompeian graffito, but provide no source. Presumably, they are drawing upon Deissmann.

5. Benary, "Interpretation of the Number 666," 84–86; Bousset, *Antichrist Legend*, 11–12; Bousset, *Offenbarung*, 105–6, 369–74; Swete, *Apocalypse*, 174–76; Charles, *Revelation*, 1:364–68; Lohse, *Offenbarung*, 81–82; Bauckham, *Climax of Prophecy*, 384–407; Giesen, *Offenbarung*, 315–18; Aune, *Revelation 6–16*, 769–73; Boxall, *Revelation*, 198–99; Koester, *Revelation*, 538–40, 596–99; Koester, "Number of the Beast," 2–5. G. K. Beale (*The Book of Revelation: A Commentary on the Greek Text* [Grand Rapids: Eerd-

these scholars note that the beast's calculated name equals what John calls him. If one transliterates the Greek term for beast, θηρίον, into Aramaic/Hebrew, then the total equals 666: θηρίον = *trywn*: $t = 400 + r = 200 + y = 10 + w = 6 + n = 50 = 666$.[6]

On the other hand, a few scholars eschew the above name calculation with numbers, preferring a more canonical interpretation of the beast's name. G. K. Beale argues that given the number of names of the beast proposed throughout history and that John the prophet uses numbers symbolically, the number of the beast is figurative. Because seven is a complete number in Revelation, 666 signifies the trifecta of incompletion, imperfection, and evil.[7] Edmondo F. Lupieri seems to come to this conclusion when he notes that there is a connection between six and Satan:

> To identify the number 666 with the name of a particular Roman emperor is to oversimplify and to run against the grain of a text that strives to be cosmic in its application. There may be some meaning in numbers' correspondence with a particular name, but this contingent aspect of the prophecy should remain secondary to its broader application. The beast is the incarnation of Satan, who is the sum and source of evil in all earthly power.[8]

---

mans, 1999], 718–28) argues against this interpretation by noting that the Aramaic/Hebrew word for Caesar (*qsr*) must be spelled "defectively" since it is spelled with a *yod* (*qsyr*) in the Mishnah. Such an argument stems from an incorrect understanding of ancient linguistics based on literary texts that scribes have groomed and harmonized throughout the years. The Dead Sea Scrolls attest to the spelling of Caesar as *qsr*: DJD 2.18.1; DJD 38.9.11 (lower text). For more examples see Koester, *Revelation*, 596–97. Even if the beast's number is 616, the Latin spelling of Nero Caesar transliterated into Aramaic/Hebrew still equals 616: *Nero Caesar* = *nrw qsr*: $n = 50 + r = 200 + w = 6 + q = 100 + s = 60 + r = 200 = 616$.

6. This interpretation also addresses the variant number 616. The transliteration of the genitive of θηρίον, θηρίου, into Aramaic/Hebrew equals 616: *tryw*: $t = 400 + r = 200 + y = 10 + w = 6 = 616$. See Bauckham, *Climax of Prophecy*, 389–90; Koester, "Number of the Beast," 11.

7. Beale, *Revelation*, 718–28.

8. Lupieri, *Apocalypse*, 212–18. See also Brian K. Blount (*Revelation: A Commentary* [Louisville: Westminster John Knox, 2009], 262), who concludes that the beast is Nero but that six is an incomplete number. However, Adela Yarbro Collins ("Numerical Symbolism in Jewish and Early Christian Apocalyptic Literature," *ANRW* II.21.2 [1984]: 1272–84) points out that six is never called an incomplete, imperfect, or Satanic number in Jewish and Christian apocalypses. Peter J. Leithart (*Revelation 12–22*, ICC [London: Bloomsbury T&T Clark, 2018], 78–81) suggests that the beast's number evokes the amount of gold that King Solomon imported into Israel yearly during his reign,

Inscriptional evidence indicates that the first proposal is correct, and that John uses Greco-Roman name calculation to cipher and to demonstrate that the beast is Nero Caesar. However, there are two limitations to this interpretation as most scholars articulate it, both of which are associated with reliance on Deissmann's work. First, NT scholars are only working with a fraction of the evidence for Greek name calculation with numbers. There are twenty-one more epigraphic instances of calculating Greek names with numbers than exegetes currently acknowledge, bringing the current total (2018) to twenty-three (and more discoveries are probably forthcoming). These cases exemplify that the practice was more widespread than scholars realize.[9] Second, exegetes are not exploiting this evidence to its fullest potential because Deissmann was unconcerned with treating inscriptions for what they are, archaeological artifacts. From the archaeological contexts of some epigraphic number calculations of Greek names, I show that it is a practice geared toward insiders who possessed enough information to decipher them.

II. Numerical Calculations in Epigraphy

Unlike the Romans, who had their numerals (I, II, III, IV, etc.), Greek (as well as Aramaic and Hebrew) speakers living in the Roman Empire used letters to signify numbers. The numerical system that they employed was taken

666 talents (1 Kgs 10:14). John uses this Solomonic number to condemn the Romans of apostasy and filling the land with idolatry (as well as *porneia* and the shedding of innocent blood).

9. Koester ("Number of the Beast," 7–13) has attempted to introduce more data into the conversation by pointing to the graffiti from Smyrna's recently excavated basilica that contain several examples of name calculation with numbers. His attempt, however, overlooks other examples of the Greco-Roman practice and Koester misinterprets this evidence by arguing that graffiti are subversive acts of noncompliance by members of the lower classes and that these graffiti resemble John's coding of the beast's name in Rev 13:18. Koester (7) notes: "Graffiti has (*sic*) a subversive quality. The large structures in the agora [of the basilica at Smyrna] and elsewhere in the city were created by people of means, whose names were formally inscribed in dedicatory inscriptions. Graffiti run counter to that sense of propriety. Those who create the graffiti assert their views in a manner and place of their own choosing. The subject matter is sometimes crude and the sketches and sayings may be grotesque. Graffiti reflect a sense of non-compliance toward the more dignified ordering of society." As I have shown in chapter 1.IV.2.6, Koester's negative conception of graffiti, prevalent in older scholarship, is a view that current historians and epigraphers reject.

from the so-called Milesian system, which needed twenty-seven letters to function. However, the Greek alphabet used in the Roman Empire had only twenty-four letters. Consequently, the Milesian system incorporated three to four archaic Greek letters that had fallen out of use by the Hellenistic period to reach the needed twenty-seven: digamma ϝ/stigma ϛ (not sigma ς) for six, koppa ϙ for ninety, and sampi ϡ for nine hundred. To account for numbers one thousand or above, Greeks placed a mark ͵ before the letter/number: ͵A (see Table 6.1).[10]

Table 6.1: Greek Letters/Numbers

Α, α = 1	Η, η = 8	Ξ, ξ = 60	Υ, υ = 400
Β, β = 2	Θ, θ = 9	Ο, ο = 70	Φ, φ = 500
Γ, γ = 3	Ι, ι = 10	Π, π = 80	Χ, χ = 600
Δ, δ = 4	Κ, κ = 20	Ϙ, ϙ = 90	Ψ, ψ = 700
Ε, ε = 5	Λ, λ = 30	Ρ, ρ = 100	Ω, ω = 800
Ϝ, ϝ / Ϛ, ϛ = 6	Μ, μ = 40	Σ, Ϲ, σ = 200	Ϡ, ϡ = 900
Ζ, ζ = 7	Ν, ν = 50	Τ, τ = 300	͵Α = 1000

The result of this method is that letters conveyed something as fundamental as dates and thus their use for numbers was widespread. For example, a statue base on which an image of the emperor Claudius stood in the Macedonian city of Pella (44 CE) begins with these words: “In the 76th year of Augustus and the 192nd year [of the Macedonian province]” (ἔτους ϚΟʹ Σεβαστοῦ τοῦ καὶ ΒϘΡʹ) (*SEG* 51.837). In this text letters signify 76 and 192. The former are ϚΟ: Ϛ = 6 + Ο = 70 = 76, while the latter are ΒϘΡ: Β = 2 + Ϙ = 90 + Ρ = 100 = 192. The 76th year of Augustus is 44 CE, for it is 76 years after the battle of Actium (31 BCE) that left Augustus (then Octavian) the sole ruler of the Roman Empire. The 192nd year of the province of Macedonia is 44 CE, for it is 192 years after the Romans established the province (146 BCE).[11]

10. Rodney Ast and Julia Lougovaya, “The Art of Isopsephism in the Greco-Roman World,” in *Ägyptische Magie und ihre Umwelt*, ed. Joachim Hengstl et al., Philippika: Altertumswissenschaftliche Abhandlungen Contributions to the Study of Ancient World Cultures 80 (Wiesbaden: Harrassowitz, 2015), 82–83.

11. For more on dates used in inscriptions see McLean, *Introduction to Greek Epigraphy*, 149–78.

Given this basic connection between letters and numbers, a Greek word, a group of words, or even a complete sentence has a numerical value, the sum of which Greeks called a calculation (ψῆφος) or a number (ἀριθμός). If two words, two groups of words, two sentences, or a number and a word, a number and a group of words, or a number and a sentence have the same numerical value, Greek speakers called this phenomenon an equal-calculation (ἰσόψηφος).[12] This practice of name calculation with numbers is found in literary and epigraphic texts beginning in the early Roman Empire and continuing into late antiquity.[13] While many exegetes of Revelation refer to the calculation of the beast's name as gematria, I prefer the terms that most ancient Greek sources, including Irenaeus, use: calculation and equal calculation.

To provide an example from the inscriptional record demonstrating how complex calculations and equal calculations can be, a young man named Leonteus (second century CE) who served as the leader of the youth (βοαγὸς) of Sparta (in modern-day Greece) dedicated the object of his victory, an iron sickle, as an ex-voto (see chapter 1.IV.2.3) to the goddess Artemis Orthia (Laconia) after he won the local musical contest called Moa.[14] The ex-voto is a gable-topped marble stele found in the sanctuary of the goddess (1868) (see Figure 6.1) that says: "The leader of the young men Leonteus dedicated (this) gift to (Artemis) Orthia: 2,730. After he won the

12. Paul Perdrizet, "Isopsephie," *REG* 17 (1904): 350–60; Maurice H. Farbridge, *Studies in Biblical and Semitic Symbolism* (London: Kegan Paul, Trench, Trubner, 1923), 87–156, esp. 95–96; Franz Dornseiff, *Das Alphabet in Mystik und Magie*, 2nd ed. (Leipzig: Teubner, 1925), 91–118; Ast and Lougovaya, "Art of Isopsephism," 82–98.

13. For literary name calculations see Lucian, *Alex.* 10–12; *PGM* 8.61; *Sib. Or.* 1.324–329; 8:148–150; Testament of Solomon 15:11; *Historia Alexandri Magni* 1.33.11–12; Artemidorus Daldianus, *Onir.* 3.28; 4.22, 24. For name calculations in papyri see: *O. Claud.* 2.414; *P. Oxy* 55.3239 = T. C. Skeat, "A Table of Isopsephisms (P. Oxy XLV. 3239)," *ZPE* 31 (1978): 45–54; Julia Lougovaya, "Isopsephisms in P. Jena II 15a-b," *ZPE* 176 (2011): 200–204. For other instances in inscriptions see *CIG* 5113; *IPergamon* 333, 339, 587. For Christian name calculations see Stephen R. Llewelyn, "ΣΔ, a Christian Isopsephism," *ZPE* 109 (1995): 125–27; Joel Kalvesmaki, "Isopsephic Inscriptions from Iasos ('Inschriften von Iasos' 419) and Shnān ('IGLS' 1403)," *ZPE* 161 (2007): 261–68.

14. The Moa were vocal, noninstrumental, musical festivities at which Spartan boys competed. For more information see R. M. Dawkins, "The Sanctuary," in *The Sanctuary of Artemis Orthia at Sparta*, ed. R. M. Dawkins, The Society for the Promotion of Hellenic Studies Paper No. 5 (London: MacMillan, 1926), 1–51; H. J. Rose, "The Cult of Orthia," in Dawkins, *Sanctuary of Artemis*, 399–407; A. M. Woodward, "Inscriptions," in Dawkins, *Sanctuary of Artemis*, 285–93.

musical (Moa) contest and he received this prize: 2,730. And (my) father honors me with equal number of lines: 2,730" (Ὀρθείῃ δῶρον Λε|οντεὺς ἀνέθη|κε βοαγὸς ͵βψλ| μῶαν νικήσας|| καὶ τάδε ἔπαθλα| λαβὼν ͵βψλ| *v.*| καὶ μ' ἔστεψε πα|τὴρ εἰσαρίθμοις| ἔπεσι ͵βψλ.) (*IG* V.1 257).[15]

Figure 6.1. Picture of Leonteus's votive with an iron sickle containing three sets of equal calculations (© Wikimedia Commons: Public Domain).

The words in each set of three lines equal 2,730. "The leader of the young men Leonteus dedicated (this) gift to (Artemis) Orthia" = 2,730: Ο = 70 + ρ = 100 + θ = 9 + ε = 5 + ι = 10 + η = 8 + δ = 4 + ω = 800 + ρ = 100 + ο = 70 + ν = 50 + Λ = 30 + ε = 5 + ο = 70 + ν = 50 + τ = 300 + ε = 5 + υ = 400 + ς = 200 + α = 1 + ν = 50 + ε = 5 + θ = 9 + η = 8 + κ = 20 + ε = 5 + β = 2 + ο

15. Woodward, "Inscriptions," 299–300, no. 7. Such votives are the most numerous of inscriptions dedicated to Artemis Orthia, numbering 130. Most are engraved on marble stelae, dedicated to either Orthia or Artemis Orthia, never Artemis, and have a groove by which iron sickles were attached to them. See Woodward, "Inscriptions," 285–86.

= 70 + α = 1 + γ = 3 + ο = 70 + ς = 200 = 2,730. "After he won the musical (Moa) contest and he received this prize" = 2,730. μ = 40 + ω = 800 + α = 1 + ν = 50 + ν = 50 + ι = 10 + κ = 20 + η = 8 + σ = 200 + α = 1 + ς = 200 + κ = 20 + α = 1 + ι = 10 + τ = 300 + α = 1 + δ = 4 + ε = 5 + ε = 5 + π = 80 + α = 1 + θ = 9 + λ = 30 + α = 1 + λ = 30 + α = 1 + β = 2 + ω = 800 + ν = 50 = 2,730.

"And (my) father honors me with equal number of lines" = 2,730. κ = 20 + α = 1 + ι = 10 + μ = 40 + ε = 5 + σ = 200 + τ = 300 + ε = 5 + ψ = 700 + ε = 5 + π = 80 + α = 1 + τ = 300 + η = 8 + ρ = 100 + ε = 5 + ι = 10 + σ = 200 + α = 1 + ρ = 100 + ι = 10 + θ = 9 + μ = 40 + ο = 70 + ι = 10 + ς = 200 + ε = 5 + π = 80 + ε = 5 + σ = 200 + ι = 10 = 2,730.

III. Name Calculations and Equal Calculations in Epigraphy

Greco-Roman calculations and equal calculations of names resemble John's use of the practice and relate to disguising individuals' names with numbers. These calculations are found only in Greek and appear most often in graffiti. Their authors vary. Some are slaves, others are freedmen and gladiators, and still others are the elite of society. Despite differences in occupation and social status, the authors of these texts follow what appears to be a standardized form irrespective of their geographical location in the Mediterranean, e.g., Pompeii, Ephesus, Smyrna, etc. Therefore, calculating names of individuals with numbers was a widespread, cross-cultural practice in which members of society who could read and write participated.

The most common form in which name calculations appear is the nominative singular ἀριθμός with the numerical value following: ἀριθμὸς + number. Sometimes the definite article, ὁ, appears before ἀριθμός and often the female demonstrative pronoun ἧς is found, removing any doubt that the inscription refers to a woman (see Table 6.2).

Table 6.2: Pan-Mediterranean Formula in Texts Calculating Names 1

Greek Text	City
ἧς ὁ ἀριθμὸς ͵αξε′	Mylasa
ἧς ἀριθμὸς φμέ	Pompeii

ἧς ὁ ἀριθμὸς μέ (or ͵αλέ)	Pompeii
ἧς ἀριθμὸς . . .	Pompeii
ὁ ἀριθμὸς νά	Pompeii
ἧς ἀριθμὸς υϙ΄	Stabiae
οὗ ἀριθμὸς φμε΄	Stabiae
ἧς ἀριθμὸς ͵αρα΄	Stabiae
ἧς ἀριθυ[ὸς - -]	Smyrna
ἧς ὁ [ἀριθμὸς] ψν	Smyrna
ἧς ὁ ἀρι[θμὸς] χις	Smyrna
ἧς [. . .] ΤΩΝ ὁ ἀριθμọ̀[ς . . .]	Smyrna
ἧς ὁ <ἀ>ριθμὸς Ατη	Smyrna
ο]ὗ ἀριθμὸς τνα	Smyrna
ὁ ἀριθ(μὸς) αυοε΄	Ephesus
ἧς ὁ ἀριθμὸς ͵ασξς΄	Ephesus
ὁ φιλῶν . . . ͵αϡϟε΄	Ephesus
ἧς ὁ ἀριθμὸς ωξε΄	Ephesus
ἧς ὁ ἀριθμὸς ωξε΄	Ephesus
ἧς . . .	Ephesus
τὴν ψῆφον . . . ͵ατνδ	Messania
. . . ρο΄	Catania

This standardized form—found in two of the seven cities to which John writes, Ephesus and Smyrna—resembles John's description of the beast's identity: ὁ ἀριθμὸς αὐτοῦ ΧΞϹ (Rev 13:18). For this reason, there is no doubt that when John's audience read or, for most of them, heard (Rev 1:1–3), Rev 13:18's reference to the beast's number they would have interpreted it as a calculation of the name of an individual, specifically of a man (ἄνθρωπος), and would not have thought that the beast's name was symbolic.[16]

Most graffitists are men who boast of their love for women and many follow what appears to be another standardized form, φιλῶ ἧς ὁ ἀριθμὸς + number (Table 6.3).[17]

16. Contra Beale, *Revelation*, 720–28.
17. Skeat, "Table of Isopsephisms," 45.

Table 6.3: Pan-Mediterranean Formula in Texts Calculating Names 2

Greek Text	City
φιλῶ ἧς ἀριθμὸς φμέ	Pompeii
φιλῶ ἧς ἀριθμὸς	Pompeii
ἡς φιλῶ ὁ ἀριθμὸς νά	Pompeii
ἐφίλει οὗ ἀριθμὸς φμέ	Stabiae
φιλ[ῶ] ἧς ἀριθυ[ὸς - - -]	Smyrna
φιλῶ ἧς ἀρι[θμὸς] χις	Smyrna
φιλῶ ἧς . . . ὁ ἀριθμὸς ψλα	Smyrna
φιλῶ ἧς <ἀ>ριθμὸς ατη	Smyrna
[φιλῶ ο]ὗ̣ ἀ̣ριθμὸς τνα	Smyrna
φιλῶ ἧς ὁ ἀριθμὸς ͵ασξς´	Ephesus
φιλῶ . . . ἧς ἀριθμὸς ωξε´	Ephesus
φιλῶ ἧς ἀριθμὸς ωξε´	Ephesus

There are exceptions, however—two men boast of their love for other men. This means that while it is more common to calculate a woman's name in inscriptions than a man's, the latter type of name calculation is not novel. Therefore, John's use of calculating the name of an emperor is a bit unusual, but not unheard of.

The archaeological contexts of some of these graffiti, most of which were found in the latter part of the twentieth century, are known. The majority of these inscriptions have been discovered in the more private spaces of elite houses in Pompeii, Stabiae, and Ephesus, but a few are from public space, like the graffiti from Smyrna's basilica. The evidence suggests that ciphering a lover's name was a way to publicize the graffitist's devotion, but only to a group of insiders: the graffitist, his lover, and associates aware of the relationship. Most exegetes of Revelation know the two Pompeian graffiti that Deissmann discusses, but these are not the only examples of name calculation with numbers from Pompeii. Archaeologists found a name calculation graffito in the House of Maius Castricius (Unit 16), which is on the western edge of the excavated city in a region called Regio VII.[18] The

18. The house is found on the Via delle Terme in Pompeii. Excavators originally assumed that Maius Castricius's house was part of the House of Fabius Rufus, which is

house was at least four stories high and, unlike most Pompeian homes, faced the Bay of Naples. The residence contains a garden, a reception room with mosaic floors and painted walls, and a private heated bath complex. To date, eighty-five graffiti and dipinti (wall drawings) have been found in the residence, the contents of which differ widely. They do, however, share some characteristics. All graffiti are written in Latin (except one) and many were composed in a cursive script suggesting experience with writing.[19] Most graffiti are found in heavily trafficked areas of the house.

The largest concentration of graffiti is in a central peristyle known as Room 2, which is the first room that those coming from the alley known as Vico dei Soprastanti entered.[20] Several other rooms (Rooms 1, 3–12) surround the peristyle and one in particular, Room 7, is located on its northern side. Around the entryway to Room 7 archaeologists found eighteen graffiti, one of which, the only one in Greek, disguises a lover's name with numbers: "I love the woman whose number is 51" (ἧς φιλῶ ὁ ἀριθμὸς να).[21] The graffitist's script is non-cursive, suggesting inexperience with composing.[22] The context of this graffito implies that someone who either lived in the house or frequented it left the message. Due to the prominent location of the graffito—visible as one entered the central peristyle—the graffitist wanted others to see and to decipher the text.

The woman's name is probably Thalia. On the northeast corner of the peristyle there is another room (known as Room 5). There is a staircase on Room 5's southern wall, beside which archaeologists found another cluster of graffiti totaling eleven texts. One of these is a Latin graffito that says: "Epaphroditus was here with Talia" (*Epaphroditus cum Talia hac*).[23] Epaphroditus is a Greek name, indicating that he is a Greek. Given that he composed in Latin, he is probably bilingual. Most graffiti in this cluster are written in a cursive Latin script, but Epaphroditus composed his text in uncial Latin letters, which suggests a lack of experience in composing in the language that supports his identification as a Greek. In addition, Talia is the Latinized

---

located directly to the south. Unfortunately, the archaeological discoveries from Maius Castricius's house have yet to be published. See Rebecca R. Benefiel, "Dialogues of Ancient Graffiti in the House of Maius Castricius in Pompeii," *AJA* 114 (2010): 62–65.

19. Ibid., 69, 89–96.

20. Ibid., 62–65.

21. Ibid., 92, no. 28. In the original publication, Carlo Giordano ("Le iscrizioni della casa di M. Fabio Rufo," *Rendiconti della Accademia di archeologia, lettere e belle arti* 41 [1966]: 80, no. 31) incorrectly ascribes this graffito to the House of Fabius Rufus.

22. Benefiel, "Dialogues of Ancient Graffiti," 69–72.

23. Ibid., 92, no. 35; Giordano, "iscrizioni della casa di M. Fabio Rufo," 83, no. 39.

spelling of the Greek name Θαλία, which has the numerical value of 51: Θ = 9 + α = 1 + λ = 30 + ι = 10 + α = 1 = 51.

The close proximity of this Latin graffito to the Greek one, literally in the next room, is more than coincidental. The Italian epigrapher Enzo Puglia identifies the woman whose number is 51 as Thalia. Provided that he is correct, then Thalia's lover is Epaphroditus.[24] The name Thalia reveals that she is a Greek and probably a slave or freedwoman who lived and served in Maius Castricius's house.[25] That Epaphroditus "was here with" may suggest that the two had a sexual encounter in that location.[26] Provided that this is correct, Epaphroditus disguises his love for Thalia in the graffito most visible in the house, but declares that he had a sexual encounter with the same woman openly in the less visible space of the next room. In short, Epaphroditus's calculation of Thalia's name is aimed at insiders who had enough information to decipher the name in question: Epaphroditus, Thalia, and probably their associates.

A similar situation comes from another town near Pompeii on the Bay of Naples, Stabiae. In 2007, excavators uncovered a bedroom (*cubiculum*) with two alcoves in the residential portion of a house known as the Villa Arianna, inside which they found two first-century-CE Greek graffiti containing four name calculations. The graffitists are two freedmen of Nero's second wife, Poppea Sabina, indicating that she owned the villa at one time. Both of their names are Caius Poppaeus and only one of the freedmen's last names is known, Hymetus.[27] The first inscription is found on the southern wall of the bedroom among other clustered graffiti, is in Latin and Greek, and contains three name calculations in Greek: "Caius Poppaeus Hymetus [l]ived here and he loved his own whose name is Euhodia. Her number is 490. He loves the man whose number is 545 as well as the [man?/woman?] whose number is 772" (*C(aius) Poppaeus Hymetus hic [ha]|bitavit et amavit cuius nomen*[28] *Euhodia*| ἧς ἀριθμὸς υϙ´, ἐφίλει οὗ ἀριθμὸς φμε´, καὶ ἅμ᾽

---

24. Enzo Puglia, "Mulierum nomina numeris dissimulata nei graffiti pompeiani," in *Minima epigraphica et papyrologica, taccuini della Cattedra e del Laboratorio di epigrafia e papirologia giuridica dell Universit degli studi di Catanzaro Magna Graecia* 7–8 (2004): 303–5. Epaphroditus had a proclivity to write graffiti, especially his name in Latin. See Benefiel, "Dialogues of Ancient Graffiti," 93, nos. 40, 41.

25. Puglia, "Mulierum nomina," 303–5.

26. Several Pompeian graffiti attest to sexual encounters in the same way: *CIL* 4.2060, 4066, 8792a; Antonio Varone, *Erotica Pompeiana: Love Inscriptions on the Walls of Pompeii*, trans. Ria P. Berg (Rome: L'erma di Bretschneider, 2002), 45–47.

27. Antonio Varone, "Le iscrizioni graffite di *Stabiae* alla luce dei nuovi rinvenimenti," *Rendiconti* 86 (2013–2014): 375–427.

28. This Latin construction corresponds to the Greek: φιλῶ ἧς ἀριθμὸς . . .

ἀριθ(μὸς) ψοβ´).[29] Hymetus provided the name (Euhodia) and the number (490) of the woman he loved. The graffitist lived in a bilingual environment and expected readers to transliterate the Latin spelling of Euhodia's name into Greek (Εὐοδία) to calculate her number: Ε = 5 + υ = 400 + ο = 70 + δ = 4 + ι = 10 + α = 1 = 490.[30] Hymetus proclaimed his love for two other people: a man whose number was 545 and a person of indeterminate gender whose number was 772.[31] Given the location of this graffito, in the bedroom and thus the private space of the Villa Adrianna, the graffitist and his lovers probably lived in the house.[32]

A second graffito found on the same wall is another Latin and Greek inscription. This one says: "C(aius) Poppaeus lived here with Hymetus and Phylacion and he loved and will love forever the woman whose number is 1,101" (*C(aius) Poppaeys hic habitavit cum| Hymeto et Phylacione| et amat amaturusque est| in aevom* ἧς ἀριθμὸς, αρα´).[33] This graffito confirms that the previous graffitist, Hymetus, lived in the Villa Arianna, along with a certain Phylacion. The graffitist, Hymetus, and Phylacion are all Greeks. The former two are freedmen and Phylacion is a slave because his name derives from the Greek term φύλαξ, meaning guard.[34] Phylacion's name does not add up to 545 or 772 so he cannot be either of the persons mentioned in the previous graffito. Nevertheless, Caius Poppaeus declares his eternal love for the woman whose number is 1,101, who may be someone who lived in the house with him.[35]

---

29. Varone, "iscrizioni graffite di *Stabiae*," 406–10, no. 26. My reading of this graffito, including the number 490 and "whose number is 545 as well as" follows Enzo Puglia's ("Tre graffiti da *Stabiae* di recente pubblicazione," *Papyrologica Lupiensia* 24 [2015]: 127–30) reconstruction of the text, which is an improvement of Varone's ("iscrizioni graffite di *Stabiae*," 406–10, no. 26) original publication as follows: ἀριθμὸς τϙ´, ἐφίλει οὗ ἀριθμὸς φμε´, κλίμα ἀριθμ(ὸς) ψοβ´. Varone notes the difficulty in his transcription because τφ´ equals 390, not 490, and κλίμα's meaning is uncertain, for it could refer to years or astral movements.

30. Puglia, "Tre graffiti da *Stabiae*," 127–30.

31. Varone, "iscrizioni graffite di *Stabiae*," 408–10.

32. Puglia, "Tre graffiti da *Stabiae*," 129–30.

33. My transcription of the graffito follows Puglia's ("Tre graffiti da *Stabiae*," 130–31) improved reading of the text. Varone's ("iscrizioni graffite di *Stabiae*," 410–12, no. 27) publication of the text as follows: *C(aius) Poppaeys hic habitavit cum| Hymeto ete* η´ (ὀκτώ) *fac<t>ione| et amat amaturusque est* να´ *euom* ἧς ἀριθμὸς ϡρα´, which has to add a letter to a word, the T in *factione*, to make the graffito sensible.

34. Puglia ("Tre graffiti da *Stabiae*," 130) proposes that Phylacion is a slave and notes that his name calculates to 1,811 (Φυλακίων), indicating that Phylacion is not the man of the previous graffito.

35. Ibid., 131.

Moving from Italy to the eastern Mediterranean, archaeologists working in Ephesus have found eight name calculations in two apartment units (insula) in what is known as Terrace House 2.[36] The Ephesian Terrace Houses are an elite set of domiciles located on one of the main streets in Ephesus, Curetes Street, which is the ancient Ephesian equivalent of apartments on Manhattan's Fifth Avenue or, given its closeness to the political center of Ephesus, Pennsylvania Avenue in Washington, D.C. While units existed in the Hellenistic period, Terrace House 2 was remodeled between 10 and 20 CE to make seven units, which were used until the end of the third century CE and sporadically remodeled throughout this period. The units with name calculations are 4 and 7, but I have chosen to focus on Unit 7.

Unit 7 is found in the northwest portion of Terrace House 2 and most of its graffiti postdate a renovation that occurred around 120 CE. Like the House of Maius Castricius in Pompeii, much graffiti are found in the unit's main peristyle (Room 38b). The peristyle's surrounding walls were covered with painted plaster on which the graffiti were written and scratched in clusters.[37] Among this lot of graffiti are seven name calculations, some of which are clearly in conversation with others. The first name calculation says: "I love the woman whose number is 1,266" (Φιλῶ ἧς ὁ ἀριθμὸς| ͵ασξς´) (U7 GR 309). The calculated name remains unknown, but Hans Taeuber suggests three possibilities: Stephanis (Στεφανίς), Sosiklea (Σωσικλέα), and Antidora (Ἀντιδώρα).[38] Another graffitist responded directly to this graffito, as the script of another hand is clearly visible, providing the name calculation of the man who loves the women in question: "And now the lover has (the number of) 1,995" (Καὶ ὁ φιλῶν δὲ ἔχει, ͵αϡϟε´) (U7 GR 310). This second graffitist knew not only the previous graffitist's lover, but also the previous graffitist's identity. Taeuber notes that one name from Ephesian epigraphy equals 1,995, Euphosunus (Εὐφρόσυνος) (*IEph* 20.53, 1078.5, 4217.3).[39]

---

36. For more information on the Terrace Houses see Sabine Ladstätter with Barbara Beck-Brandt, Martin Steskal, and Norbert Zimmermann, *Terrace House 2 in Ephesos: An Archaeological Guide*, trans. Nicole M. High with Emma Sachs (Istanbul: Homer Kitabevi, 2013), 75–83.

37. This unit was built between 50 and 75 CE. It was renovated around 120 CE and a new water system was installed, which provided water to a fountain, latrine, and a hot water bath inside. Room 38b measures 143 m square and had eight Doric columns surrounding it. See Elisabeth Rathmayr, "Zusammenfassung—Summary—Özet," in *Hanghaus 2 in Ephesos Die Wohneinheit 7. Baubefund, Ausstattung, Funde*, ed. Elisabeth Rathmayr, Forschungen in Ephesos VIII.10 (Vienna: Paul Gerin GmbH & Co, 2016), 773–82.

38. Hans Taeuber, "Graffiti und Inschriften," in Rathmayr, *Hanghaus 2*, 235.

39. Ibid., 236.

A third name calculation provides a number/name and invites a certain person to solve the cipher. "Now again I love the woman among the gods whose number is 865. If you are Gorgus who finds it, then write it below. [Second Hand] Clodia" (Νῦν πάλι φιλῶ νὴ θεοὺς γυναῖκα ἧς ὁ ἀριθμὸς| ωξε΄| ἐάν ἦς Γόργος ὁ εὕρων, ὑπόγραψον.| [Second Hand] Κλωδία) (GR 311).[40] Gorgus or someone else was up to the challenge and solved the name calculation of this woman, for in a second hand directly underneath the graffito another graffitist wrote the answer, Clodia, $\kappa = 20 + \lambda = 30 + \omega = 800 + \delta = 4 + \iota = 10 + \alpha = 1 = 865$.[41] One probable reason for this is that the above graffitist, his lover, and Gorgus are part of the same circle of friends who lived in or frequented Unit 7.

The graffitists in Unit 7 are probably elite Ephesians. Ephesian epigraphy attests to two Ephesian men named Gorgus, both of whom were elites.[42] In addition, archaeologists have discovered inscriptions and graffiti inside two units of Terrace House 2 identifying two of the second-century-CE occupants: Caius Flavius Furius Aptus and Caius Vibius Salutaris. The latter set up the 568-line inscription on one of the walls of the Ephesian theater that I noted in chapter 1. Both of these men were local elites with connections to Rome.[43] Therefore, Nobert Zimmermann and Sabine Ladstätter conclude that the evidence is incontrovertible that "well-known and prosperous Ephesian citizens" lived in Terrace House 2.[44] In fact, due to the large concentration of name calculating graffiti in the peristyles of these units Taeuber concludes that elite participants at banquets played these word games to amuse themselves.[45]

40. Ibid.

41. Clodia is a name attested in Ephesus during Tiberius's reign (*IEph* 1687). See D. Knibbe, H. Engelmann, and B. Iplikcioglu, "Neue Inschriften aus Ephesos XII," *JÖAI* 62 (1993): 136, no. 37.

42. The first is Gorgus the son of Sosus, who is found in a list of a group of musicians (μολποί) who made a dedication (*IEph* 901.30), and the second is Titus Flavius Claudius Gorgus, whose statue was set up in the city (*IEph* 673). This second Gorgus lived in the second century CE around the same time as the above graffito from Unit 7. Taeuber ("Graffiti," 236) proposes that this Gorgus may be the one in question.

43. The former lived in Unit 2, was a priest of Dionysus in Ephesus, and his son, Titus Flavius Lollianus Aristobulus, was a Roman senator (*IEph* 1267). The latter, Salutaris, lived in Unit 6 and had personal connections with the emperor Trajan (cf. *GIBM* 481 = *IEph* 27). See Hilke Thür, "Die WE 4—Zusammenfassung und Ergebnisse," in *Hanghaus 2 in Ephesos. Die Wohneinheit 4 Baubefund, Ausstattung, Funde. Textband*, ed. Hilke Thur, Forschungen in Ephesos VIII.6 (Vienna: Osterreichische Akademie der Wissenschaften, 2005), 434.

44. Norbert Zimmermann and Sabine Ladstätter, *Wall Painting in Ephesos from the Hellenistic to the Byzantine Period* (Istanbul: Ege Yayinlari, 2011), 54.

45. Taeuber, "Graffiti," 235.

One of the few public locations in which inscriptions calculating names of individuals have been found is Smyrna. The graffiti from Smyrna were found between 2003 and 2007 in the basement of the basilica that stood in the city's agora. The building was originally a stoa constructed in the second century BCE and converted into a multistory basilica between 75 and 125 CE. It was used until the seventh century CE. The ground level of the structure was the seat of the Roman tribunal. The basilica had a basement with four galleries or naves (4.4 m high and 5 m wide) running east to west. The first and second galleries are not separated from each other and are made from a series of piers and arches supporting the first floor of the basilica. These galleries were open to the public at all times and provided a shady spot for individuals to gather. The third gallery has sixty-three rooms (each measuring 1.6 x 2.15 m with a door measuring .70 m) that may have held shops, workshops, and/or offices. The fourth gallery is the northernmost of the four and its decoration differed from the others in that its walls had marble plating, which is called revetment. Archaeologists propose that this gallery may have had an official function like a reception hall. In addition, there was a spring of water in the basement of the basilica that caused people to gather there and this water was said to have healing properties.[46]

The piers and arches of the first and second naves were covered with plaster and archaeologists have found numerous graffiti that people visiting the basement scratched or wrote on them.[47] The contents of these texts vary. Some express love, others civic pride, and still others refer to the spring's healing waters.[48] Precise dating of the graffiti is impossible, but most probably date to the late second to early third century CE.[49] Five, maybe six, of these 104 graffiti (close to 6 percent) use name calculations to disguise the names of lovers with numbers, following the same formula found at Pompeii, Stabiae, and Ephesus: φιλῶ ἧς / οὗ ἀριθμὸς . . . (see Table 6.4).[50]

---

46. Akin Ersoy, "Introduction," in *Graffiti from the Basilica in the Agora of Smyrna*, ed. Roger S. Bagnall et al. (New York: New York University Press, 2016), 1–20; Roger S. Bagnall, *Everyday Writing in the Graeco-Roman East* (Berkeley: University of California Press, 2011), 7–46.

47. Ersoy, "Introduction," 1–20; Bagnall, *Everyday Writing*, 7–46.

48. Roger S. Bagnall, "General Characteristics of the Graffiti," in *Graffiti from the Basilica*, 20–22.

49. See Roger S. Bagnall, "Dating the Graffiti," in *Graffiti from the Basilica*, 36–40.

50. Roger S. Bagnall, "Isopsephisms of Desire," in *Graffiti from the Basilica*, 48–52; Roger S. Bagnall et al., "The Graffiti," in *Graffiti from the Basilica*, 55–462.

Table 6.4: Name Calculations from Smyrna

Greek Text	Translation
μίαν φιλ[ῶ]| ἧς ἀριθυ[ὸς - -]	I love one woman whose number is . . . (T5.1)
ΗΣ Ο| ΨΝ [φιλῶ?] ἧς ὁ [ἀριθμὸς] ψν.	[I love] the woman whose number is 750 (T12.7)
φιλῶ ἧς ὁ ἀρι[θμὸς]| χις ọπọλ̣λ̣ . . .	I love the woman whose number is 616 (T22.1)
φιλῶ ἧς [. . .] ΤΩΝ| ὁ ἀριθμọ̀[ς . . .] . ΗΝ.| ψλα [- 7 -] .	I love the woman whose number is 731 (T24.2)
φιλῶ ἧς ὁ <ἀ>ριθμὸς| Ατη	I love the woman whose number is 1,308 (T27.3)
[φιλῶ ο]ὗ̣ ạ̓ριθμὸς τνα	I love the man whose number is 351 (T42.2)

These texts appear in clusters near other graffiti and dipinti indicating that they are parts of ongoing dialogues. Two are written in cursive (T5.1; 24.2) and four graffiti are in capital letters (T12.7; T22.1; T27.3; T42.2). The graffitists are probably men, even the one who claims to love a man. Roger Bagnall points out that the graffito that encodes the name of a man with a number is incised near a picture of two male heads and that one of these may be the graffitist. As noted above, some exegetes of Revelation conclude that John's cipher of 666 is almost impossible to figure out.[51] Bagnall, however, has deciphered three names in these graffiti and proposes possible names for the two others.[52] Using prosopography from Smyrna in the Roman period, Bagnall proposes that 750 is probably Secounda (Σεκουνδα): Σ = 200 + ε = 5 + κ = 20 + ο = 70 + υ = 400 + ν = 50 + δ = 4 + α = 1 = 750, 731 is probably Anthousa (Ανθουσα): Α = 1 + ν = 50 + θ = 9 + ο = 70 + υ = 400 + σ = 200 + α = 1 = 73,[53] and 1,308 is probably Tyche (Τυχη): Τ = 300 + υ = 400 + χ = 600 + η = 8 = 1,308.[54] He is not as sure about 616, suggesting that the name may be Pheria, Eupolla, Metullika, or an unattested name. Similarly, 731 could be Cuparion, Filainon, or Tation. There is no way

51. Beale, *Revelation*, 720–21; Lupieri, *Apocalypse*, 212.

52. Bagnall (*Everyday Writing*, 15) asks and answers, "How hard were these names to figure out? Not very, I would guess."

53. Bagnall, "Graffiti," 236.

54. Ibid., 267.

to know the exact social class of these graffitists, but use of cursive script suggests that some were familiar with writing. Bagnall concludes that the graffitists are "from families capable of affording some level of education, and probably from a fairly wide range within that population."[55] Given that these name calculations appear in clusters of graffiti, they are dialogues occurring among insiders.[56]

IV. Revelation 13:18 and Greco-Roman Name Calculation

The archaeological contexts of the epigraphic name calculations above suggest that graffitists composed them for insiders who possessed enough information to calculate the names in question: the author, a group of associates, and possibly the person whose name is calculated. Similarly, John provides the context that his audience needs to decipher his calculation of the beast's name. The most explicit and detailed description of Roman imperial divine honors in Revelation prefaces John's reference to the beast and his number.[57] John notes that the inhabitants of the earth worship the seven-headed beast from the sea who has ten crowns that the Dragon/Satan has empowered (Rev 13:4, 8). The beast from the land compels people to worship the beast from the sea (Rev 13:12), especially his statue (εἰκών) (Rev 13:15).[58] Furthermore, John provides enough evidence for his audience to connect the beast to Nero. He points out that one of the heads, probably the one on which there are ten diadems and blasphemous names, received a death blow that was

55. Bagnall, "General Characteristics," 22.

56. These graffiti are not the result of anti-imperial actions as Koester ("Number of the Beast," 7–11) proposes. The basement was designed to be filled with people taking shelter from the Mediterranean heat, gathering for conversations, purchasing items from shops, or passing through on their way to draw water from the spring. If these graffiti are signs of noncompliance, the graffitists chose a highly populated place to express their discontent with society. In addition, the ground floor of the basilica was the Roman tribunal and the fourth gallery may have been used for official governmental purposes.

57. For imperial divine honors in Revelation see Simon R. F. Price, *Rituals and Power: The Roman Imperial Cult in Asia Minor* (Cambridge: Cambridge University Press, 1984); Steven J. Friesen, *Imperial Cults and the Apocalypse of John: Reading Revelation in the Ruins* (Oxford: Oxford University Press, 2001).

58. The reason that John provides for this worship is the beast from the sea's martial prowess and *pax Romana* (Rev 13:4).

healed (Rev 13:3), which probably refers to the Nero *redivivus* myth that the emperor would rise from the dead.[59]

There are, however, two aspects of John's name calculation that Revelation's audience would have considered unusual. First, unlike other epigraphic name calculations, John's encodes the name of an emperor, not that of a lover. This use of name calculation for an emperor may be a survival of the evidence, however, for Suetonius says that during Nero's reign negative "verses" (*carminibus*) about the emperor were published (*proscripta*) and circulated (*vulgate*), including the famous name calculation, "A new calculation: Nero killed his own mother" (Νεόψηφον. Νέρων ἰδίαν μητέρα ἀπέκτεινε) (*Nero* 39.1–2).

Second, John's audience had to transliterate the number from Greek into Aramaic/Hebrew to calculate it. For this reason, John calls for wisdom (σοφία) and understanding (νοῦς) on the part of his audience. The only other time he alerts his audience to the need of wisdom (σοφία) and understanding (νοῦς) is in his interpretation of the seven heads as seven kings of Rome (Rev 17:9). This is also the only other time νοῦς appears in Revelation. John connects wisdom and understanding with matters associated with the imperial purple. It may seem odd that John expects his readers and auditors to transliterate this Greek name calculation into Aramaic/Hebrew, but the prophet's use of the OT remains an enigma to most scholars. There is general agreement that while John does not explicitly quote the OT in Revelation his prophecies are filled with allusions to scripture.[60] Certainly, John expects his audience to grasp his reference to Armageddon (Rev 16:16).[61] At the very least, John expected that there would be people in the seven churches who could decipher his name calculation. Significantly, one of the graffitists from Stabiae discussed above expected that readers of his graffito would transliterate the name of his lover from Latin to Greek to calculate her name accurately.

---

59. For the most in-depth discussion still to date see Bauckham, *Climax of Prophecy*, 407–31. This Nero-like figure is probably Domitian. Juvenal (*Sat.* 4.38) called Domitian a bald-headed Nero (*caluus Nero*). I am grateful for Prof. Richard E. Oster for this reference.

60. Koester (*Revelation*, 123) notes, "John assumed that his readers would be acquainted with biblical narratives and prophetic texts. . . . Revelation employs biblical language and imagery in every chapter, but the author never quotes texts exactly." For a recent discussion of the OT in Revelation see C. Thomas Fraatz, "Blessed Is the One Who Reads and Those Who Hear the Words of Prophecy: Rome and Revelation's Use of Scripture," (PhD diss., Boston College, 2017).

61. Koester (*Revelation*, 597) notes that at least one mid-third to fourth century CE Jew in Sardis probably transliterated the Latin name Severus into Hebrew (*sbyrws*) in an inscription from the synagogue in that city.

Finally, John's audience would have been attuned to the possibility that the beast's name/number is not a mere calculation but an equal calculation. Some would have noted the connection between the beast's name, Nero Caesar, and the numerical value of the Greek term "beast" transliterated into Aramaic/Hebrew. Therefore, John's audience would have been aware that John's name calculation is an equal one that demonstrates Nero's beastliness.[62]

V. Conclusion

To summarize, inscriptions have the ability to shed new light on exegetically difficult NT texts. Using the number and name of the beast of Rev 13:18 as a test case, I have demonstrated that inscriptions indicate that John's use of name calculation of the beast resembles a common Greco-Roman practice. I have marshalled more cases of inscriptional name calculations than most scholars currently acknowledge. To date (2018), there are twenty-three such texts known to me in Greek epigraphy and more are probably forthcoming. The practice of name calculation was geared toward a group of insiders: the one who produced the name calculation, the one whose name is ciphered, and their associates. Similarly, John provides all the necessary background information for his audience to grasp that the beast's name is Nero Caesar.

VI. Appendix of Epigraphic Examples of Calculations and Equal Calculations

Greek Text	Translation	City
Ἀμέριμνος ἐμνήσθη Ἁρμονίας τῆς εἰδίας κυρίας| ἐπ᾽ ἀγαθῷ ἧς ὁ ἀριθμὸς μέ (or ͵αλέ) τοῦ καλοῦ ὀνόματος.	Amerimnus remembered for a good cause the harmony of his own girlfriend, the number of her beautiful name is 45 (or 1035) (*CIL* 4.4839).	Pompeii
φιλῶ ἧς ἀριθμὸς φμέ	I love the woman whose number is 545 (*CIL* 4.4861).	Pompeii

62. Bauckham, *Climax of Prophecy*, 389; Aune, *Revelation 6–16*, 769; Koester, *Revelation*, 598.

φιλῶ ἧς ἀριθμὸς	I love her whose number is . . .[1]	Pompeii
ἧς φιλῶ ὁ ἀριθμὸς νά	I love the woman whose number is 51.[2]	Pompeii
C(aius) Poppaeus Hymetus hic [ha]|bitavit et amavit cuius nomen Euhodia|ἧς ἀριθμὸς υϙ΄, ἐφίλει οὗ ἀριθμὸς φμε΄, καὶ ἅμ'| ἀριθ(μὸς) ψοβ΄	Caius Poppaeus Hymetus [l]ived here and he loved his own whose name is Euhodia. Her number is 490. He loves the man whose number is 545 as well as the [man?/woman?] whose number is 772.[3]	Stabiae
C(aius) Poppaeys hic habitavit cum| Hymeto et Phylacione| et amat amaturusque est| in aevom ἧς ἀριθμὸς ͵αρα΄	C(aius) Poppaeus lived here with Hymetus and Phylacion and he loved and will love forever the woman whose number is 1,101.[4]	Stabiae
ἐμνήσθη ὁ καλὸς τῆς καλῆς ἧς ὁ ἀριθ(μὸς) αυοε΄	The beauty of the beautiful woman whose number is 1,475 is remembered (U4 GR 2).[5]	Ephesus
Φιλῶ ἧς ὁ ἀριθμὸς| ͵ασξς΄	I love the woman whose number is 1,266 (U7 GR 309).	Ephesus
Καὶ ὁ φιλῶν δὲ ἔχει, ͵αϡϟε΄.	And now the lover has (the number of) 1,995 (U7 GR 310).	Ephesus
Νῦν πάλι φιλῶ νὴ θεοὺς γυναῖκα ἧς ὁ ἀριθμὸς ωξε΄| ἐάν ἦς Γόργος ὁ εὕρων, ὑπόγραψον.| [Second Hand] Κλωδία	Now again I love the woman among the gods whose number is 865. If you are Gorgus who finds it, then write it below. [Second Hand] Clodia (U7 GR 311).	Ephesus
Φιλῶ ἧς ὁ ἀριθμὸς ωξε΄| (Second Hand) Κλωδία	I love the woman whose number is 865. (Second Hand) Clodia (U7 GR 312).	Ephesus

1. G. Minervini, "Studii Pompeiani – Caserma de' Gladiatori," *Bullettino archeologico Napoletano N.S.* 7 (1859): 116–20, esp. 119.

2. Benefiel, "Dialogues of Ancient Graffiti," 92, no. 28.

3. Puglia, "Tre graffiti da *Stabiae*," 129.

4. Ibid., 131.

5. Hans Taeuber, "Graffiti," in *Hanghaus 2 in Ephesos. Die Wohneinheit 4 Baubefund, Ausstattung, Funde. Textband*, ed. Hilke Thür, Forschungen in Ephesos VIII.6 (Vienna: Österreichische Akademie der Wissenschaften, 2005), 132–43.

<table>
<tr><td>Φιλῶ . . .</td><td>I love . . . (U7 GR 316).</td><td>Ephesus</td></tr>
<tr><td>Φιλῶ ἧς [---]|| ι̣ωνο</td><td>I love the woman . . . (U7 GR 320).</td><td>Ephesus</td></tr>
<tr><td>Φιλ(ῶ ---)</td><td>I love . . . (U7 GR 323).</td><td>Ephesus</td></tr>
<tr><td>γρ(αμματεὺς) Ἀπολλώνιος Πτολε|μαίου ἐμνήσθη| τῆς συνβίου ἧς ὁ ἀρι|θμὸς ͵αξε′.</td><td>The sc(ribe) Apollonius son of Ptolemaius remembered his wife/concubine whose number is 1,065 (IMylasa 369).</td><td>Mylasa</td></tr>
<tr><td>Ζητῶν μου τὴν ψῆφον| παροδεῖτα| γνώση̣ τὸν κείμενον| ἐνθάδε με|| κεῖμαι δ' ἐν γαίῃ τῇ με| ἀναθρεψαμένη̣| ͵ατνδ′</td><td>Traveler seeking my calculation you will see me lying here. Now I am lying in the cherished ground that is over me. (I am) 1,354 (IG V.1 1368).</td><td>Messenia</td></tr>
<tr><td>Ἐμνήσθη Ἀσπεὶ[ς] τῆς κυρίας| ἧς Θαλλί(σ)κος ρο′</td><td>Aspeis and Thalliskos remembered the lady (whose number is?) 170.[1]</td><td>Catania, Italy</td></tr>
<tr><td>μίαν φιλ[ῶ]| ἧς ἀριθυ[ὸς - -]</td><td>I love one woman whose number is . . . (T5.1).</td><td>Smyrna</td></tr>
<tr><td>ΗΣ Ο
ΨΝ This may spell [φιλῶ] ἧς ὁ [ἀριθμὸς] ψν.</td><td>[I love] the woman whose number is 750 (T12.7).</td><td>Smyrna</td></tr>
<tr><td>φιλῶ ἧς ὁ ἀρι[θμὸς]
χις ϙπ̣ο̣λ̣λ̣</td><td>I love the woman whose number is 616 (T22.1).</td><td>Smyrna</td></tr>
<tr><td>φιλῶ ἧς [. . .] ΤΩΝ
ὁ ἀριθμὸ̣[ς . . .] . ΗΝ.
ψλα [- 7 -] .</td><td>I love the woman whose number is 731 (T24.2).</td><td>Smyrna</td></tr>
<tr><td>φιλῶ ἧς ὁ <ἀ>ριθμὸς
Ατη</td><td>I love the woman whose number is 1,308 (T27.3).[2]</td><td>Smyrna</td></tr>
<tr><td>[φιλῶ ο]ὗ̣ ἀ̣ριθμὸς τνα</td><td>I love the man whose number is 351 (T42.2).[3]</td><td>Smyrna</td></tr>
</table>

1. Giacomo Manganaro, "Graffiti e iscrizioni funerarie della Sicilia orientale," *Helikon* 3–4 (1962): 485–93.

2. This graffito is found in Bay 27 to the right of a picture of a ship.

3. This graffito is from Bay 42 and is near the picture of two bald men (DP54.1). Roger S. Bagnall et al., "The Graffiti," in *Graffiti from the Basilica*, 55–462.

Conclusion

The inhabitants of the Greco-Roman world created myriads of inscriptions to serve as durable advertisements for future generations to read. The individuals responsible for these epigraphs had no way of knowing that two thousand years hence we would put their inscriptions to use in the interpretation and historical reconstruction of an obscure faction of Judaism that began in Roman Judea in the mid 30s CE, Christianity. Nevertheless, throughout this book, I have shown the benefits of using inscriptions in the interpretation of the NT. In the second chapter, I demonstrated how inscriptions aid in the reconstruction of theological developments of early Christianity such as Christology. Greek and Semitic inscriptions from the southern Levant support that the title lord was a royal title particular to the region during the formation of the earliest Christology. The similarities between the use of lord in these inscriptions and the use of *kyrios* for Jesus in Paul's letters suggest that Jesus was first called *kyrios* in the southern Levant and that this title was royal, messianic, and not exclusively divine.

In the third chapter, I showed the philological ability of inscriptions to determine the meaning of a word at a given place and time. Through an epigraphic survey of the Greek verb προλαμβάνω, I demonstrated that the verb most probably carried a temporal meaning in the first century CE. Therefore, the most appropriate translation of προλαμβάνω in 1 Cor 11:21 is "go ahead with," which means that the problem that Paul's addresses with the Lord's Banquet in Corinth (1 Cor 11:17–34) is that some richer Corinthians "are going ahead with" their own banquet (1 Cor 11:21), not waiting on the less affluent members of their congregation to join them.

In the fourth chapter, I demonstrated the benefit of proper contextualization of inscriptions for interpreting the NT. I examined the proposal that Luke's reference to Christians in Thessalonica "opposing Caesar's decrees" refers to imperial loyalty oaths. Through analyses of these oaths, I showed that they are not imperial decrees, but decisions of local communities. Therefore, "Caesar's decrees" cannot be imperial loyalty oaths. Instead, I proposed that "Caesar's decrees" probably relates to Thessalonica's status as a "free city" in the Roman Empire. Using comparative inscriptional evidence,

I argued that "Caesar's decrees" refers to letters and edicts from the emperor Augustus and successive emperors affirming and reaffirming Thessalonica's status as a "free city."

In the fifth chapter, I showed the value of inscriptions in illuminating the lives of people in the Greco-Roman world who were not elite males. The information inscriptions provide suggests that Lydia, Syntyche, Euodia, and other women of high social standing were probably benefactresses, deacons, and possibly overseers in the church in Philippi. In my sixth chapter, I demonstrated how inscriptions illuminate certain difficult NT texts by generating more data to interpret them. I gathered a total of twenty-three cases of the calculation of a person's Greek name with numbers in the Roman Empire, most of which are largely unknown to NT scholars, that resemble John the prophet's calculation of the beast's name with a number. The archaeological contexts of some of these inscriptions indicate that the calculation of a person's Greek name was geared toward a group of insiders: the one who made the calculation, sometimes the one about whom the calculation is made, and their associates. Similarly, John provides his audience with the context necessary to calculate the beast's name as Nero Caesar.

One of the aims of Adolf Deissmann in his many erudite publications was to convince NT scholars to approach the NT through social history: to use inscriptions (and papyri) to interpret the NT in light of its cultural context. Deissmann longed for a time when all NT scholars used these sources in their historical reconstructions of the NT:

> Some day, when yet stronger waves of light come flooding over to us from the East, it will be recognised that the restoration of the New Testament to its native home, its own age and social level, means something more than the mere repatriation of our sacred Book. It brings with it new life and depth to all our conceptions of Primitive Christianity.[1]

By "social level" Deissmann means interpreting early Christianity as if most of its adherents were from the lower social classes of the Roman world, which he wrongly believed were responsible for some inscriptions but almost all our extant papyri.

While I disagree with Deissmann that early Christians and the authors of most extant papyri were from the lower social classes of the Roman world,

1. Adolf Deissmann, *Light from the Ancient East: The New Testament Illustrated by Recently Discovered Texts of the Graeco-Roman World*, trans. Lionel R. M. Strachan, 4th ed. (New York: Hodder & Stoughton, 1910; repr. Grand Rapids: Baker Books, 1978), 402.

I share his dream that one day more students of NT will use inscriptions in their interpretation of its documents and in the historical reconstruction of early Christianity.[2] However, one of my goals in this book has not been merely to encourage the reader to use inscriptions, but to use them properly. To approach epigraphs as what they are: archaeological artifacts; semi-permanent documents that local communities and people living in specific parts of the Greco-Roman world produced at specific times and for specific purposes. Therefore, the material on which inscriptions were engraved, where they were set up in Greco-Roman cities, when they were taken down, and the circumstances surrounding their discovery in the modern period can and often do provide information about inscriptions as important as their content.

Given that there are more than half a million Greek, Latin, and Semitic inscriptions that have survived from the Hellenistic and Roman periods and more are discovered every year, Deissmann is certainly correct that this corpus of material can bring "new life and depth" to the study of the NT. There is no doubt that hitherto unknown solutions to the numerous problems associated with the historical reconstruction of early Christianity, as well as the exegetical difficulties of certain NT texts, are waiting to be discovered in these vastly untapped primary sources directly from the world of the NT. It is even possible and probable that new solutions to problems that scholars consider settled await the student of the NT who dares to delve into the contextualized study of inscriptions.

To conclude, at the end of *Light from the Ancient East*, Deissmann challenges the reader that to be a "good" exegete of the NT, to be a "good" preacher, or to be a "good" pastor they must spend time learning about "the age of the New Testament" from inscriptions (and papyri).[3] The context of Deissmann's comment is his encouragement for the reader to spend more time in primary sources contemporary to the writing of the NT than in modern secondary ones about the early Roman Empire. As a pastor myself, I am well aware of the constraints of ministry. Much of my time is devoted to pastoral, teaching, and preaching responsibilities, and I do not have as much time for research as I would like (who among us does?). Nevertheless, I contend that today's student of the NT in graduate school or seminary

---

2. For a more balanced approach to the social classes of early Christians see Wayne A. Meeks, *The First Urban Christians: The Social World of the Apostle Paul*, 2nd ed. (New Haven: Yale University Press, 2003).

3. Deissmann, *Light from the Ancient East*, 403.

and/or the pastor serving in a parish must aspire to be as well-informed as possible about the NT. I agree with Deissmann that one of the best ways to educate oneself about the early Roman Empire is to spend time reading and studying the actual documents that individuals living in it produced: inscriptions. The time spent in this activity will bountifully reward the reader in their work, whether it be in graduate studies or in a local parish. They will see some of the benefits that inscriptions bring to the study of the NT and, as Louis Robert notes, that inscriptions are "a perpetual contribution that enlivens the history of antiquity."[4] Such enlightenment will alter one's perspective of the NT, transforming its documents from black-and-white to full HD color.

4. Louis Robert ("Les épigraphies et L'épigraphie grecque et romaine," in *Opera minora selecta. Epigraphie et antiquités grecque* [Amsterdam: AM Hakkert, 1990], 5:75) notes that epigraphy is "*[u]n perpétuel apport vivifie l'histoire de l'Antiquité . . .*"

APPENDIX 1

Important Printed Collections of Inscriptions[1]

Bulletin épigraphique (*BE*) is a journal published yearly reviewing newly discovered Greek inscriptions. It began in 1888 and is still being produced.

Corpus Inscriptionum Graecarum (*CIG*) is the first modern corpus of inscriptions. It is produced in six volumes from 1828 to 1877 and contains all published Greek inscriptions up to 1877 in one collection that is organized geographically.

Corpus Inscriptionum Iudaeae/Palestinae (*CIIP*) is a corpus of all Latin, Greek, and Semitic inscriptions that have been discovered in ancient Palestine and its environs from the Hellenistic period to the seventh century CE. Four volumes have been published from 2010 to 2018 and two more are expected in the near future.

Corpus Inscriptionum Latinarum (*CIL*) is a corpus of Latin inscriptions that began to be produced in 1862 and is still in production. The volumes are organized geographically and thematically.

Corpus Inscriptionum Semiticarum (*CIS*) is a corpus of Semitic inscriptions that was produced from 1881 to 1962. The two volumes that will most interest the student of the NT are *CIS* 2 (Aramaic and Nabataean inscriptions) and *CIS* 3 (Jewish inscriptions).

1. My discussion on epigraphic collections was informed by John Bodel, "Appendix: A Brief Guide to Some Standard Collections," in *Epigraphic Evidence: Ancient History from Inscriptions*, ed. John Bodel (London: Routledge, 2001), 153–74; Christer Bruun, "The Major Corpora and Epigraphic Publications," in *The Oxford Handbook of Roman Epigraphy*, ed. Christer Bruun and Jonathan Edmondson (Oxford: Oxford University Press, 2015), 66–77.

Inscriptiones Graecae (*IG*) is a corpus of Greek inscriptions that began to be produced in 1903 and is still in production. It is organized around geographic locations and supplements *CIG*.

Inscriptiones graecae ad res romanas pertinentes (*IGRR*) is an anthology of select Greek inscriptions from the Mediterranean basin dating to the Greco-Roman period in four volumes that were produced from 1901 to 1927.

Inscriptiones Latinae Selectae (*ILS*) is an anthology of select Latin inscriptions that was produced in three volumes from 1892 to 1916.

L'Année épigraphique (*AE*) is a journal published yearly reviewing newly discovered Latin inscriptions. It began in 1888 and is still in production.

Orientis Graeci Inscriptiones Selectae (*OGIS*) is an anthology of select Greek inscriptions from the eastern Mediterranean that date to the Hellenistic and Roman periods in two volumes that were produced from 1903 to 1905.

Sylloge Inscriptionum Graecarum (*Syll* or *SIG*) is a corpus of select Greek inscriptions in four volumes that has undergone three editions. The first edition appeared in 1883 and the second and third editions between 1915 and 1924. Volumes one and two cover inscriptions from the Peloponnesian War (405/404 BCE) to the sixth century CE, the third volume contains epigraphs covering various categories of ancient life from antiquity, and the fourth volume is an index.

Supplementum Epigraphicum Graecum (*SEG*) is a corpus published yearly containing newly discovered Greek inscriptions. It began in 1923 and is still in production.

Epigraphic Bulletin for Greek Religion (*EBGR*) is an online journal published yearly chronicling newly discovered Greek inscriptions related to Greek religion (http://journals.openedition.org/kernos/605?lang=en).

APPENDIX 2

Online Search Engines and Collections of Inscriptions[1]

The Ancient Graffiti Project is a digital collection and search engine of graffiti from Pompeii and Herculaneum allowing one to search for graffiti by location, with a number of filters such as language, writings style, etc., or by Latin terms and English translations. This database is a work in progress (http://ancientgraffiti.org).

Archive.org contains many digitized, older corpora of inscriptions: *CIG*, *CIL*, *CIS*, *IG*, *IGRR*, *ILS*, *OGIS*, *SIG*, and *TNSI*.

Centre for the Study of Ancient Documents (CSAD) is a digital collection operated by Oxford University, providing access to inscriptions at Oxford, which consist mostly of Greek epigraphs from Chios, Samos, Priene, Rhodes, and Samothrace, and Latin inscriptions from Britain (http://www.csad.ox.ac.uk).

Corpus Inscriptionum Latinarum (*CIL*) has an online companion to its published volumes that include related bibliographies and photographs of inscriptions (https://cil.bbaw.de).

The Electronic Archive of Greek and Latin Epigraphy Project (EAGLE) is a digital collection of Greek and Latin inscriptions from Europeana, which is a multilingual digital collection of about 1.5 million items digitized by European museums, libraries, and archives from twenty-five countries in the European Union. The project's goal is to make available most inscriptions from the Greek and Roman world along with information about them, including photographs and English translations. The search engine filters include: text of an inscription, the place it was found, type of inscription,

1. For a discussion of some of these epigraphic internet sources see Tom Elliott, "Epigraphy and Digital Resources," in Bruun and Edmondson, *Oxford Handbook*, 78–85.

location, material, decoration, and bibliography. In addition, EAGLE has a mobile application that allows one to scan an inscription found on site or in a museum to discover information about it (https://www.eagle-network.eu).

The Epigraphic Database Heidelberg (EDH) is part of the EAGLE project (see above) and focuses on Latin and bilingual (i.e., Latin and Greek) inscriptions (along with photographs) from the Roman Empire. The filters for the search engine include: current location, language, type of monument, engraving technique, date, historically relevant data, literature about an inscription, commentary, persons mentioned in an inscription, and the text of an inscription (https://edh-www.adw.uni-heidelberg.de/home).

The Epigraphic Database Rome (EDR) is part of the EAGLE project (see above), but allows one to search for inscriptions only from Rome. The filters for the search engine include: the region of Rome, bibliography, and the text of an inscription (http://www.edr-edr.it).

Epigraphik-Datenbank Clauss-Slaby (EDCS) is an online collection of over 500,000 Latin inscriptions, including photographs, from all over the Mediterranean basin. The search engine filters include: province, place, type of inscription, and the text of an inscription (http://www.manfredclauss.de/gb/index.html).

Epigraphische Datenbank zum antiken Kleinasien (EDK) is a working collection of Greek and Latin inscriptions from Asia Minor produced by the University of Hamburg. The digital collection includes inscriptions, descriptions of them, and commentaries. The filters for the search engine include: text of an inscription, category of inscription, region, language, type of object, and date (https://www.epigraphik.uni-hamburg.de).

Die Inschriften von Philippi is an online companion containing pictures of Greek and Latin inscriptions from Philippi that are in the epigraphic catalogue that Peter Pilhofer has edited and published: *Philippi II: Katalog der Inschriften von Philippi*.

InscriptiFact is a digital library of almost 70,000 high-resolution photographs of Semitic inscriptions from the ancient Near East and the Greco-Roman world as well as some of the Dead Sea Scrolls. It is not an online search engine, but one that can be downloaded and used free of charge (http://www.inscriptifact.com).

Inscriptiones Graecae (*IG*) is an online edition of some of the recently published volumes of *IG*, beginning with *IG* IX I^2 4 (2001), that contains the texts of inscriptions and their German translations (http://pom.bbaw.de/ig).

Inscriptions of Aphrodisias (*IAph2007*) is an online digital edition of published inscriptions and photographs of them from Aphrodisias that King's College London has produced (http://insaph.kcl.ac.uk/iaph2007).

Searchable Greek Inscriptions is an online, searchable database of Greek inscriptions from antiquity produced by the Packard Humanities Institute. The search engine allows one to search the text of Greek inscriptions by region or to browse inscriptions (https://epigraphy.packhum.org).

The U.S. Epigraphy Project is a working digital collection of Greek and Latin inscriptions located in the United States of America arranged by collections and publications. The database is accessible through a search engine with the following filters: language, date, origin, type, and material (http://usepigraphy.brown.edu/projects/usep).

APPENDIX 3

Abbreviations in Inscriptions

Most Common Roman Names

Praenomen	Latin Abbreviation	Greek Abbreviation
Appius	Ap	Απ
Aulus	A	Α, Αυ, Αυλ
Caius/Gaius	C	Γ, Γα, Γαι
Gnaeus	Cn	Γν, Γνα
Decimus	D	Δ, Δεκ
Lucius	L	Λ, Λου, Λουκ
Marcus	M, Mar	Μ, Μαρ
Manius	M´	Μαν
Publius	P	Π, Πο, Ποπ
Quintus	Q	Κ, Κο
Sergius	Ser	Σερ
Sextus	Sex	Σ, Σε, Σεξ
Titus	T	Τ, Τι, Τιτ
Tiberius	Ti, Tib	Τ, Τι, Τιβ

Greek Numbers

Greek Letter	Number
Α, α	1
Β, β	2
Γ, γ	3
Δ, δ	4
Ε, ε	5
Ϝ, ϝ / Ϛ, ϛ	6

Ζ, ζ	7
Η, η	8
Θ, θ	9
Ι, ι	10
Κ, κ	20
Λ, λ	30
Μ, μ	40
Ν, ν	50
Ξ, ξ	60
Ο, ο	70
Π, π	80
Ϙ, ϙ	90
Ρ, ρ	100
Σ, Ϲ, σ	200
Τ, τ	300
Υ, υ	400
Φ, φ	500
Χ, χ	600
Ψ, ψ	700
Ω, ω	800
Ϡ, ϡ	900
͵Α	1000

Common Abbreviations in Latin Inscriptions[1]

Abbreviation	Latin Term	English Translation
AED	*aedilis*	aedile
ANN	*annos*	year(s)
AVG	*Augustalis*	priests of Augustus
C V	*clarissimus vir*	distinguished man
COH	*cohors*	cohort
COL	*colonia*	colony

1. Table adapted from Lawrence Keppie, *Understanding Roman Inscriptions* (Baltimore: Johns Hopkins University Press, 1991), 138–39.

COS	*consul*	consul
C R	*cives Romani*	Roman citizens
D D	*decreto decurionum*	by decree of the decurions
DEC	*decurio*	decurion
DED	*dedit*	he or she gave
D M	*Dis Manibus*	to the deceased spirits
D S	*de suo*	from his or her own funds
EQ	*eques*	knight
EX S C	*ex senatus consulto*	by senatorial decree
F	*filius/filia*	son/daughter
FEC	*fecit*	he or she did
GEN	*genius*	life force
H	*hic*	here
H S E	*hic situs/sita est*	he or she lies here
IMP	*imperator*	victorious general or emperor
I O M	*Iuppiter Optimus Maximus*	Jupiter Best and Greatest
L	*libertus/liberta*	freedperson
LEG	*legio*	legion
L D D D	*locus datus decreto decurionum*	site given by decree of the decurions
MIL	*miles/militavit*	soldier/he served in the army
NAT	*natus*	born
OPT	*optimus*	best
PAT PAT/ P P	*pater patriae*	father of his country
P M	*pontifex maximus*	high priest
POS	*posuit*	he or she set (this) up
P P	*primus pilus*	chief centurion
PRAEF	*praefectus*	prefect
PRAET	*praetor*	praetor
PROCON	*proconsul*	proconsul
Q	*quaestor*	quaestor
REST	*restituit*	he or she restored
R P	*res publica*	republic
S C	*senatus consultum*	by senatorial decree

S P	*sua pecunia*	with his or her own money
S P Q R	*senatus populusque Romanus*	the senate and the Roman people
S T T L	*sit tibi terra levis*	may the earth lie lightly on you
TEST	*testamentum*	will
TRIB POT/ TR P	*tribunicia potestate*	with tribunican power
TR MIL	*tribunus militum*	military tribune
TR PL	*tribunus plebis*	tribune of the people
TRIB	*tribunus*	tribune
V	*vir/vixit/vovit*	man/he or she lived/he or she vowed
V C	*vir clarissimus*	most distinguished man
VOT	*votum/vota*	vow
V S	*votum solvit*	he or she paid their vow

Glossary

agora. The civic, political, and social heart of a Greek city that is most often centrally located.

augur. A Roman priest specializing in augury, or divining the will of the gods, most often from the flight of birds.

augury. Divining the will of the gods, most often from the flight of birds.

autopsy. Firsthand inspection and examination of an inscription.

epigraph. A message most often engraved, scratched, or written on a durable surface.

epigrapher. A specialist who studies inscriptions.

epigraphy. The science of the study of inscriptions.

forum. An open square that was the commercial, judicial, political, and religious center of Rome, Italian municipalities, and colonies of Rome.

inscription. A message most often engraved, scratched, or written on a durable surface.

pomerium. The religious boundary of Rome, an Italian municipality, or a colony of Rome in which augury could be practiced.

temple *(naos)*. The literal house in which a god's image resides.

temple complex/sanctuary (*temenos*). A sacred boundary containing at least an altar of a god and often the deity's temple and other sacred buildings as well.

Bibliography

Abrahamsen, Valerie A. "Priestesses and Other Female Cult Leaders at Philippi in the Early Christian Era." Pages 25–62 in *The People Beside Paul: The Philippian Assembly and History from Below*. Edited by Joseph A. Marchal. Atlanta: SBL Press, 2015.

———. *Women and Worship at Philippi: Diana/Artemis and Other Cults in the Early Christian Era*. Portland, ME: Astarte Shell Press, 1995.

———. "Women at Philippi: The Pagan and Christian Evidence." *JFSR* 3 (1987): 17–30.

Adam-Veleni, P. "Thessalonike." Pages 545–62 in *Brill's Companion to Ancient Macedon: Studies in the Archaeology and History of Macedon, 650 BC–300 AD*. Edited by Robin J. Lane Fox. Leiden: Brill, 2015.

Aitken, James K. "Psalms." Pages 320–34 in *T&T Clark Companion to the Septuagint*. Edited by James K. Aitken. London: Bloomsbury T&T Clark, 2015.

Alföldy, Géza. "Augustus und die Inschriften: Tradition und Innovation Die Geburt der imperialen Epigraphik." *Gymnasium* 98 (1991): 289–324.

Allamani-Souri, Victoria. "The Province of Macedonia in the Roman Imperium." Pages 67–79 in *Roman Thessaloniki*. Thessaloniki Archaeological Museum Publications 1. Edited by D. V. Grammenos. Translated by David Hardy. Thessaloniki: Archaeological Museum, 2003.

Amandry, Michael, et al, eds. *Roman Provincial Coinage*. 10 vols. London: British Museum Press, 1992–.

Aristotle. *Art of Rhetoric*. Translated by J. H. Freese. LCL. Cambridge: Harvard University Press, 1926.

Arnaoutoglou, Ilias. *Ancient Greek Laws: A Sourcebook*. London: Routledge, 1998.

Ascough, Richard S. *Lydia: Paul's Cosmopolitan Hostess*. Collegeville, MN: Liturgical Press, 2009.

———. *Paul's Macedonian Associations*. WUNT 2/161. Tübingen: Mohr Siebeck, 2003.

Ast, Rodney, and Julia Lougovaya. "The Art of Isopsephism in the Greco-Roman World." Pages 82–98 in *Ägyptische Magie und ihre Umwelt*.

Edited by Joachim Hengstl et al. Philippika: Altertumswissenschaftliche Abhandlungen Contributions to the Study of Ancient World Cultures 80. Wiesbaden: Harrassowitz, 2015.

Aune, David E. *Revelation 6–16*. WBC 52B. Nashville: Nelson, 1998.

Badian, Ernst. "History from 'Square Brackets.'" *ZPE* 79 (1989): 59–70.

Bagnall, Roger S. "Dating the Graffiti." Pages 36–40 in *Graffiti from the Basilica in the Agora of Smyrna*. Edited by Roger S. Bagnall et al. New York: New York University Press, 2016.

———. *Everyday Writing in the Graeco-Roman East*. Berkeley: University of California Press, 2011.

———. "General Characteristics of the Graffiti." Pages 20–22 in *Graffiti from the Basilica in the Agora of Smyrna*. Edited by Roger S. Bagnall et al. New York: New York University Press, 2016.

———. "Isopsephisms of Desire." Pages 48–52 in *Graffiti from the Basilica in the Agora of Smyrna*. Edited by Roger S. Bagnall et al. New York: New York University Press, 2016.

Bagnall, Roger S., and Peter Derow, eds. *The Hellenistic Period: Historical Sources in Translation*. Malden, MA: Blackwell, 2004.

Bagnall, Roger S., et al. "The Graffiti." Pages 55–462 in *Graffiti from the Basilica in the Agora of Smyrna*. Edited by Roger S. Bagnall et al. New York: New York University Press, 2016.

Baird, J. A., and Claire Taylor. "Ancient Graffiti in Context: Introduction." Pages 1–19 in *Ancient Graffiti in Context*. Edited by J. A. Baird and Claire Taylor. New York: Routledge, 2011.

Balz, Horst, and Gerhard Schneider, eds. *Exegetical Dictionary of the New Testament*. 3 vols. Grand Rapids: Eerdmans, 1990–1993.

Barclay, John M. G. "Conflict in Thessalonica." *CBQ* 55 (1993): 512–30.

———. "Thessalonica and Corinth: Social Contrasts in Pauline Christianity." *JSNT* 47 (1992): 49–74.

Barrett, C. K. *A Commentary on the First Epistle to the Corinthians*. HNTC. New York: Harper & Row, 1968.

———. *A Critical and Exegetical Commentary on the Acts of the Apostles*. ICC. 2 vols. Edinburgh: T&T Clark, 1998.

Bauckham, Richard. *The Climax of Prophecy: Studies on the Book of Revelation*. Edinburgh: T&T Clark, 1993.

———. *Jesus and the God of Israel: God Crucified and Other Studies on the New Testament's Christology of Divine Identity*. Grand Rapids: Eerdmans, 2008.

Baudissin, W. G. *Kyrios als Gottesname im Judentum und seine Stelle in der Religionsgeschichte.* 4 vols. Giessen: Töpelmann, 1926–1929.

Baunack, Johannes, et al., eds. *Sammlung der griechischen Dialekt-Inschriften II.* Göttingen: Vandenhoeck & Ruprecht, 1885–1899.

Beale, G. K. *The Book of Revelation: A Commentary on the Greek Text.* Grand Rapids: Eerdmans, 1999.

Beard, Mary, John North, and Simon R. F. Price. *Religions of Rome.* 2 vols. Cambridge: Cambridge University Press, 1998.

Benary, Ferdinand. "Interpretation of the Number 666 (χξς) in the Apocalypse (13:18) and the Various Reading 616 (χις)." Translated by Henry Boynton Smith. *Bibliotheca Sacra and Theological Review* 1 (1844): 84–86.

Benefiel, Rebecca R. "Dialogues of Ancient Graffiti in the House of Maius Castricius in Pompeii." *AJA* 114 (2010): 59–101.

Benoit, P., J. T. Milik, and R. de Vaux. *Les grottes de Murabbaât.* DJD 2. Oxford: Clarendon, 1961.

Betz, Hans Dieter. *Galatians: A Commentary on Paul's Letter to the Churches in Galatia.* Hermeneia. Philadelphia: Fortress, 1979.

———, ed. *The Greek Magical Papyri in Translation: Including the Demotic Spells.* 2nd ed. Chicago: University of Chicago Press, 1992.

Biblia Hebraica Stuttgartensia. 4th ed. Edited by Karl Elliger, Wilhelm Rudolph, et al. Stuttgart: Deutsche Bibelgesellschaft, 1997.

Birdsall, J. Neville. "Irenaeus and the Number of the Beast: Revelation 13,18." Pages 349–59 in *New Testament Textual Criticism and Exegesis.* Edited by A. Denaux. Leuven: Leuven University Press, 2002.

Blount, Brian K. *Revelation: A Commentary.* Louisville: Westminster John Knox, 2009.

Blue, Bradley B. "Acts and the House Church." Pages 119–222 in *The Book of Acts in Its Graeco-Roman Setting.* Vol. 2 of *The Book of Acts in Its First Century Setting Volume 2.* Edited by David W. Gill and Conrad Gempf. Grand Rapids: Eerdmans, 1994.

———. "The House Church at Corinth and the Lord's Supper: Famine, Food Supply, and the *Present Distress.*" *CTR* 5 (1991): 229–39.

Blümel, Wolfgang, ed. *Die Inschriften von Iasos.* 2 vols. Bonn: Habelt, 1985.

———, ed. *Die Inschriften von Mylasa.* 2 vols. Inschriften griechischer Städte aus Kleinasien 34–35. Bonn: Habelt, 1987–1988.

Bockmuehl, Markus. *The Epistle to the Philippians.* BNTC. Peabody, MA: Hendrickson, 1998.

Bodel, John. "Appendix: A Brief Guide to Some Standard Collections." Pages 153–74 in *Epigraphic Evidence: Ancient History from Inscriptions*. Edited by John Bodel. London: Routledge, 2001.

———, ed. *Epigraphic Evidence: Ancient History from Inscriptions*. London: Routledge, 2001.

———. "Epigraphy and the Ancient Historian." Pages 1–56 in *Epigraphic Evidence: Ancient History from Inscriptions*. Edited by John Bodel. London: Routledge, 2001.

———. "Inscriptions and Literacy." Pages 745–63 in *The Oxford Handbook of Roman Epigraphy*. Edited by Christer Bruun and Jonathan Edmondson. Oxford: Oxford University Press, 2015.

Boeckh, August, ed. *Corpus Inscriptionum Graecarum*. 4 vols. Berlin, 1828–1877.

Botterweck, G. Johannes, and Helmer Ringgren, eds. *Theological Dictionary of the Old Testament*. Translated by John T. Willis et al. 8 vols. Grand Rapids: Eerdmans, 1974–2006.

Bousset, Wilhelm. *The Antichrist Legend: A Chapter in Christian and Jewish Folklore*. Translated by A. H. Keane. London, 1896.

———. *Die Offenbarung Johannis*. Göttingen: Vandenhoeck & Ruprecht, 1906.

———. *Kyrios Christos: A History of the Belief in Christ from the Beginnings of Christianity to Irenaeus*. Translated by John E. Staley. Nashville: Abingdon, 1970.

Bowersock, G. W. *Augustus and the Greek World*. Oxford: Clarendon, 1965.

Boxall, Ian. *The Revelation of Saint John*. BNTC. Peabody, MA: Hendrickson, 2006.

Brélaz, Cédric, ed. *Corpus des Inscriptions grecques et latines de Philippes. Tome II La colonie romaine, Part 1 La vie publique de la colonie*. Athens: École française d'Athènes, 2014.

———. "'Outside the City Gate': Center and Periphery in Paul's Preaching in Philippi." Pages 123–40 in *The Urban World and the First Christians*. Edited by Steve Walton, Paul R. Trebilco, and David W. J. Gill. Grand Rapids: Eerdmans, 2017.

———. *Philippes, colonie romaine d'Orient. Recherches d'histoire institutionnelle et sociale*. BCHSup 59. Athens: École française d'Athènes, 2018.

Bremen, Riet van. *The Limits of Participation: Women and Civic Life in the Greek East in the Hellenistic and Roman Periods*. Amsterdam: J. C. Gieben, 1996.

Brocke, Christoph vom. *Thessaloniki—Stadt des Kassander und Gemeinde des Paulus*. WUNT 2/125. Tübingen: Mohr Siebeck, 2001.

Brown, Francis, S. R. Driver, and Charles A. Briggs. *A Hebrew and English Lexicon of the Old Testament*. Oxford: Clarendon, 1952.

Brown, Raymond E. "*Episkopē* and *Episkopos*: The New Testament Evidence." *TS* 41 (1980): 322–38.

Bruce, F. F. *1 and 2 Thessalonians*. WBC 45. Waco, TX: Word, 1982.

———. *The Acts of the Apostles: The Greek Text with Introduction and Commentary*. 3rd ed. Grand Rapids: Eerdmans, 1990.

Bruun, Christer. "Latin Inscriptions." Pages 78–82 in vol. 4 of *The Oxford Encyclopedia of Ancient Greece and Rome*. 6 vols. Edited by Michael Gagarin. Oxford: Oxford University Press, 2010.

———. "The Major Corpora and Epigraphic Publications." Pages 66–77 in *The Oxford Handbook of Roman Epigraphy*. Edited by Christer Bruun and Jonathan Edmondson. Oxford: Oxford University Press, 2015.

Bruun, Christer, and Jonathan Edmondson, eds. *The Oxford Handbook of Roman Epigraphy*. Oxford: Oxford University Press, 2015.

Buckler, W. H., and David Robinson. *Sardis VII, Part 1: Greek and Latin Inscriptions*. Publications of the American Society of the Excavation of Sardis. Leiden: Brill, 1932.

Buckler, W. H., William Moir Calder, and William Keith Chambers Guthrie. *Monuments and Documents from Eastern Asia and Western Galatia*. MAMA 4. Manchester: Manchester University Press, 1933.

Bultmann, Rudolf. *Theology of the New Testament*. 2 vols. Translated by Kendrick Grobel. New York: Scribner's Sons, 1951, 1955.

Bureth, Paul. *Les Titulatures imperiales dans les papyrus, les ostraca et les inscriptoins d'Égypte (30 a.C.–284 p.C.)*. Brussells: Foundation égyptologique reine Elisabeth, 1964.

Burnett, D. Clint. *Christ's Enthronement at God's Right Hand and Its Greco-Roman Cultural Context*. BZNW. Berlin: de Gruyter, forthcoming.

———. "Divine Titles for Julio-Claudian Imperials in Corinth: Neglected Factors in Reconstructions of Corinthian Imperial Worship and Its Connections to the Corinthian Church." *CBQ* 82 (2020), forthcoming.

———. "Imperial Divine Honours in Julio-Claudian Thessalonica: A Reassessment of Thessalonian Imperial Cultic Activity." *JBL*, forthcoming.

Cagnat, René, et al, eds. *Inscriptiones graecae ad res romanas pertinentes*. 4 vols. Paris: Ernest Leroux, 1901–1927.

Caird, G. B. *A Commentary on the Revelation of St. John the Divine*. HNTC. New York: Harper & Row, 1966.

Caldelli, Maria Letizia. "Women in the Roman World." Pages 582–604 in *The Oxford Handbook of Roman Epigraphy*. Edited by Christer Bruun and Jonathan Edmondson. Oxford: Oxford University Press, 2015.

Calder, William Moore. "Colonia Caesareia Antiocheia." *JRS* 2 (1912): 79–109.

Calpino, Teresa J. *Women, Work and Leadership in Acts*. WUNT 2/361. Tübingen: Mohr Siebeck, 2014.

Cameron, A. "Inscriptions Relating to Sacral Manumission and Confession." *HTR* 32 (1939): 143–79.

Campbell, Douglas. "Possible Inscriptional Attestation to Sergius Paul[l]us (Acts 13:6–12), and the Implications for Pauline Chronology." *JTS* 56 (2005): 1–29.

Cancik, Hubert. "Der Kaiser-Eid: Zur Praxis der römischen Herrscherverehrung." Pages 29–45 in *Die Praxis der Herrscherverehrung in Rom und seinen Provinzen*. Edited by Hubert Cancik and Konrad Hitzl. Tübingen: Mohr Siebeck, 2003.

Caneva, Stefano G., and Aurian Delli Pizzi. "Given to a Deity? Religious and Social Reappraisal of Human Consecrations in the Hellenistic and Roman East." *ClQ* 65 (2015): 167–91.

Carcopino, Jérôme. *Daily Life in Ancient Rome*. Translated by E. O. Lorimer. 2nd ed. New Haven: Yale University Press, 2003.

Cerfaux, Lucien. "Le titre Kyrios et la dignité royale de Jésus." Pages 3–63 in vol. 1 of *Recueil Lucien Cerfaux: Études d'Exégèse et d'Histoire Religieuse de Monseigneur Cerfaux*. 3 vols. Gembloux: Duculot, 1954.

Charles, R. H. *A Critical and Exegetical Commentary on the Revelation of St. John*. ICC. 2 vols. Edinburgh: T&T Clark, 1920.

Charlesworth, James, et al. *Miscellaneous Texts from the Judaean Desert*. DJD 38. Oxford: Clarendon, 2000.

Chioffi, Laura. "[---] *Capys* [---] *cum moenia sulco signaret* [---]. Un nuovo termine di pomerium da Capua." Pages 231–41 in *Se déplacer dans l'Empire romain Approches épigraphiques. XVIIIe rencontre franco-italienne d'épigraphie du monde romain, Bordeaux 7–8 octobre 2011*. Edited by Ségolène Demougin and Milagros Navarro Caballero. Paris: de Boccard, 2014.

Cicero. *The Verrine Orations*. Translated by L. H. G. Greenwood. 2 vols. LCL. Cambridge: Harvard University Press, 1928, 1935.

Clarke, Edward Daniel. *Travels in Various Countries of Europe, Asia, and Africa*. London, 1816.

Cohick, Lynn H. *Women in the World of the Earliest Christians: Illuminating Ancient Ways of Life*. Grand Rapids: Baker Academic, 2009.

Collart, Paul. *Philippes ville de Macédoine depuis ses origines jusqu'à la fin de l'époque romaine*. 2 vols. Paris: de Boccard, 1937.

Collart, Paul, and Pierre Ducrey. "Catalogue." BCHSup 2 (1975): 27–196.

———. "Étude des types et de leur representation." BCHSup 2 (1975): 197–251.

Collingwood, R. G., and R. P. Wright, eds. *The Roman Inscriptions of Britain*. Vol. 1, *Inscriptions on Stone*. Oxford: Clarendon, 1965.

Collins, Raymond F. *First Corinthians*. SP 7. Collegeville, MN: Liturgical Press, 1999.

Connolly, Serena. "Ὀμνύω αὐτὸν τὸν Σεβαστὸν: The Greek Oath in the Roman World." Pages 203–16 in *Horkos: The Oath in Greek Society*. Edited by Alan H. Sommerstein and Judith Fletcher. Exeter: Bristol Phoenix Press, 2007.

Conzelmann, Hans. *1 Corinthians: A Commentary on the First Epistle to the Corinthians*. Translated by James W. Leitch. Hermeneia. Minneapolis: Fortress, 1975.

———. *Acts of the Apostles: A Commentary on Acts of the Apostles*. Translated by James Limburg, A. Thomas Kraabel, and Donald H. Juel. Hermeneia. Philadelphia: Fortress, 1987.

Cook, B. F. *Greek Inscriptions*. Berkeley: University of California Press, 1987.

Cooley, Alison E. *The Cambridge Manual of Latin Epigraphy*. Cambridge: Cambridge University Press, 2012.

———, ed. *Res Gestae Divi Augusti: Text, Translation and Commentary*. Cambridge: Cambridge University Press, 2009.

Corpus Inscriptionum Semiticarum. 5 vols. Paris: Reipublicae Typographeo, 1881–1962.

Cotton, Hannah M., et al., eds. *Corpus Inscriptionum Iudaeae/Palaestinae: A Multilingual Corpus of Inscriptions from Alexander to Muhammad*. 6 vols. Berlin: de Gruyter, 2008–.

Crampa, Jonas, ed. *Greek Inscriptions*. Labraunda: Swedish Excavations and Researches III.1–2. Lund and Stockholm: 1969, 1972.

Crawford, M. H., ed. *Roman Statutes*. 2 vols. London: Institute of Classical Studies, 1996.

Cullmann, Oscar. *The Christology of the New Testament*. Translated by Shirley Guthrie and Charles A. M. Hall. Rev. ed. Philadelphia: Westminster, 1963.

Cumont, Franz. "Un serment de fidélité à l'empereur Auguste." *REG* 14 (1901): 26–45.

Cyriac of Ancona. *Later Travels*. The I Tatti Renaissance Library. Edited and translated by Edward W. Bodnar with Clive Foss. Cambridge: Harvard University Press, 2003.

———. *Life and Early Travels*. The I Tatti Renaissance Library. Edited and translated by Charles Mitchell, Edward W. Bodnar, and Clive Foss. Cambridge: Harvard University Press, 2015.

D'Ambra, Eve. *Roman Women*. Cambridge: Cambridge University Press, 2007.

D'Angelo, Mary Rose. "Women Partners in the New Testament." *JFSR* 6 (1990): 65–86.

Dahl, Nils A. "Euodia and Syntyche and Paul's Letter to the Philippians." Pages 3–15 in *The Social World of the First Christians: Essays in Honor of Wayne A. Meeks*. Edited by L. Michael White and O. Larry Yarbrough. Minneapolis: Fortress, 1995.

Dalman, Gustaf. *The Words of Jesus: Considered in the Light of Post-Biblical Jewish Writings and the Aramaic Language*. Translated by D. M. Kay. Edinburgh: T&T Clark, 1902.

Danker, Frederick W., Walter Bauer, William F. Arndt, and F. Wilbur Gingrich. *Greek-English Lexicon of the New Testament and Other Early Christian Literature*. 3rd ed. Chicago: University of Chicago Press, 2000.

Dawkins, R. M. "The Sanctuary." Pages 1–51 in *The Sanctuary of Artemis Orthia at Sparta*. Edited by R. M. Dawkins. The Society for the Promotion of Hellenic Studies Paper No. 5. London: MacMillan, 1926.

Deissmann, Adolf. *Light from the Ancient East: The New Testament Illustrated by Recently Discovered Texts of the Graeco-Roman World*. Translated by Lionel R. M. Strachan. 4th ed. London: Hodder & Stoughton, 1910. Repr., Grand Rapids: Baker Books, 1978.

Delacoulonche, Alfred. "Mémoire sur le berceau de la puissance macédonienne des bords de l'Haliacmon et ceux de l'Axius." *Archives des missions scientifiques et littéraires* 8 (1859): 67–288.

Dessau, Hermann, ed. *Inscriptiones latinae selectae*. 3 vols. Berlin: Weidmannos, 1892–1916.

Dibelius, Martin, and Hans Conzelmann. *The Pastoral Epistles: A Commentary on the Pastoral Epistles*. Translated by Philip Buttolph and Adela Yarbro. Hermeneia. Philadelphia: Fortress, 1972.

Dio Cassius. *Roman History*. Translated by Earnest Cary. 9 vols. LCL. Cambridge: Harvard University Press, 1914–1927.

Dittenberger, Wilhelm, ed. *Orientis Graeci Inscriptiones Selectae*. 2 vols. Leipzig: Hirzel, 1903–1905.

Dittenberger, Wilhelm, et al, eds. *Sylloge Inscriptionum Graecarum*. 4 vols. 3rd ed. Leipzig: Hirzel, 1915–1924.

Dobschütz, Ernst von. *Die Thessalonischer-Briefe*. KEK 7. Göttingen: Vandenhoeck & Ruprecht, 1909.

Dodd, C. H. *According to the Scriptures: The Sub-Structure of New Testament Theology*. London: Nisbet, 1952.

Donfried, Karl Paul. "The Cults of Thessalonica and the Thessalonian Correspondence." *NTS* 31 (1985): 336–56.

———. "The Theology of 1 Thessalonians." Pages 1–79 in *The Theology of the Shorter Pauline Letters*. Cambridge: Cambridge University Press, 1993.

Dornseiff, Franz. *Das Alphabet in Mystik und Magie*. 2nd ed. Leipzig: Teubner, 1925.

Dreyer, Boris, and Helmut Engelmann. "Augustus und Germanicus im ionischen Metropolis." *ZPE* 158 (2006): 173–82.

Dunbabin, Katherine M. D. *The Roman Banquet: Images of Conviviality*. Cambridge: Cambridge University Press, 2003.

———. "Ut Graeco More Biberetur: Greeks and Romans on the Dining Couch." Pages 81–101 in *Meals in Social Context: Aspects of the Communal Meal in the Hellenistic and Roman World*. Edited by Inge Nielsen and Hanne Sigismund Nielsen. Oxford: Aarhus University Press, 1998.

Dunbabin, Katherine M. D., and William J. Slater. "Roman Dining." Pages 438–66 in *The Oxford Handbook of Social Relations in the Roman World*. Edited by Michael Peachin. Oxford: Oxford University Press, 2011.

Dunn, James D. G. *The Theology of Paul the Apostle*. Grand Rapids: Eerdmans, 1998.

Eckstein, Arthur M. "Macedonia and Rome, 221–146 BC." Pages 225–50 in *A Companion to Ancient Macedonia*. Edited by Joseph Roismas and Ian Worthington. Malden, MA: Blackwell, 2010.

Edelstein, Emma J., and Ludwig Edelstein. *Asclepius: A Collection and Interpretation of the Testimonies*. 2 vols. Baltimore: Johns Hopkins University Press, 1945.

Edmondson, Jonathan. "Inscribing Roman Texts: *Officinae*, Layout, and Carving Techniques." Pages 111–30 in *The Oxford Handbook of Roman Epigraphy*. Edited by Christer Bruun and Jonathan Edmondson. Oxford: Oxford University Press, 2015.

Edson, Charles, ed. *Inscriptiones Graecae, X: Inscriptiones Epiri, Macedoniae, Thraciae, Scythiae. Pars II.1. Inscriptiones Thessalonicae et viciniae*. Berlin: de Gruyter, 1972.

Elliger, Winfried. *Paulus in Griechenland: Philippi, Thessaloniki, Athen, Korinth*. Stuttgart: Katholisches Bibelwerk, 1987.

Elliott, Tom. "Epigraphic Evidence for Boundary Disputes in the Roman Empire." PhD diss., University of North Carolina at Chapel Hill, 2004.

———. "Epigraphy and Digital Resources." Pages 78–85 in *The Oxford Handbook of Roman Epigraphy*. Edited by Christer Bruun and Jonathan Edmondson. Oxford: Oxford University Press, 2015.

Erskine, Andrew. "The Romans as Common Benefactors." *Historia* 43 (1994): 70–87.

Ersoy, Akin. "Introduction." Pages 1–20 in *Graffiti from the Basilica in the Agora of Smyrna*. Edited by Roger S. Bagnall et al. New York: New York University Press, 2016.

Farbridge, Maurice H. *Studies in Biblical and Semitic Symbolism*. London: Kegan Paul, Trench, Trubner, 1923.

Fee, Gordon D. *The First Epistle to the Corinthians*. Rev. ed. NICNT. Grand Rapids: Eerdmans, 2014.

———. *Paul's Letter to the Philippians*. NICNT. Grand Rapids: Eerdmans, 1995.

Ferguson, Everett. "Bishop." Pages 182–85 in *Encyclopedia of Early Christianity*. Edited by Everett Ferguson. 2nd ed. New York: Routledge, 1999.

Fitzmyer, Joseph A. *The Acts of the Apostles: A New Translation with Introduction and Commentary*. AB 31. New York: Doubleday, 1998.

———. *First Corinthians: A New Translation with Introduction and Commentary*. AYB 32. New Haven: Yale University Press, 2008.

———. "Kyrios and Maranatha and Their Aramaic Background." Pages 218–35 in *To Advance the Gospel: New Testament Studies*. New York: Crossroad, 1981.

———. "The Semitic Background of the New Testament *Kyrios*-Title." Pages 115–42 in *A Wandering Aramean: Collected Aramaic Essays*. Missoula, MT: Scholars Press, 1979.

Foerster, Werner, and Gottfried Quell. *Lord*. Bible Key Words. Translated by H. P. Kingdon. London: Black, 1933.

Fournier, Julien, ed. *Philippes, de la Préhistoire à Byzance: études d'archéologie et d'histoire*. BCHSup 55. Athènes: École française d'Athènes, 2016.

Fraatz, C. Thomas. "Blessed Is the One Who Reads and Those Who Hear the Words of Prophecy: Rome and Revelation's Use of Scripture." PhD diss., Boston College, 2017.

Fränkel, Max, ed. *Die Inschriften von Pergamon*. Altertümer von Pergamon 8.1, 2. 2 vols. Berlin: W. Spemann, 1890–1895.

Freedman, David Noel, ed. *Anchor Bible Dictionary*. 6 vols. New York: Doubleday, 1992.

Frenschkowski, Marco. "Kyrios in Context: Q 6:46, the Emperor as 'Lord,' and the Political Implications of Christology in Q." Pages 95–114 in *Zwischen den Reichen: Neues Testament und Römische Herrschaft*. Edited by Michael Labahn and Jürgen Zangenberg. Tübingen: Francke, 2002.

Frey, Jean-Baptiste, ed. *Corpus of Jewish Inscriptions: Jewish Inscriptions from the Third Century B.C. to the Seventh Century A.D.* Sussidi allo studio delle antichità cristiane 1. New York: Ktav, 1975.

Friesen, Steven J. *Imperial Cults and the Apocalypse of John*. Oxford: Oxford University Press, 2001.

Fujii, Takashi. *Imperial Cult and Imperial Representation in Roman Cyprus*. Heidelberger Althistorische Beiträge und Epigraphische Studien 53. Stuttgart: Steiner, 2013.

Fuller, Reginald. *Foundations of New Testament Christology*. New York: Scribner's Sons, 1965.

Furnish, Victor Paul. *II Corinthians: Translated with Introduction, Notes, and Commentary*. AB 32A. Garden City: Doubleday, 1984.

Gaertringen, Friedrich Hiller von, ed. *Inschriften von Priene*. Berlin: Reimer, 1906.

Gager, John G., ed. *Curse Tablets and Binding Spells from the Ancient World*. Oxford: Oxford University Press, 1992.

Galli, Marco. "Pilgrimage as Elite *Habitus*: Educated Pilgrims in Sacred Landscapes during the Second Sophistic." Pages 253–90 in *Pilgrimage in Graeco-Roman and Early Christian Antiquity: Seeing the Gods*. Edited by Jaś Elsner and Ian Rutherford. Oxford: Oxford University Press, 2005.

Gargola, Daniel J. "Grain Distribution and the Revenue of the Temple of Hera on Samos." *Phoenix* 46 (1992): 12–28.

Garland, David E. *1 Corinthians*. BECNT. Grand Rapids: Baker Academic, 2003.

Gauthier, Philippe. *Les cites grecques et leurs bienfaiteurs*. BCHSup 12. Paris: École française d'Athènes, 1985.

Gerber, Albrecht. *Deissmann the Philologist*. BZNW 171. Berlin: de Gruyter, 2009.

Getty-Sullivan, Mary Ann. *Women in the New Testament*. Collegeville, MN: Liturgical Press, 2001.

Gibson, John C. L. *Textbook of Syrian Semitic Inscriptions*. Vol. 3, *Phoenician Inscriptions Including Inscriptions in the Mixed Dialect of Arslan Tash*. Oxford: Oxford University Press, 1982.

Giesen, Heinz. *Die Offenbarung des Johannes*. RNT. Regensburg: Pustet, 1997.
Gillman, Florence M. *Women Who Knew Paul*. Collegeville, MN: Liturgical Press, 1992.
Giordano, Carlo. "Le iscrizioni della casa di M. Fabio Rufo." *Rendiconti della Accademia di archeologia, lettere e belle arti* 41 (1966): 73–89.
Girone, Maria. *Ἰάματα: Guarigioni miracolose di Asclepio in testi epigrafici*. Bari, Italy: Levante, 1998.
Goldsworthy, Adrian. *Augustus: First Emperor of Rome*. New Haven: Yale University Press, 2014.
———. *Caesar: Life of a Colossus*. New Haven: Yale University Press, 2006.
———. *In the Name of Rome: The Men Who Won the Roman Empire*. New Haven: Yale University Press, 2003.
———. *Pax Romana: War, Peace and Conquest in the Roman World*. London: Weidenfeld & Nicolson, 2016.
González, Julián. "The First Oath *pro salute Augusti* Found in Baetica." *ZPE* 72 (1988): 113–27.
Gradel, Ittai. "Roman Apotheosis." Pages 186–99 in vol. 2 of *Thesaurus Cultus et Rituum Antiquorum (ThesCRA)*. Los Angeles: Getty, 2004.
Graf, Fritz. "Oath/Serment/Eid/Giuramento." Pages 237–46 in vol. 3 of *Thesaurus Cultus et Rituum Antiquorum (ThesCRA)*. Los Angeles: Getty, 2005.
Grammenos, D. V., ed. *Roman Thessaloniki*. Translated by David Hardy. Thessaloniki Archaeological Museum Publications 1. Thessaloniki: Archaeological Museum, 2003.
Grenfell, Bernard, et al., eds. *The Oxyrhynchus Papyri*. London: Egypt Exploration Fund, 1898–.
Habicht, Christian. *Divine Honors for Mortal Men in Greek Cities: The Early Cases*. Translated by John Noël Dillon. Ann Arbor: Michigan Classical Press, 2016.
———. "Samische Volksbeschlüsse der hellenistischer Zeit." *MDAI(A)* 72 (1957): 152–274.
Haenchen, Ernst. *Acts of the Apostles: A Commentary*. Philadelphia: Westminster, 1971.
Hahn, Ferdinand. *The Titles of Jesus in Christology: Their History in Early Christianity*. Translated by Harold Knight and George Ogg. Cleveland, OH: World Publishing Company, 1969.
Hallo, William H., ed. *The Context of Scripture*. 3 vols. Leiden: Brill, 1997–2002.
Hamilton, Mary. *Incubation or the Cure of Disease in Pagan Temples and Church Christians*. London: Henderson, 1906.

Harland, Philip A., ed. *Greco-Roman Associations: Texts, Translations, and Commentary*. Vol. 2, *North Coast of the Black Sea, Asia Minor*. BZNW 204. Berlin: de Gruyter, 2014.

Harris, B. F. "Oaths of Allegiance to Caesar." *Prudentia* 14 (1982): 109–22.

Harris, William V. *Ancient Literacy*. Cambridge: Harvard University Press, 1989.

Harrison, James K. *Paul and Imperial Authorities at Thessalonica and Rome: A Study in the Conflict of Ideology*. WUNT 273. Tübingen: Mohr Siebeck, 2011.

Hasluck, F. W. *Cyzicus*. Cambridge: Cambridge University Press, 1910.

Hawthorne, Gerald F., and Ralph P. Martin. *Philippians*. Rev. ed. WBC 43. Grand Rapids: Zondervan, 2004.

Hawthorne, Gerald F., Ralph P. Martin, and Daniel G. Reid, eds. *Dictionary of Paul and His Letters*. Downers Grove, IL: InterVarsity Press, 1993.

Hay, David. *Glory at the Right Hand: Psalm 110 in Early Christianity*. Nashville: Abingdon, 1973.

Hays, Richard B. *First Corinthians*. IBC. Louisville: Westminster John Knox, 1997.

Healey, John F. *The Nabataean Tomb Inscriptions of Mada'in Salih*. JSSSup 1. Oxford: Oxford University Press, 1993.

———. *Textbook of Syrian Semitic Inscriptions*. Vol. 4, *Aramaic Inscriptions and Documents of the Roman Period*. Oxford: Oxford University Press, 2009.

Hendrix, Holland Lee. "Thessalonicans Honour Romans." PhD Thesis, Harvard University, 1984.

Hengel, Martin. *The "Hellenization" of Judaea in the First Century After Christ*. Translated by John Bowdon. London: SCM, 1989.

———. *Judaism and Hellenism: Studies in Their Encounter in Palestine during the Early Hellenistic Period*. Translated by John Bowden. 2 vols. Philadelphia: Fortress, 1974.

Herrmann, Peter. "Die Inschriften römischer Zeit aus dem Heraion von Samos." *MDAI(A)* 77 (1960): 63–183.

———. *Die römische Kaisereid: Untersuchungen zu seiner Herkunft und Entwickung*. Hypomnemeta 20. Göttingen: Vanderhoeck & Ruprecht, 1968.

Hofius, Otfried. "The Lord's Supper and the Lord's Supper Tradition: Reflections on 1 Corinthians 11:23b–25." Pages 75–115 in *One Loaf, One Cup: Ecumenical Studies on 1 Cor. 11 and other Eucharistic Texts*. Edited by B. F. Meyer. Macon, GA: Mercer University Press, 1993.

Holloway, Paul A. *Philippians*. Hermeneia. Minneapolis: Fortress, 2017.

Holmes, Michael W. *The Apostolic Fathers: Greek Texts and English Translations*. 3rd ed. Grand Rapids: Baker Academic, 2007.

Horrell, David G. "Domestic Space and Christian Meetings at Corinth: Imagining New Contexts and the Buildings East of the Theatre." *NTS* 50 (2004): 349–69.

Horsley, G. H. R., and Stephen R. Llewelyn, eds. *New Documents Illustrating Early Christianity*. North Ryde, NSW: The Ancient History Documentary Research Centre, Macquarie University, 1981–.

Horster, Marietta. "Urban Infrastructure and Euergetism outside the City of Rome." Pages 515–36 in *The Oxford Handbook of Roman Epigraphy*. Edited by Christer Bruun and Jonathan Edmondson. Oxford: Oxford University Press, 2015.

Hossfeld, Frank-Lothar, and Erich Zenger. *Psalms 3: A Commentary on Psalms 101–150*. Hermeneia. Translated by Linda M. Maloney. Minneapolis: Fortress, 2011.

Humann, Carl, et al., eds. *Altertümer von Hierapolis*. Jahrbuch des Kaiserlich Deutschen Archäologischen Instituts Ergänzungsheft 4. Berlin, 1898.

Hunt, A. S., C. C. Edgar, and D. L. Page, eds. *Select Papyri*. 3 vols. Cambridge: Harvard University Press, 1932, 1942.

Hurtado, Larry W. "Lord." Pages 560–69 in *Dictionary of Paul and his Letters*. Edited by Gerald F. Hawthorne, Ralph P. Martin, and Daniel G. Reid. Downers Grove, IL: InterVarsity Press, 1993.

———. *Lord Jesus Christ: Devotion to Jesus in Earliest Christianity*. Grand Rapids: Eerdmans, 2003.

———. "New Testament Christology: A Critique of Bousset's Influence." *TS* 40 (1979): 306–17.

Jewett, Robert. *The Thessalonian Correspondence: Pauline Rhetoric and Millenarian Piety*. Philadelphia: Fortress, 1986.

Johnson, Luke Timothy. *The First and Second Letters to Timothy: A New Translation with Introduction and Commentary*. AB 35A. New York: Doubleday, 2001.

Josephus. Translated by Henry St. J. Thackeray et al. 10 vols. LCL. Cambridge: Harvard University Press, 1926–1965.

Judge, E. A. "The Decrees of Caesar at Thessalonica." *RTR* 30 (1971): 1–7.

Juel, Donald. *Messianic Exegesis: Christological Interpretation of the Old Testament in Early Christianity*. Philadelphia: Fortress, 1992.

Juvenal. *Satires*. Translated by Susanna Morton Braund. LCL. Cambridge: Harvard University Press, 2004.

Kalvesmaki, Joel. "Isopsephic Inscriptions from Iasos ('Inschriften von Iasos' 419) and Shnān ('IGLS' 1403)." *ZPE* 161 (2007): 261–68.

Keegan, Peter. *Graffiti in Antiquity*. London: Routledge, 2014.

Keener, Craig S. *Acts: An Exegetical Commentary*. Vol. 3, *15:1–23:35*. Grand Rapids: Baker Academic, 2014.

Kent, John Harvey, ed. *Corinth VIII, Part III The Inscriptions 1926–1950*. Princeton, NJ: The American School of Classical Studies at Athens, 1966.

Keppie, Lawrence. *Understanding Roman Inscriptions*. Baltimore: Johns Hopkins University Press, 1991.

Kilgallen, John J. "Persecution in the Acts of the Apostles." Pages 143–60 in *Luke and Acts*. Edited by Gerald O'Collins and Gilberto Marconi. Translated by Matthew J. O'Connell. New York: Paulist, 1993.

Kirchner, Johannes, and Ericus Sironen, eds. *Inscriptiones Graecae II et III: Inscriptiones Atticae Euclidis anno posteriores*. 2nd ed. Berlin: de Gruyter, 1913–1940, 2008.

Kittel, Gerhard, and Gerhard Friedrich, eds. *Theological Dictionary of the New Testament*. Translated by Geoffrey W. Bromiley. 10 vols. Grand Rapids: Eerdmans, 1964–1976.

Kittredge, Cynthia Briggs. *Community and Authority: The Rhetoric of Obedience in the Pauline Tradition*. HTS 45. Harrisburg, PA: Trinity, 1998.

Klauck, Hans-Josef. "Do They Never Come Back? 'Nero Redivivus' and the Apocalypse of John." *CBQ* 63 (2001): 683–98.

———. *Herrenmahl und Hellenistischer Kult: Eine religionsgeschichtliche Untersuchung zum ersten Korintherbrief*. Münster: Aschendorff, 1982.

Klauser, Theodor, et al., eds. *Reallexikon für Antike und Christentum*. Stuttgart: Hiersemann, 1950–.

Knibbe, D., H. Engelmann, and B. Iplikcioglu, "Neue Inschriften aus Ephesos XII." *JÖAI* 62 (1993): 113–50.

Koester, Craig. "The Number of the Beast in Revelation 13 in Light of Papyri, Graffiti, and Inscriptions." *Journal of Early Christian History* 6 (2016): 1–21.

———. *Revelation: A New Translation with Introduction and Commentary*. AYB 38A. New Haven: Yale University Press, 2014.

Kolbe, Walter, ed. *Inscriptiones Graecae, V,1. Inscriptiones Laconiae et Messeniae*. Berlin: de Gruyter, 1913.

Kraemer, Ross Shepherd. *Her Share of the Blessings: Women's Religions among Pagans, Jews, and Christians in the Greco-Roman World*. New York: Oxford University Press, 1992.

Kraus, Hans-Joachim. *Psalms 60–150*. Translated by Hilton Osward. Minneapolis: Augsburg Fortress, 1989.

Kroll, W., ed. *Historia Alexandri Magni (Pseudo-Callisthenes). Resensio vetusta*. Berlin: Weidmann, 1926.

La Regina, Adriano. *Archaeological Guide to Rome*. Translated by Richard Sadleir. Milan: Electa, 2017.

Ladstätter, Sabine, with Barbara Beck-Brandt, Martin Steskal, and Norbert Zimmermann. *Terrace House 2 in Ephesos: An Archaeological Guide*. Translated by Nicole M. High with Emma Sachs. Istanbul: Homer Kitabevi, 2013.

Lampe, Peter. "Das korinthische Herrenmahl im Schnittpunkt hellenistisch-römischer Mahlpraxis und paulinischer Theologia Crucis (1Kor 11,17–34)." *ZNW* 82 (1991): 183–213.

———. "The Eucharist: Identifying with Christ on the Cross." *Int* 48 (1994): 36–49.

Lattimore, Richmond, ed. *Themes in Greek and Latin Epitaphs*. Urbana, IL: University of Illinois Press, 1962.

Leithart, Peter J. *Revelation 12–22*. ICC. London: Bloomsbury T&T Clark, 2018.

Levick, Barbara. "Some Augustan Oaths." Pages 245–56 in *Scritti di storia per Mario Pani*. Edited by Silvana Cagnazzi et al. Bari, Italy: Edipuglia, 2011.

Levine, Lee I. *The Ancient Synagogue: The First Thousand Years*. 2nd ed. New Haven: Yale University Press, 2000.

Liddell, Henry George, Robert Scott, Henry Stuart Jones. *A Greek-English Lexicon*. 9th ed. with revised supplement. Oxford: Clarendon, 1996.

Lim, Timothy H. "Deuteronomy in the Judaism of the Second Temple Period." Pages 6–26 in *Deuteronomy and the New Testament: The New Testament and the Scriptures of Israel*. Edited by Steve Moyise and Maarten J. J. Menken. LSTS 358. New York: T&T Clark, 2007.

Limentani, Ida Calabi. *Epigrafia Latina*. 4th ed. Bologna: Cisalpino, 1989.

Lindars, Barnabas. *New Testament Apologetic: The Doctrinal Significance of the Old Testament Quotations Study Edition*. London: SCM, 1973.

Livy. *History of Rome*. Translated by B. O. Foster et al. 14 vols. LCL. Cambridge: Harvard University Press, 1919–1952.

Llewelyn, Stephen R. "ΣΔ, a Christian Isopsephism." *ZPE* 109 (1995): 125–27.

Lloris, Francisco Beltán. "The 'Epigraphic Habit' in the Roman World." Pages 131–48 in *The Oxford Handbook of Roman Epigraphy*. Edited by

Christer Bruun and Jonathan Edmondson. Oxford: Oxford University Press, 2015.

———. "Latin Epigraphy: The Main Types of Inscriptions." Pages 89–110 in *The Oxford Handbook of Roman Epigraphy*. Edited by Christer Bruun and Jonathan Edmondson. Oxford: Oxford University Press, 2015.

Lohse, Eduard. *Die Offenbarung des Johannes*. NTD 11. Göttingen: Vandenhoeck & Ruprecht, 1983.

Lougovaya, Julia. "Isopsephisms in P. Jena II 15a-b." *ZPE* 176 (2011): 200–204.

Luck, George. *Arcana Mundi: Magic and Occult in the Greek and Roman Worlds; A Collection of Ancient Texts*. 2nd ed. Baltimore: Johns Hopkins University Press, 2006.

Lührmann, Dieter. "The Beginnings of the Church at Thessalonica." Pages 237–41 in *Greeks, Romans, and Christians: Essays in Honor of Abraham J. Malherbe*. Edited by David L. Balch, Everett Ferguson, and Wayne A. Meeks. Minneapolis: Fortress, 1990.

Lupieri, Edmondo F. *A Commentary on the Apocalypse of John*. Translated by Maria Poggi Johnson and Adam Kamesar. Grand Rapids: Eerdmans, 1999.

Ma, John. "Epigraphy and the Display of Authority." Pages 133–58 in *Epigraphy and the Historical Sciences*. Proceedings of the British Academy 177. Edited by John Davies and John Wilkes. Oxford: Oxford University Press, 2012.

MacMullen, Ramsay. "The Epigraphic Habit in the Roman Empire." *AJP* 103 (1982): 233–46.

Malherbe, Abraham J. *The Letters to the Thessalonians: A New Translation with Introduction and Commentary*. AB 32B. New York: Doubleday, 2000.

Malinowski, Francis X. "The Brave Women of Philippi." *BTB* 15 (1985): 60–64.

Manganaro, Giacomo. "Graffiti e iscrizioni funerarie della Sicilia orientale." *Helikon* 3–4 (1962): 485–501.

Marshall, I. Howard. *A Critical and Exegetical Commentary on the Pastoral Epistles*. ICC. Edinburgh: T&T Clark, 1999.

———. "Palestinian and Hellenistic Christianity: Some Critical Comments." *NTS* 19 (1973): 271–87.

Martínez, Florentino García, and Eibert J. C. Tigchelaar. *The Dead Sea Scrolls: Study Edition*. 2 vols. Grand Rapids: Eerdmans, 1997–1998.

Mau, August. *Pompeii: Its Life and Art*. Translated by Francis W. Kelsey. London, 1899.

McLean, B. H. *An Introduction to Greek Epigraphy of the Hellenistic and Roman Periods from Alexander the Great down to the Reign of Constantine (323 B.C.–A.D. 337)*. Ann Arbor: University of Michigan Press, 2002.

Meeks, Wayne A. *The First Urban Christians: The Social World of the Apostle Paul*. 2nd ed. New Haven: Yale University Press, 2003.

Meier, P. Gabriel, ed. *Catalogus codium manu scriptorum qui in Bibliotheca Monasterii Einsidlensis O.S.B. servantur: Tomus I complectens centurias quinque priores*. Einsidlae, Switzerland, 1899.

Meiggs, Russell, and David M. Lewis, eds. *A Selection of Greek Historical Inscriptions to the end of the Fifth Century B.C.* Rev. ed. Oxford: Clarendon, 1988.

Merkelbach, Reinhold, ed. *Die Inschriften von Assos*. Inschriften griechischer Städte aus Kleinasien 4. Bonn: Habelt, 1976.

Merklein, Helmut. "*Marānā* (»unser Herr«) als Bezeichnung des nabatäischen Königs: Eine Analogie zur neutestamentlichen Kyrios-Bezeichnung?" Pages 25–41 in *Von Jesus zum Christus: Christologische Studien*. Edited by Erich Gräßer. BZNW 93. Berlin: de Gruyter, 1998.

Merritt, Benjamin Dean, ed. *Corinth VIII, Part I Greek Inscriptions 1896–1927*. Cambridge: Harvard University Press, 1931.

Metzger, Bruce. *A Textual Commentary on the Greek New Testament*. 2nd ed. Stuttgart: Deutsche Bibelgesellschaft, 1994.

Meyer, Elizabeth. "Explaining the Epigraphic Habit in the Roman Empire: The Evidence of Epitaphs." *JRS* 80 (1990): 74–96.

Michael, Michael George. "666 or 616 (Rev. 13:18)." *BBS* 19 (2000): 77–83.

Migne, Jacques-Paul, ed. *Patrologia Graeca*. 161 vols. Paris: Imprimerie Catholique, 1857–1866.

Millar, Fergus. *The Emperor and the Roman World (31 BC–AD 337)*. London: Duckworth, 1977.

Milligan, George. *St Paul's Epistles to the Thessalonians: The Greek Text with Introduction and Notes*. London: Macmillan, 1908.

Minervini, G. "Studii Pompeiani – Caserma de' Gladiatori." *Bullettino archeologico Napoletano N.S.* 7 (1859): 116–20.

Mitchell, Stephen, and David French, ed. *The Greek and Latin Inscriptions of Ankara (Ancyra)*. Vol. 1, *From Augustus to the End of the Third Century AD*. Beiträge zur Alten Geschichte Band 62. Munich: Beck, 2012.

Mitford, T. B. "A Cypriot Oath of Allegiance to Tiberius." *JRS* 50 (1960): 75–79.

Mommsen, Theodore, et al. *Corpus Inscriptionum Latinarum*. Berlin: Reimer and de Gruyter, 1862–.

Moulton, James H., and George Milligan. *The Vocabulary of the Greek Testament Illustrated from the Papyri and Other Non-Literary Sources*. London: Hodder & Stoughton, 1914–1929.

Murphy-O'Connor, Jerome. "House Churches and the Eucharist." *TBT* 22 (1984): 32–38.

———. "House Churches and the Eucharist." Pages 183–93 in *Keys to First Corinthians: Revisiting the Major Issues*. Oxford: Oxford University Press, 2009.

———. *Paul the Letter-Writer: His World, His Options, His Skills*. *GNS* 41. Collegeville, MN: Liturgical Press, 1995.

———. *St. Paul's Corinth: Texts and Archaeology*. Wilmington, DE: Glazier, 1983.

Nasrallah, Laura S. *Archaeology and the Letters of Paul*. Oxford: Oxford University Press, 2019.

———. "'You Were Bought with a Price': Freedpersons and Things in 1 Corinthians." Pages 54–73 in *Corinth in Contrast: Studies in Inequality*. Edited by Steven J. Friesen, Sarah A. James, and Daniel N. Schowalter. Leiden: Brill, 2014.

Nelis-Clément, Jocelyne, and Damien Nelis. "Petronius' Epigraphic Habit." *Dictynna* 2 (2005): 1–16.

Newton, Charles Thomas, ed. *The Collection of Greek Inscriptions in the British Museum*. 5 vols. London: British Museum, 1874–1916.

Novenson, Matthew V. *Christ among the Messiahs: Christ Language in Paul and Messiah Language in Ancient Judaism*. Oxford: Oxford University Press, 2012.

Novum Testamentum Graecae. 28th Rev. edition. Edited by Barbara and Kurt Aland et al. Stuttgart: Deutsche Bibelgesellschaft, 2012.

Noy, David. "Inscriptions and Papyri: Jewish." Pages 539–41 in *The Dictionary of New Testament Background*. Edited by Craig A. Evans and Stanley E. Porter. Downers Grove, IL: InterVarsity Press, 2000.

Olcott, George N. *Thesaurus Linguae Latinae Epigraphicae: A Dictionary of the Latin Inscriptions*. Rome: Loescher, 1904.

Oliver, James H., ed. *Greek Constitutions of Early Roman Emperors from Inscriptions and Papyri*. Philadelphia: American Philological Society, 1989.

Osborne, Robin. "Greek Epigraphy and Archaeology." Pages 115–29 in *The Diversity of Classical Archaeology*. Edited by Achim Lichtenberger and Rubina Raja. Turnhout, Belgium: Brepols, 2017.

Osiek, Carolyn. *Philippians, Philemon*. ANTC. Nashville: Abingdon, 2000.

Oster, Richard E. "Women, Diaspora Synagogues (Proseuche) and Acts 16:13 (Philippi)." Pages 260–99 in *Faith in Practice: Studies in the Book of Acts; A Festschrift in Honor of Earl and Ottie Mearl Stuckenbruck*. Edited by David A. Fiensy and William D. Howden. Atlanta: European Evangelistic Society, 1995.

Parker, David C. "A New Oxyrhynchus Papyrus of Revelation: P115 (P. Oxy. 4499)." *NTS* 46 (2000): 159–74.

Paton, William R., ed. *Inscriptiones Graecae, XII. Inscriptiones insularum maris Aegaei praeter Delum, 2. Inscriptiones Lesbi, Nesi, Tenedi*. Berlin: de Gruyter, 1899.

Peek, Werner, ed. *Griechische Vers-Inschriften I, Grab-Epigramme*. Berlin: Akademie, 1955.

Perdrizet, Paul. "Isopsephie." *REG* 17 (1904): 350–60.

Peterlin, Davorin. *Paul's Letter to the Philippians in Light of Disunity in the Church*. Leiden: Brill, 1995.

Petronius. *Satyricon*. Translated by Michael Heseltine and W. H. D. Rouse. Revised by E. H. Warmington. LCL. Cambridge: Harvard University Press, 1975.

Petzl, Georg, ed. *Die Beichtinschriften Westkleinasiens*. Bonn: Habelt, 1994.

———, ed. *Tituli Asiae Minoris, V. Tituli Lydiae linguis Graeca et Latina conscripti*. Vienna: Verlag der Österreichischen Akademie der Wissenschaften, 2007.

Philo. Translated by F. H. Colson et al. 10 vols. LCL. Cambridge: Harvard University Press, 1929–1953.

Pilhofer, Peter, ed. *Philippi. Band II Katalog der Inschriften von Philippi 2. Auflage*. WUNT 119. Tübingen: Mohr Siebeck, 2009.

Portefaix, Lilian. *Sisters Rejoice: Paul's Letter to the Philippians and Luke-Acts as Seen by First-Century Philippian Women*. Stockholm: Almqvist & Wiksell, 1988.

Porter, Stanley E. "Inscriptions and Papyri: Greco-Roman." Pages 529–39 in *The Dictionary of New Testament Background*. Edited by Craig A. Evans and Stanley E. Porter. Downers Grove, IL: InterVarsity Press, 2000.

———. "Language and Translation of the New Testament." Pages 184–210 in *The Oxford Handbook of Biblical Studies*. Edited by J. W. Rogerson and Judith Lieu. Oxford: Oxford University Press, 2006.

Preisendanz, Karl, ed. *Papyri Graecae Magicae: Die griechischen Zauberpapyri*. 2nd ed. Stuttgart: Teubner, 1973–1974.

Prêtre, Clarisse, and Philippe Charlier. *Maladies humaines, thérapies divines: analyse épigraphique et paléopathologique de textes de guérison grecs*. Villeneuve d'Ascq: Presses Universitaries du Septentrion, 2009.

Price, Simon R. F. *Rituals and Power: The Roman Imperial Cult in Asia Minor*. Cambridge: Cambridge University Press, 1984.

Pritchard, James B., ed. *The Ancient Near East: Supplementary Texts and Pictures Relating to the Old Testament*. Princeton: Princeton University Press, 1969.

Puglia, Enzo. "Mulierum nomina numeris dissimulata nei graffiti pompeiani." *Minima epigraphica et papyrologica, taccuini della Cattedra e del Laboratorio di epigrafia e papirologia giuridica dell Universit degli studi di Catanzaro Magna Graecia* 7–8 (2004): 303–10.

———. "Tre graffiti da *Stabiae* di recente pubblicazione." *Papyrologica Lupiensia* 24 (2015): 127–36.

Rathmayr, Elisabeth. "Zusammenfassung—Summary—Özet." Pages 773–82 in *Hanghaus 2 in Ephesos Die Wohneinheit 7. Baubefund, Ausstattung, Funde. Texteband 2*. Forschungen in Ephesos VIII.10. Edited by Elisabeth Rathmayr. Vienna: Paul Gerin GmbH & Co, 2016.

Reimer, Ivoni Richter. *Women in the Acts of the Apostles: A Feminist Liberation Perspective*. Translated by Linda M. Maloney. Minneapolis: Fortress, 1995.

Renberg, Gil. *Where Dreams May Come: Incubation Sanctuaries in the Greco-Roman World*. Leiden: Brill, 2016.

Reumann, John. "Church Offices in Paul, Especially in Philippians." Pages 82–91 in *Origins and Method: Toward a New Understanding of Judaism and Christianity; Essays in Honour of John C. Hurd*. Edited by John Coolidge Hurd and B. H. McLean. Sheffield: JSOT Press, 1993.

———. *Philippians: A New Translation with Introduction and Commentary*. AYB 33B. New Haven: Yale University Press, 2008.

Reynolds, Joyce, Charlotte Roueché, and Gabriel Bodard, eds. *Inscriptions of Aphrodisias* (2007). http://insaph.kcl.ac.uk/iaph2007.

Richards, E. Randolph. *Paul and First-Century Letter Writing: Secretaries, Composition and Collection*. Downers Grove, IL: InterVarsity Press, 2004.

Richardson, Peter. *Herod the Great: King of the Jews and Friend of the Romans*. Columbia: University of South Carolina Press, 1996.

Ricl, Marijana, ed. *The Inscriptions of Alexandreia Troas*. Österreichische Akademie der Wissenschaften Nordrhein-Westfälische Akademie der Wissenschaften 53. Bonn: Habelt, 1997.

Riesner, Rainer. *Paul's Early Period: Chronology, Mission Strategy, Theology*. Translated by Doug Stott. Grand Rapids: Eerdmans, 1998.

Ritti, Tullia. *An Epigraphic Guide to Hierapolis of Phrygia (Pamukkale): An Archaeological Guide*. Translated by Paul Arthur. Istanbul: Ege Yayinlari, 2006.

Robert, Louis. "Les épigraphies et L'épigraphie grecque et romaine." Pages 65–109 in vol. 5 of *Opera minora selecta. Epigraphie et antiquités grecque*. 7 vols. Amsterdam: AM Hakkert, 1990.

Rogers, Guy MacLean. *The Sacred Identity of Ephesos: Foundation Myths of a Roman City*. London: Routledge, 1991.

Romiopoulou, Catherine. "Un nouveau milliaire de la Via Egnatia." *BCH* 98 (1974): 813–16.

Rose, H. J. "The Cult of Orthia." Pages 399–407 in *The Sanctuary of Artemis Orthia at Sparta*. Edited by R. M. Dawkins. The Society for the Promotion of Hellenic Studies Paper No. 5. London: MacMillan, 1926.

Rösel, Martin. "The Reading and Translation of the Divine Name in the Masoretic Tradition and the Greek Pentateuch." *JSOT* 31 (2007): 411–28.

Rougement, Georges, et al., eds. *Corpus des inscriptions de Delphes*. Paris: de Boccard, 1977–.

Rowe, C. Kavin. *World Upside Down: Reading Acts in the Graeco-Roman Age*. Oxford: Oxford University Press, 2009.

Rowe, Greg. *Princes and Political Cultures: The New Tiberian Senatorial Decrees*. Ann Arbor: University of Michigan Press, 2002.

———. "The Roman State: Laws, Lawmaking, and Legal Documents." Pages 299–318 in *The Oxford Handbook of Roman Epigraphy*. Edited by Christer Bruun and Jonathan Edmondson. Oxford: Oxford University Press, 2015.

Royse, James R. "Philo, ΚΥΡΙΟΣ, and the Tetragrammaton." SPhiloA 3 (1991): 167–83.

Salomies, Olli. "Names and Identities: Onomastics and Prosopography." Pages 73–94 in *Epigraphic Evidence: Ancient History from Inscriptions*. Edited by John Bodel. London: Routledge, 2001.

Scharf, Ralf. "Conobaria 5 v. Chr.–Der erste römische 'Kaisereid.'" Pages 415–24 in *Hommages à Carl Deroux, III. Histoire et épigraphie, Droit*. Edited by Pol Defosse. Latomus 270. Leuven: Peeters, 2003.

Scheid, John. *An Introduction to Roman Religion*. Translated by Janet Lloyd. Bloomington: Indiana University Press, 2003.

———. "The Religious Roles of Roman Women." Pages 377–408 in *A History of Women in the West*. Vol. 1, *From Ancient Goddesses to Christian Saints*. Edited by Pauline Schmitt Pantel. Cambridge: Belknap Press of Harvard University Press, 1992.

Scherrer, Peter. "The City of Ephesos: From the Roman Period to Late Antiquity." Pages 1–25 in *Ephesos: Metropolis of Asia; An Interdisciplinary Approach to its Archaeology, Religion, and Culture*. Edited by Helmut Koester. HTS 41. Cambridge: Harvard University Press, 1995.

Septuaginta. Rev. ed. Edited by Alfred Rahlfs and Robert Hanhart. Stuttgart: Deutsche Bibelgesellschaft, 2006.

Septuaginta: Psalmi cum Odis. Edited by Alfred Rahlfs. Göttingen: Vandenhoeck & Ruprecht, 1979.

Sève, Michel. *1914–2014 Philippes Φιλιπποι Philippi. 100 ans de recherches françaises 100 χρονια γαλλικων επευνων 100 Years of French Research*. Athens: École française d'Athènes, 2014.

Sève, Michel, and Patrick Weber. *Guide du forum de Philippes*. Sites et Monuments 18. Athens: École française d'Athenes, 2012.

———. "Un monument honorifique au forum de Philippes." *BCH* 112 (1988): 467–79.

Sherk, Robert K., ed. *The Municipal Decrees of the Roman West*. Buffalo: State University of New York at Buffalo, 1970.

———, ed. *Roman Documents from the Greek East: Senatus Consulta and Epistulae to the Age of Augustus*. Baltimore: Johns Hopkins University Press, 1969.

———, ed. *Rome and the Greek East to the Death of Augustus*. Cambridge: Cambridge University Press, 1984.

Sherwin-White, A. N. *Roman Society and Roman Law in the New Testament*. Oxford: Clarendon, 1963.

Shipley, Graham. *A History of Samos: 800–188 BC*. Oxford: Clarendon, 1987.

Skeat, T. C. "A Table of Isopsephisms (P. Oxy XLV. 3239)." *ZPE* 31 (1978): 45–54.

Smith, Dennis E. *From Symposium to Eucharist: The Banquet in the Early Christian World*. Minneapolis: Fortress, 2003.

Sogliano, A. "Isopsepha Pompeina." *Rendiconti della Reale Accademia dei Lincei, Classe di scienze morali, storiche e filologiche* 10 (1901): 256–59.

Solin, Heikki, and Marja Itkonen. *Graffiti del Palatino, I Paedagogium*. Helsinki: Institutum Romanum Finlandiae, 1966.

Sørensen, Søren Lund. "A Re-examination of the Imperial Oath from Vezirköprü." *Philia* 1 (2015): 14–32.

Sterck-Degueldre, Jean-Pierre. *Eine Frau namens Lydia*. WUNT 2/176. Tübingen: Mohr Siebeck, 2004.

Sterrett, J. R. S. "Inscriptions of Assos." *Papers of the American School of Classical Studies at Athens* 1 (1882–1883): 1–90.

Still, Todd D. *Conflict at Thessalonica: A Pauline Church and Its Neighbours*. JSNTSup 183. Sheffield: Sheffield Academic, 1999.

Suetonius. *The Lives of the Caesars*. 2 vols. Translated by J. C. Rolfe and K. R. Bradley. LCL. Cambridge: Harvard University Press, 1914.

Supplementum Epigraphicum Graecum. Vols. 1–11. Edited by Jacob E. Hondius. Leiden: Brill, 1923–1954. Vols. 12–25. Edited by Arthur G. Woodhead. Leiden: Brill, 1955–1971. Vols. 26–41. Edited by Henry W. Pleket and Ronald S. Stroud. Amsterdam: Brill, 1979–1994. Vols. 42–44. Edited by Henry W. Pleket, Ronald S. Stroud, and Johan H. M. Strubbe. Amsterdam: Brill, 1995–1997. Vols. 45–49. Edited by Henry W. Pleket, Ronald S. Stroud, Angelos Chaniotis, and Johan H. M. Strubbe. Amsterdam: Brill, 1998–2002. Vols. 50–. Edited by Angelos Chaniotis, Ronald S. Stroud, and Johan H. M. Strubbe. Amsterdam: Brill, 2003–.

Susini, Giancarlo. *The Roman Stonecutter: An Introduction to Latin Epigraphy*. Translated by A. M. Dabrowski. Oxford: Blackwell, 1973.

Swete, Henry Barclay. *The Apocalypse of St John: The Greek Text with Introduction, Notes and Indices*. 3rd ed. London: MacMillan, 1911.

———. *An Introduction to the Old Testament in Greek*. Cambridge: Cambridge University Press, 1900.

———. *The Psalms in Greek According to the Septuagint with the Canticles*. 2nd ed. Cambridge, 1896.

Tacitus. *Annals*. Translated by Clifford H. Moore and John Jackson. 2 vols. LCL. Cambridge: Harvard University Press, 1931, 1937.

Taeuber, Hans. "Ephesische Graffiti als Zeugnisse des Lebensgefühls in der hohen Kaiserzeit." Pages 61–68 in *Epigraphik und Neues Testament*. Edited by Thomas Corsten, Markus Öhler, and Joseph Verheyden. WUNT 365. Tübingen: Mohr Siebeck, 2016.

———. "Graffiti." Pages 132–43 in *Hanghaus 2 in Ephesos. Die Wohneinheit 4. Baubefund, Ausstattung, Funde. Textband*. Edited by Hilke Thür. Forschungen in Ephesos VIII.6. Vienna: Österreichische Akademie der Wissenschaften, 2005.

———. "Graffiti und Inschriften." Pages 233–58 in *Hanghaus 2 in Ephesos Die Wohneinheit 7. Baubefund, Ausstattung, Funde*. Forschungen in Ephesos VIII.10. Edited by Elisabeth Rathmayr. Vienna: Paul Gerin GmbH & Co, 2016.

Theissen, Gerd. *The Social Setting of Pauline Christianity: Essays on Corinth*. Edited and translated by John H. Schütz. Philadelphia: Fortress, 1982.

Thiselton, Anthony C. *The First Epistle to the Corinthians: A Commentary on the Greek Text*. NIGTC. Grand Rapids: Eerdmans, 2000.

Thomas, Rosalind. "Writing, Law, and Written Law." Pages 41–60 in *The Cambridge Companion to Ancient Greek Law*. Edited by Michael Gagarin and David Cohen. Cambridge: Cambridge University Press, 2005.

Thomas, W. Derek. "The Place of Women in the Church at Philippi." *ExpTim* 83 (1971–1972): 117–20.

Thür, Gerhard, and Christian Koch. "Prozessrechtlicher Kommentar zum 'Getreidegesetz' aus Samos." *Anzeiger* 118 (1981): 61–88.

Thür, Hilke. "Die WE 4—Zusammenfassung und Ergebnisse." Pages 427–38 in *Hanghaus 2 in Ephesos. Die Wohneinheit 4. Baubefund, Ausstattung, Funde. Textband*. Forschungen in Ephesos VIII.6. Edited by Hilke Thür. Vienna: Österreichische Akademie der Wissenschaften, 2005.

Tov, Emanuel. *Hebrew Bible, Greek Bible, and Qumran*. TSAJ 121. Tübingen: Mohr Siebeck, 2008.

Towner, Philip. *The Letters to Timothy and Titus*. NICNT. Grand Rapids: Eerdmans, 2006.

Tribulato, Olga. "The Stone-Cutter's Bilingual Inscription from Palermo (*IG* XIV 297 = *CIL* X 7296): A New Interpretation." *ZPE* 177 (2011): 131–40.

Vanderspoel, John. "*Provincia Macedonia*." Pages 251–75 in *A Companion to Ancient Macedonia*. Edited by Joseph Roismas and Ian Worthington. Malden, MA: Blackwell, 2010.

Varone, Antonio. *Erotica Pompeiana: Love Inscriptions on the Walls of Pompeii*. Translated by Ria P. Berg. Rome: L'erma di Bretschneider, 2002.

———. "Le iscrizioni graffite di *Stabiae* alla luce dei nuovi rinvenimenti." *Rendiconti* 86 (2013–2014): 375–427.

Verheyden, Joseph, Markus Öhler, and Thomas Corsten. "Introduction." Pages 1–4 in *Epigraphik und Neues Testament*. Edited by Thomas Corsten, Markus Öhler, and Joseph Verheyden. WUNT 365. Tübingen: Mohr Siebeck, 2016.

Vos, Craig Steven de. *Church and Community Conflicts: The Relationships of the Thessalonian, Corinthian, and Philippian Churches with Their Wider Civic Communities*. SBLDS 168. Atlanta: Scholars Press, 1997.

Wallace, Daniel B. *Greek Grammar Beyond the Basics: An Exegetical Syntax of the New Testament*. Grand Rapids: Zondervan, 1996.

Wallace-Hadrill, Andrew. *Houses and Society in Pompeii and Herculaneum*. Princeton: Princeton University Press, 1994.

Wankel, Hermann, et al, eds. *Die Inschriften von Ephesos*. 8 vols. Bonn: Habelt, 1979–1984.

Weima, Jeffrey A. D. "The Political Charges against Paul and Silas in Acts 17:6–7: Roman Benefaction in Thessalonica." Pages 241–68 in *Stones, Bones, and the Sacred: Essays on Material Culture and Ancient Religion in Honor of Dennis E. Smith*. Edited by Alan H. Cadwallader. ECL 21. Atlanta: SBL Press, 2016.

Weinfeld, Moshe. *Deuteronomy 1–11: A New Translation with Introduction and Commentary*. AB 5. New York: Doubleday, 1991.

———. "The Loyalty Oath in the Ancient Near East." Pages 2–44 in *Normative and Sectarian Judaism in the Second Temple Period*. LSTS 54. London: T&T Clark, 2005.

Welles, C. Bradford, ed. *Royal Correspondence in the Hellenistic Period: A Study of Greek Epigraphy*. Studia Historica 28. Rome: L'erma di Bretschneider, 1966.

West, Allen Brown, ed. *Corinth*. Vol. 8.2, *Latin Inscriptions 1896–1926*. Princeton: American School of Classical Studies at Athens, 1931.

Wiegand, Theodore, and Ulrich von Wilamowitz-Moellendorff. "Ein Gesetz von Samos über die Beschaffung von Brotkorn aus öffentlichen Mitteln." *Sitzungsberichte der königlich preussischen Akademie der Wissenschaften* 1 (1904): 917–31.

Wilamowitz-Moellendorff, Ulrich von. *Isyllos von Epidauros*. Berlin, 1886.

Winter, Bruce W. *After Paul Left Corinth: The Influence of Secular Ethics and Social Change*. Grand Rapids: Eerdmans, 2001.

———. *Divine Honours for Caesars: The First Christians' Responses*. Grand Rapids: Eerdmans, 2015.

———. "The Lord's Supper at Corinth: An Alternative Reconstruction." *RTR* 37 (1978): 73–82.

Wise, Michael Owen. *Language and Literary in Roman Judaea: A Study of the Bar Kokhba Documents*. AYBRL. New Haven: Yale University Press, 2015.

Witherington, Ben, III. *Making a Meal of It: Rethinking the Theology of the Lord's Supper*. Waco, TX: Baylor University Press, 2007.

———. *Women in the Earliest Churches*. SNTSMS 59. Cambridge: Cambridge University Press, 1988.

Woodhead, A. Geoffrey. *The Study of Greek Inscriptions*. 2nd ed. London: Bristol Classical Press, 1992.

Woodward, A. M. "Inscriptions." Pages 285–377 in *The Sanctuary of Artemis Orthia at Sparta*. Edited by R. M. Dawkins. The Society for the Promotion of Hellenic Studies Paper No. 5. London: MacMillan, 1926.

Woolf, Greg. "Literacy." Pages 875–97 in *The High Empire, AD 70–192*. Vol. 11 of *Cambridge Ancient History*. Edited by Alan Bowman, Peter Garnsey, and Dominic Rathbone. Cambridge: Cambridge University Press, 2000.

———. "Monumental Writing and the Expansion of Roman Society in the Early Empire." *JRS* 86 (1996): 22–39.

Wright, N. T. *Paul and the Faithfulness of God*. 2 vols. Minneapolis: Fortress, 2013.

Wright, Robert B. *Psalms of Solomon: A Critical Edition of the Greek Text*. London: T&T Clark, 2007.

Yadin, Yigael, et al. *The Documents from the Bar Kokhba Period in the Cave of Letters: Hebrew, Aramaic, and Nabatean-Aramaic Paypri*. JDS 3. Jerusalem: Israel Exploration Society, 2002.

Yarbro Collins, Adela. *Mark: A Commentary*. Hermeneia. Minneapolis: Fortress, 2007.

———. "Numerical Symbolism in Jewish and Early Christian Apocalyptic Literature." *ANRW* 21.2:1221–87. Part 2, *Principat*, 21.2. Edited by Wolfgang Haase. New York: de Gruyter, 1984.

Zimmermann, Norbert, and Sabine Ladstätter. *Wall Painting in Ephesos from the Hellenistic to the Byzantine Period*. Istanbul: Ege Yayinlari, 2011.

Index of Modern Authors

Abrahamsen, Valerie A., 123n6, 126, 131n36, 133nn45–46, 135
Adam-Veleni, P., 111n51, 113n57
Aitken, James K., 61n9
Alföldy, Géza, 16n16
Allamani-Souri, Victoria, 118n61
Arnaoutoglou, Ilias, 87n27
Ascough, Richard S., 122n5, 124n10
Ast, Rodney, 145n10, 146n12
Aune, David E., 141n3, 160n62

Badian, Ernst, 54
Bagnall, Roger S., 86, 156nn46–50, 157–58, 162n70
Baird, J. A., 45n68
Barclay, John M. G., 99nn7–8, 100n9
Barrett, C. K., 78n2, 98n5
Bauckham, Richard, 64n22, 65, 74, 141n3, 143n6, 159n59, 160n62
Baudissin, W. G., 65n24
Beale, G. K., 142n5, 143, 149n16, 157n51
Beard, Mary, 26n34, 34n50, 36n57, 47n72, 125n17, 129n28, 129n30, 131n38, 132n40, 133n43
Benary, Ferdinand, 141n3, 142n5
Benefiel, Rebecca R., 45n68, 47n71, 151n18, 151n22, 152n24, 161n64
Betz, Hans Dieter, 47n73, 70n47
Birdsall, J. Neville, 141n2
Blount, Brian K., 143n8
Blue, Bradley, 79n6, 123n6
Bockmuehl, Markus, 123n7
Bodel, John, 9n1, 11n4, 16nn15–16, 39n59, 48n76, 49n78, 50n81, 51n85, 167n1
Bousset, Wilhelm, 61n11, 62–63, 64n19, 66, 75, 141n3
Boxall, Ian, 141n3
Brélaz, Cédric, 125n17, 127n23, 128n25, 129n27, 132n42
Bremen, Riet van, 131n38
Brocke, Christoph vom, 98n4
Brown, Raymond E., 124n13
Bruce, F. F., 99n6, 100n10, 101n16
Bruun, Christer, 9, 51n85, 167n1
Bultmann, Rudolf, 63n14, 64n19
Bureth, Paul, 68n37
Burnett, D. Clint, 49n79, 61n10, 91n39, 115n60

Caird, G. B., 142n4
Caldelli, Maria Letizia, 121n1
Calpino, Teresa J., 122n5
Cameron, A., 80n8
Campbell, Douglas, 54n88
Cancik, Hubert, 101n17
Caneva, Stefano, 132n42
Carcopino, Jérôme, 92n43
Cerfaux, Lucien, 67n35, 68n37, 69, 73n62, 74n65, 76n74
Charles, R. H., 141n3
Charlier, Philippe, 80n11, 83n15, 84
Chioffi, Laura, 34n51
Clarke, Edward Daniel, 115n58
Cohick, Lynn H., 121n1, 122n5
Collart, Paul, 125n17, 134nn47–48, 134n52, 135n53, 135nn56–57
Collins, Raymond F., 78n2
Connolly, Serena, 101n17, 102n18, 104n28
Conzelmann, Hans, 79, 84n21, 91n38, 123n6, 124n12
Cook, B. F., 9n1, 50n81
Cooley, Alison E., 9n1, 21n24, 22n25, 24nn32–33, 29n41, 31n47, 35n53, 38n58, 39n60, 41n62, 43n64, 50n81, 55n89, 56n91
Crawford, M. H., 28n40
Cullmann, Oscar, 62
Cumont, Franz, 101n17, 103n22, 103n24 104n30, 106n34

Dahl, Nils A., 122n5, 138n65
Dalman, Gustaf, 62–64, 66
D'Ambra, Eve, 131n38
D'Angelo, Mary Rose, 126n19
Dawkins, R. M., 146n14
Deissmann, Adolf, 2–3, 4n8, 11n7, 44, 56, 142, 144, 150, 164–66

Delacoulonche, Alfred, 132n42
Derow, Peter, 86
Dessau, Hermann, 52
Dibelius, Martin, 124n13
Dobschütz, Ernst von, 99nn7–8
Dodd, C. H., 76n72
Donfried, Karl Paul, 99n7, 100, 101n16, 115n60
Dornseiff, Franz, 146n12
Dreyer, Boris, 88n32
Ducrey, Pierre, 134n52, 135n53, 135nn56–57
Dunbabin, Katherine M. D., 91nn40–41, 92
Dunn, James D. G., 59n3, 78n2

Eckstein, Arthur M., 111n50
Edelstein, Emma J., 80n11, 83n19
Edelstein, Ludwig, 80n11, 83n19
Edmondson, Jonathan, 9n1, 17n18
Elliger, Winfried, 98n4
Elliott, Tom, 33n49, 53n86, 169n1
Engelmann, Helmut, 88n32, 155n41
Erskine, Andrew, 112
Ersoy, Akin, 156nn46–47

Farbridge, Maurice H., 146n12
Fee, Gordon D., 79n6, 123n7, 125n16
Ferguson, Everett, 122n4
Fitzmyer, Joseph A., 64–68, 72n54, 73–74, 76n73, 78n8, 90n35, 98n5, 99n6, 101n16
Foerster, Werner, 59n2, 62n13, 68n37, 73n62, 74n65
Fraatz, C. Thomas, 159n60
Frenschkowski, Marco, 59n2, 68n37, 69, 73n62
Friesen, Steven J., 158n57
Fujii, Takashi, 101n17
Fuller, Reginald, 63n14
Furnish, Victor Paul, 1n2, 70n48

Galli, Marco, 80n11, 83n15, 83n19
Gargola, Daniel J., 84nn22–23, 85n24
Garland, David E., 79n6, 84n21
Gauthier, Philippe, 29n42
Gerber, Albrecht, 2n4, 4n8
Getty-Sullivan, Mary Ann, 122n5, 125n16
Giesen, Heinz, 141n3
Gillman, Florence M., 122n5, 123nn8–9
Giordano, Carlo, 151n21, 151n23
Girone, Maria, 80n11
Goldsworthy, Adrian, 16n16, 110nn47–49, 113nn55–56
Gonzalez, Julián, 101n17, 102nn18–19, 103n22
Gradel, Ittai, 115n59
Graf, David F., 70n45
Graf, Fritz, 101n17

Habicht, Christian, 84n22, 111
Haenchen, Ernst, 98n5, 99n6, 123n6
Hahn, Ferdinand, 63n14
Hamilton, Mary, 80n11, 83
Harland, Philip A., 51n83
Harris, B. F., 101n17, 102n19
Harris, William V., 48–49
Harrison, James K., 101n16
Hasluck, F. W., 119n63
Hawthorne, Gerald F., 59n2, 123n9, 125n14, 137
Hay, David, 61n10
Hays, Richard B., 79
Healey, John F., 69
Hendrix, Holland Lee, 98n4, 115n60
Hengel, Martin, 63
Herrmann, Peter, 101n17, 102nn18–19, 103nn22–26, 104n27, 104n29, 104n30, 105nn31–33, 106nn34–35, 106nn37–38, 107nn39–42, 108n43
Hofius, Otfried, 78n2
Holloway, Paul A., 122n2
Horrell, David G., 95n49
Horster, Marietta, 29n42
Hossfeld, Frank-Lothar, 61n8
Hurtado, Larry W., 59nn2–3, 60n4, 61, 63n16, 64, 65nn24–25, 75

Itkonen, Marja, 13n10

Jewett, Robert, 99nn7–8, 101n16
Johnson, Luke Timothy, 124n13
Judge, E. A., 101n12
Juel, Donald, 76n71

Kalvesmaki, Joel, 146n13
Keegan, Peter, 45n68, 46
Keener, Craig S., 99n6, 101n16, 122n5, 125n16
Keppie, Lawrence, 9n1, 17n18, 35n53, 174n1
Kilgallen, John J., 99n6
Kittredge, Cynthia Briggs, 122n5, 124n10, 138n64
Klauck, Hans-Josef, 78n2, 141n3
Koch, Christian, 84n22, 87
Koester, Craig, 141n3, 142n5, 143n6, 144n9, 158n56, 159nn60–61, 160n62
Kraemer, Ross Shepherd, 121n1
Kraus, Hans-Joachim, 61n8

La Regina, Adriano, 34n52
Ladstätter, Sabine, 154n36, 155
Lampe, Peter, 78n2, 90n36
Leithart, Peter J., 143n8
Levick, Barbara, 101n17, 104n28
Levine, Lee I., 136n60
Lewis, David M., 51n84
Lim, Timothy H., 103n21
Limentani, Ida Calabi, 21n24
Lindars, Barnabas, 76n72
Llewelyn, Stephen R., 146n13
Lloris, Francisco Beltán, 16n14, 16n16, 20n22, 29n43, 36n56
Lohse, Eduard, 141n3
Lougovaya, Julia, 145n10, 146n12
Luck, George, 80n11, 83n15, 83n19
Lührmann, Dieter, 99nn6–7
Lupieri, Edmondo F., 142n4, 143, 157n51

Ma, John, 23n27
MacMullen, Ramsay, 15n13
Malherbe, Abraham J., 60n4, 100n10
Malinowski, Francis X., 122n5
Manganaro, Giacomo, 162n68
Marshall, I. Howard, 63n17, 124n13
Martin, Ralph P., 123n9, 125n14, 137
Mau, August, 32n48, 46
McLean, B. H., 2, 9n1, 11, 17n18, 18n21, 20n22, 21n23, 22n25, 24n31, 29n41, 30n45, 35n53, 36nn55–56, 38n58, 39n60, 43n64, 44n67, 55n89, 56n91, 125n15, 140, 145n11
Meeks, Wayne A., 165n2
Meier, P. Gabriel, 51n82
Meiggs, Russell, 51n84
Merklein, Helmut, 67, 69, 75n68, 75n70
Metzger, Bruce, 141n2
Meyer, Elizabeth, 15n14
Michael, Michael George, 141n2
Millar, Fergus, 118
Milligan, George, 75, 79, 83n16, 99nn7–8, 101n15
Minervini, G., 161n63
Mitford, T. B., 101n17, 103n22, 103n25, 104nn29–30, 105n32, 106n34, 106n37
Murphy-O'Connor, Jerome, 3n5, 78n2, 94–95

Nasrallah, Laura S., 4, 44n66, 97n3
Nelis-Clément, Jocelyne, 43n65
North, John, 26n34, 34n50, 36n57, 125n17, 129n28, 129n30, 132n40, 133n43
Novenson, Matthew V., 73
Noy, David, 3n6

Osborne, Robin, 56
Osiek, Carolyn, 122n5, 124n10, 126n20, 138n66
Oster, Richard E., 136n60

Parker, David C., 141n2
Peek, Werner, 80n10
Perdrizet, Paul, 146n12
Peterlin, Davorin, 122n5, 123n9, 125n16, 137, 138n66
Petzl, Georg, 80n8
Pizzi, Aurian Delli, 132n42
Portefaix, Lilian, 122n5, 123n9, 126, 129, 133n46, 134n47, 134n51, 135
Porter, Stanley E., 3n6, 4n8, 77n1
Prêtre, Clarisse, 80n11, 83n15, 84
Price, Simon R. F., 26n34, 34n50, 36n57, 47n72, 125n17, 129n28, 129n30, 131n38, 132n40, 133n43, 158n57
Puglia, Enzo, 152, 153nn29–30, 153nn32–34, 161n65

Quell, Gottfried, 59n2, 62n13

Rathmayr, Elisabeth, 154n37
Reimer, Ivoni Richter, 122n5, 136n60
Renberg, Gil, 81n11, 82n12, 83n13
Reumann, John, 124n10, 125, 138n65
Richards, E. Randolph, 3n5
Richardson, Peter, 71n50
Ricl, Marijana, 80n9
Riesner, Rainer, 99n6, 100n9
Ritti, Tullia, 40n61
Robert, Louis, 7, 9nn1–2, 10, 11n5, 14n11, 15n12, 17n18, 22n26, 54n87, 97, 166
Rogers, Guy MacLean, 13n9
Rose, H. J., 146n14
Rösel, Martin, 65n28
Rowe, C. Kavin, 98n5
Rowe, Greg, 24n33, 101n17
Royse, James R., 66n29

Salomies, Olli, 50n80
Scharf, Ralf, 101n17
Scheid, John, 129n28, 129n30, 131–32
Scherrer, Peter, 42n63
Sève, Michel, 125n17, 128n26, 130n34, 131n35
Sherk, Robert K., 24n33, 89
Sherwin-White, A. N., 98n5, 109
Shipley, Graham, 84nn22–23
Skeat, T. C., 146n13, 149n17
Slater, William J., 92n44, 94n48
Smith, Dennis E., 79, 84n21

Sogliano, A., 142n4
Solin, Heikki, 13n10
Sørensen, Søren Lund, 101n17, 103n22, 103n24, 104nn29–30, 106n34
Sterck-Degueldre, Jean-Pierre, 122n5
Still, Todd D., 99n7, 100n9
Susini, Giancarlo, 17n18, 18n21
Swete, Henry Barclay, 61n9, 141n3

Taeuber, Hans, 141n3, 154–55, 161n67
Taylor, Claire, 45n68
Theissen, Gerd, 78nn2–3, 95n50
Thiselton, Anthony C., 79
Thomas, Rosalind, 28n39
Thomas, W. Derek, 122n5
Thür, Gerhard, 84n22, 87
Thür, Hilke, 155n43
Tov, Emanuel, 65n28
Towner, Philip, 124n13
Tribulato, Olga, 17n19

Vanderspoel, John, 111n50, 112n53
Varone, Antonio, 152nn26–27, 153n29, 153n31, 153n33
Vos, Craig Steven de, 99n7, 100n9

Wallace, Daniel B., 77n1
Wallace-Hadrill, Andrew, 92n45
Weber, Patrick, 128n26, 130n34, 131n35
Weima, Jeffrey A. D., 98n5, 100n11, 108n44
Weinfeld, Moshe, 102, 103n21
Welles, C. Bradford, 26n35
Wiegand, Theodore, 84n22, 85n24, 87
Wilamowitz-Moellendorff, Ulrich von, 80n11, 83n15, 83n17, 84n22, 85n24, 87
Winter, Bruce W., 79, 83–84, 90n37, 91, 101n16
Wise, Michael Owen, 58n1
Witherington, Ben III, 79n6, 122n5, 123n7, 125n16, 137
Woodhead, A. Geoffrey, 9n1, 24n31, 27n36, 29n41, 36n55, 38n58, 39n60, 44n67, 50n81, 54n87, 55n89
Woodward, A. M., 146n14, 147n15
Woolf, Greg, 15n14, 48–49
Wright, N. T., 64n22, 65n26, 68n37
Wright, Robert B., 61n11

Yarbro Collins, Adela, 60n6, 70n46, 92n42, 143n8

Zenger, Erich, 61n8
Zimmermann, Norbert, 154n36, 155

Index of Subjects

616, 141n2, 142n5, 143n6
666, 141–43, 157

Agrippa I, 71, 74
Agrippa II, 74
androcentricism, 121
antistes, 132–33, 137
Aretas IV, 69, 70, 72
Asclepius, 80–83, 84n21
Augustus, Caesar, 6, 10, 16, 22–23, 24, 26, 27, 34, 36, 38, 39, 50, 51, 68n37, 73, 88–89, 97, 103, 104n30, 105, 107n40, 108, 113, 114, 115, 116–17, 118, 119, 128, 129, 130n34, 145

Babatha, 70
beast, name of, 140–62
benefactress, 31, 128, 129, 137

Caesar, Julius, 10, 112, 113, 115
Caesar's decrees, 97–120
calculation, 140–62
  equal, 146, 160
  name, 140–62
Caligula (Gaius), Caesar, 68n37, 103, 105, 108
Cave of Letters, 70
Christ, 60, 61, 73, 137
church, organization of, 122–26, 136–39
Claudius, Caesar, 32, 68n37, 117, 118, 128, 129, 130, 131, 145
corpora, 3–4, 51–54, 55, 57, 167–68, 169–71
cult of Roman benefactors, 112
curse tablets, 47–48
Cynoscephalae, 110

Damascus, 63, 64n19, 70
deacon, 123–26, 138

Egnatius, Gnaeus, 35–36, 111
elders, 124
Ephesus, 12, 42, 71, 97, 149, 150, 154–55, 161–62
Euodia, 121–23, 124n10, 125–26, 136–39

forum, 11, 22, 23, 30, 31, 34, 128–31, 137
free city, 26, 97, 109, 113, 114, 117, 118, 119, 120

graffiti, 13, 15, 45–47, 140–62
Greco-Roman literature, 9, 10, 58, 61, 62, 109, 121, 140

Herod the Great, 69–71
History of Religions School, 62, 63n14
Holy Spirit Greek, 77

imperial loyalty oaths, 28, 97–120, 101–8
  ancient Near East, 102–3
  Greek, 104–7
  Latin, 107–8
inscriptions
  archaeological artifacts, 56–57, 144
  boundary markers, 9–10, 29, 32–36
  calendars, 24, 36–37
  curse tablets, 47–48
  dating, 49–50
  decrees (Greek), 23–24
  decrees (Latin), 24–26
  dedications (private), 42–43, 74, 113
  dedications (public), 36, 38
  defixio, 47–48
  direct ancient sources, 9
  domestic, 43
  epitaphs, 39–42, 69, 72, 73, 80, 129
  forma, 17
  honorific (private), 42
  honorific (public), 29–36, 128
  inventories, 23, 27
  length, 11–13
  letters, 23, 26–27, 97, 119–20
  literacy, 48–49
  material, 11, 17–18, 23–26

NT Greek, 7, 56, 77
numbers, 144–48
official documents, 20, 23–28
ordinatio, 17
paleography, 50
philology, 77–90
private, 20–22, 38–48
production of, 16–20
public, 20–22, 22–38
religious laws, 23–28
sacred (private), 42–45
sacred (public), 29–38
sculptio, 19
social history, 10, 109
Theodotus, 50
treaties, 23, 27–28, 101–8
typology, 20–48
warning inscription from the Jerusalem temple, 9–10

Koine Greek, 7, 56, 77

Livia, Augusta, 38, 74, 117, 129–30
Lord, 58–76
adon, 59, 61–62, 64–66, 69, 72, 73–76
ancient Near Eastern tradition, 58–59
historical background, 58–67
kyrios, 58–76
mr', 59, 62, 64–67, 68–69, 71, 72–76
of kings, 68
Lord's Banquet, 77–96
Lydia, 122, 123, 126n22, 136–39

Maccabeus, Judas, 69
Macedon, kingdom of, 110–11
Macedonia, province of, 111–13, 115, 117
Metellus, Quintus Caecilius, 111
mystery cults, 63

Nabatea, 66, 67n35, 68–70, 72–73
Nero, Caesar, 32, 68n37, 118, 140, 142, 143n8, 144, 152, 158–60

overseer, 122–25, 132, 138, 139

parousia, 75
Philip V, 110
Philippi, 11–12, 35, 43, 113, 114, 121–39
Pompeii, 31–32, 34, 43–44, 92–94, 140, 148–49, 150–52, 154, 160–61
Priene calendar, 38–39, 88
Pydna, 110, 111

religion, 10, 25, 34, 47, 97, 115, 117, 127–29
nonofficial, 25–26, 128, 129, 132
official, 115, 128, 129, 131–32
Roman epigraphic culture, 15–16, 48
Roman epigraphic habit, 15–16, 48
roman numerals, 144
Roman religion, 25–26, 34, 115, 117, 127, 129
female limited participation, 131–32
religio, 129
superstitio, 129

sigla, 54–56
Smyrna, basilica, 149–50, 156–58
Sparta, 146
Syntyche, 121–22, 123, 124n10, 125–26, 136–39

Tetragrammaton, 64–65
Tiberius, Caesar, 38, 55n88, 68n37, 74, 100n12, 101n17, 103, 106, 117, 118, 119, 129

Via Egnatia, 35, 36n54, 111–12, 117, 128

Index of Ancient Sources

Inscriptions

AE
(2006): 290 34

CID
2.4 27

CIG
1967 115
4039 38
5113 146n13
5554 17n19

CIIP
2 9–10
9 50
3351 64n20

CIL
2.172 103n22, 103n26, 107nn41–42, 108n43
4.2060 152n26
4.2487 45
4.4066 152n26
4.4839 160
4.4861 160
4.8792a 152n26
4.10619 47
6.896 30
6.2305 37
10.877 44
10.3825.4 34
11.5998a 103n22, 104n27, 107nn41–42

CIPh II.1
12 129n31
20 129n31
26 128, 129n27
53 130
75 127
118 129n31, 130
126 129n31, 130
135 132nn41–42

CIS
1.7 68n38
2.184 73n58
2.185 73n61
2.199 69n41, 72n55, 72n57
2.201 69n42, 72n55, 73n58
2.205 69n41, 72n55, 72n57
2.206 69n41, 72n55, 72n57
2.209 69n43, 72n55, 73n60
2.212 69n43, 72n55
2.219 70n49
2.323 72n56
2.337 72n56

Corinth 8.3
534 18

GIBM
3.418 24n29
3.420 24n29
3.449 24n29
3.481 13, 155n43
4.893 14n11

Graffiti (Ephesus)
U4 GR 2 161
U7 GR 309 154, 161
U7 GR 310 154, 161
U7 GR 311 155, 161
U7 GR 312 161
U7 GR 316 162
U7 GR 320 162
U7 GR 323 162

Graffiti (Smyrna)
T5 1 157, 162
T12 7 157, 162
T16 1 157, 162
T22 1 157, 162
T24 2 157, 162
T27 3 157, 162
T42 2 157, 162

H
1 69nn40–41, 72n55, 72n57
5 69n40
9 69n40, 69n43, 72n55
11 69n40
12 69nn40–41, 72n55, 72n57
19 69n40
28 69n40
29 69n40, 69n42, 72n55, 73n58
30 69n40
34 69n40
36 69n40
38 69n40
(i) Petra 69n40, 73n60

IAph2007
8.32 26, 117–18

IEph
20 154
27 13, 155n43
567 45
673 155n42
901 155n42
1078 154
1267 155n43

1687 155n41
3006 42
4217 154

IG
I³ 104 28
II² 1140 23n28
IV 955 81–84
IV².1 126 81–84
V.1 257 146–48
V.1 1368 162
X.2.1 4 112
X.2.1 6 113, 118
X.2.1 31 24n30, 109, 112, 115–16
X.2.1 37 24n30
X.2.1 83 113
X.2.1 109 113
X.2.1 124 113
X.2.1 128 112
X.2.1 133 112
X.2.1 134 111
X.2.1 226 112, 126
X.2.1 259 23n28
X.2.1 285 114
X.2.1 448 114
X.2.1 450 114
X.2.1 457 114
X.2.1 483 114
X.2.1 495 114
X.2.1 573 114
X.2.1 608 114
X.2.1 826 114
X.2.1 923 114
X.2.1s 1059 116
X.2.1s 1060 117
X.2.1s 1075 114
X.2.1s 1321 114
X.2.1s 1339 114
X.2.1s 1650 116–17
XII.2 510 28nn37–38
XII.2 644 80n9
XII.3 173 28n38
XII.3 174 23
XII.6.1 172 84–87
XIV 297 17n19

IGRR
II 503 17n19
III 137 103n22, 103n24, 104nn29–30, 106n34
III 157 38
III 935 54n88
IV 2 28nn37–38
IV 39 103n23, 105n33, 106n38
IV 251 103n22, 103n26, 104nn29–32, 106n35, 106n37, 107nn39–40
IV 262 24n33
IV 880 36n54
IV 1028 28n38
IV 1031 22–23
IV 1659 36n54

IHierapJ
51 40

ILabraunda
58 82n13
59 82n13
94 82n13

ILS
18 26
129 30
190 103n22, 103n26, 107nn41–42, 108n43
3785 31
5466 11n8
6368 32
7679 1n1, 17
7680 17n19
7760 41–42
8781 103n22, 103n24, 104nn29–30, 106n34

IMylasa
369 162

IPergamon
246 14n11
333 146n13
349 146n13
587 146n13

IPriene
105 24, 36, 88n32
157 38

***MAMA* 4**
4:279 80n8

OGIS
309 14n11
332 14n11
383 14–15
414 71n51
415 70–71
416 71n51
417 71n51
418 70, 71n53
419 71n52
420 71n52
421 71n52
422 71n52
423 70, 74
424 71n52
425 70
426 70, 74
427 71n51
428 71n51
429 71n51
456 103n23, 105n33, 106n38
458 24, 36, 88n32
532 103n22, 103n24, 104nn29–30, 106n34
533 38
606 74
762 23n27, 28nn37–38

Philippi II
1 130
2 130
48 127–28
57 129n30
91 134n51
92 11–12
168 136
170 136
171 136
172 129n30, 135–36
173 135–36
174 136
181 136
183 136
184 129n30, 135
207 128
208 129n31
222 130, 131n37
226 130
227 129n30
231 129n31
286 129
314 129
338 134n49
339 134n50
341 134
342 134
408 134n49
451 129n30, 132n41

512 127n24
513 129
519 127, 129n30, 133n45
524 127n24, 134n49
525 134n49
529 127n24
638 127
644 127n24
649 127

RDGE
65 88–89
67 23

Res Gestae
20.1 11n8

RIB
1.7 47

RPC
1.1551 113
1.1554 115
1.1555 115
1.1578 117
1.1579 117
1.1580 117

Sardis 7.1
4 29n44

SEG
2.396 132n42
18.578 103n22, 103n25, 104nn29–30, 105n32, 106n34, 106n37
19.765 32–33
20.302 54n88
35.761 11–12
51.837 145
52.618 132n42

***SGDI* II**
2116 44–45

***SIG*[3]**
278 24n29
585 27
588 28n37
609 23n27
616 30n46
624 29n44
630 23n27, 29n44
646 24n33
656 29n44
664 23n27, 24n33
693 28nn37–38
694 23n27
700 29n44
747 24n33
780 23
797 103n22, 103n26, 104nn29–30, 105nn31–32, 106n35, 106n37, 107nn39–40
976 84–87
1170 80–84

***TAM* 5**
3 1430 50

Old Testament

Genesis
23:6 59
24:10 59

Exodus
3:13–15 64–65

Deuteronomy
29:9–28 106n36

1 Kings
1:2 67n36, 75n67
1:17 67n36, 75n67
1:18 67n36
1:20 67n36
1:21 67n36
1:24 67n36
1:27 67n36
1:31 67n36
1:33 67n36
1:36 67n36
1:37 67n36
1:43 67n36
1:47 67n36
2:38 67n36
10:14 143n8

2 Chronicles
15:14 106n36

Psalms
110 61
110:1 61, 66n32, 75–76

Daniel
4:16 = ET 4:19 75n67
4:21 = ET 4:24 75n67

New Testament

Matthew
8:2 59, 62
8:6 62
8:8 62
8:21 62
8:25 62
9:28 62
14:28 62
14:30 62
15:25 62
15:27 62
25:34 76n72
25:37 76n72
25:40 76n72
25:44 76n72
27:37 1

Mark
1:3 60n6
2:28 60n6
5:19 60n6
6:17–29 70
6:21 91
6:21–29 91
6:22 91–92
6:24 91–92
7:28 60
11:3 60n6
11:9 60n6
12:9 60n6
12:11 60n6
12:29 60n6
12:30 60n6
12:35–37 67
12:36 60n6
12:37 60n6
13:20 60n6
13:25 60n6
15:26 1
16:19 60n6
16:20 60n6

Luke
3:1 74
23:38 1

John
19:19 1

Acts
2:34–35 65
2:34–36 59, 75, 76
6:9 136n60
9:2 136n60
9:20 136n60
13:5 136n60
13:6–12 54n88
13:14 136n60
13:43 136n60
14:1 136n60
15:21 136n60
16:11–12 35
16:11–16 122
16:11–40 123, 129
16:13 136n60
16:14–15 136
16:16 136n60
16:21 125–26
16:40 122, 136
17:1 35, 98, 136n60
17:1–10 98n4
17:2–4 98
17:5 98
17:6 24n30, 100
17:6–7 98
17:7 97
17:10 136n60
17:16 91n38
17:17 136n60
17:23 1
17:24–31 1
18:4 136n60
18:7 136n60
18:19 136n60
18:26 136n60
19:8 136n60
22:3 72
22:19 136n60
24:12 136n60
25:26 59
26:11 136n60

Romans
1:4 60, 72
4:24 72
5:1 72
5:11 72
5:21 72
6:16–20 44
6:23 72
7:25 72
8:39 72
10:9 60
10:12–13 60
12:8 124
14:8 60
15:6 72, 73
15:30 72
16:1 137, 138
16:1–2 124, 138
16:13 128
16:18 72
16:20 72

1 Corinthians
1:2 60, 72
1:3 72
1:7 72
1:8 60n5, 72
1:9 72
1:10 72
1:26 95n49
5:4 72
5:5 60n5
6:20 44
7:23 44
8:5–6 59, 65
9:1 72
11:17–34 77–96
11:21 77–96
11:26 60n5
11:30 96
11:33 79, 91, 95
11:34 95
12:3 60
15:31 72
15:57 72
16:11 91
16:15–16 124
16:22 60, 64, 72

2 Corinthians
1:2 72
1:3 72, 73
1:14 60n5
3:7–11 1
4:5 60
8:9 72
11:31 73
11:32 69, 70, 72

Galatians
1:17–18 70, 72
1:18–20 72
6:14 72
6:18 72

Philippians
1:1 125, 133, 138
1:27–2:11 138
2:9–11 59, 60, 65
3:20 60n5
3:20–4:3 138
4:2–3 121–22
4:3 126
4:5 60n5

Colossians
1:15–20 75
3:22 59
4:13 16n15, 39
4:15 137

1 Thessalonians
1:1 98
1:3 72
1:4 101n14
1:5 101n14
1:6 99
1:10 101, 119
2:1 101n14
2:2 99, 101n14
2:5 101n14
2:11 101n14
2:12 101, 119
2:14–16 99
2:16–18 99
2:17–18 119
2:19 60n5, 72, 75
3:2 137
3:2–3 137
3:3 99, 101n14
3:4 101n14
3:4–5 99
3:11 72
3:13 60n5, 72, 75
4:2 101n14
4:13–18 59, 67n35, 75, 101, 119
4:15 75
4:15–5:2 60n5
5:2 60n5, 101n14, 119
5:9 60n5, 72
5:12 124
5:15 99
5:23 60n5, 72, 75
5:28 72

2 Thessalonians
1:1 98
1:4–5 99
1:5 101, 119

2:6 101n14
2:8 60n5
3:7 101n14

1 Timothy
3:2–7 124–25
3:7–14 137
3:8–13 125
3:11–13 138

Titus
1:5–9 124

Hebrews
10:13 91n38
11:10 91n38

James
5:7 91n38

Revelation
1:1–3 149
2:17 1
3:12 1–2
13:1 2n3
13:1–10 141
13:3 159
13:4 158
13:8 158
13:11–18 141
13:12 158
13:15 158
13:18 140–62
14:1 2n3
14:11 2n3
16:16 159
17:3 2n3
17:5 2n3
17:9 159
19:12 2n3
19:16 2n3
21:12 2
21:14 2
22:4 2n3

Second Temple Jewish Works

Josephus

Ant.
13.68 65
13.375 69
13.382 69
15.107 69
15.111 69
15.112–120 70
15.147–154 70
15.155–160 70
18.109 70
18.109–112 70
18.111–115 70
20.90 65

J.W.
1.360–364 69

Philo

Abraham
121 66

Flaccus
25–35 71
36–38 71
39 71

Joseph
29 28

Moses
2.115 66
2.132 66

Old Testament Apocrypha and Pseudepigrapha

1 Maccabees
5:24–25 69
5:25–27 69
8:22–32 28n37

1 Enoch
10:9 64

Letter of Aristeas
155 65

Psalms of Solomon
18 (superscription) 61
18:7 61

Sibylline Oracles
1.148–50 146n13
1.324–29 146n13

Testament of Job
33:3 61n10

Testament of Solomon
15:11 146n13

Apostolic Fathers

Polycarp

To the Philippians
4:3 122n3
5:2–6:3 138
14 122n3

Ignatius

To the Ephesians
4:1 122n4
5:1 122n4
5:1–3 122n4
5:2 122n4
6:1 122n4
20:2 122n4

To the Magnesians
2:1 122n4
3:1 122n4
3:2 122n4
6:1 122n4
13:1 122n4
13:2 122n4

To the Philadelphians
1:1 122n4
4:1 122n4
7:1 122n4
8:1 122n4

To Polycarp
5:2 122n4
6:1 122n4

To the Smyrnaeans
8:1 122n4
8:1–2 122n4
8:2 122n4
9:1 122n4
12:2 122n4

To the Trallians
2:1 122n4
2:1–3 122n4
2:2 122n4
3:1 122n4
3:2 122n4
7:1 122n4
7:1–2 122n4

12:2 122n4
13:2 122n4

Church Fathers

Irenaeus

Against Heresies
5.30.1 141
5.30.3 141

Pagan Authors

Aristotle

Rhetoric
1361A 29n44

Artemidorus Daldianus

Onirocritica
3.28 146n13
4.22 146n13
4.24 146n13

Cassius Dio
41.18.5–6 112
41.43.1–5 112–13
41.44.1 112
47.18.2–47.19.3 115
54.7.6 119
54.8.3–5 34
54.23.7–8 119
56.46.1–5 117
58.2.1–6 129
60.5.1–5 130

Cicero

In Verrem
2.3.111–12 133n43, 137n63

Historia Alexandri Magni
1.33.11–12 146n13

Lucian

Alexander the False Prophet
10–12 146n13

Pliny the Elder

Naturalis historia
34.9 29
34.99 24n32

Strabo

Geographica
10.5.3 118
12.8.11 119

Suetonius

Divus Augustus
99.1–101.4 117

Divus Claudius
11.2 129–30

Divus Julius
88 115

Domitianus
5 1n1, 11n8

Nero
39.1–2 159

Otho
6.2 34

Tiberius
37.3 119

Vespasianus
8 24n32

Tacitus

Annales
4.36 119
5.1–2 129